OUR BODY OF WORK

OUR BODY OF WORK

Embodied Administration and Teaching

EDITED BY
MELISSA NICOLAS AND ANNA SICARI

UTAH STATE UNIVERSITY PRESS
Logan

© 2022 by University Press of Colorado

Published by Utah State University Press
An imprint of University Press of Colorado
245 Century Circle, Suite 202
Louisville, Colorado 80027

All rights reserved
Printed in the United States of America

 The University Press of Colorado is a proud member of the Association of University Presses.

The University Press of Colorado is a cooperative publishing enterprise supported, in part, by Adams State University, Colorado State University, Fort Lewis College, Metropolitan State University of Denver, University of Alaska Fairbanks, University of Colorado, University of Denver, University of Northern Colorado, University of Wyoming, Utah State University, and Western Colorado University.

∞ This paper meets the requirements of the ANSI/NISO Z39.48-1992 (Permanence of Paper).

ISBN: 978-1-64642-233-3 (paperback)
ISBN: 978-1-64642-234-0 (ebook)
https://doi.org/10.7330/9781646422340

Library of Congress Cataloging-in-Publication Data
Names: Nicolas, Melissa, editor. | Sicari, Anna, editor.
Title: Our body of work : embodied administration and teaching / edited by Melissa Nicolas and Anna Sicari.
Description: Logan : Utah State University Press, [2022] | Includes bibliographical references and index.
Identifiers: LCCN 2022013717 (print) | LCCN 2022013718 (ebook) | ISBN 9781646422333 (paperback) | ISBN 9781646422340 (epub)
Subjects: LCSH: Human body and language. | Language and culture. | Writing centers—Administration. | Rhetoric—Study and teaching—Social aspects. | Academic writing—Women authors. | Women scholars—Attitudes.
Classification: LCC P35 .O97 2022 (print) | LCC P35 (ebook) | DDC 808/.0420711—dc23/eng/20220504
LC record available at https://lccn.loc.gov/2022013717
LC ebook record available at https://lccn.loc.gov/2022013718

Cover photograph © Andrey Armyagov/Shutterstock.

Melissa—to Nan Johnson for never answering my question about what writing the body would look like
Anna—to JD for the laughter, support, and weekend donuts

CONTENTS

Acknowledgments   xi

1. Introduction: Institutional Embodiment and Our Body of Work
   Melissa Nicolas and Anna Sicari   3

1.1. Painting
   Rita Malenczyk   26

DISCOMFORT AND PAIN

2. Embracing Discomfort: Embodiment and Decolonial Writing Center Praxis
   Isaac Wang   33

2.1. An Embodied Life: My Postpartum Writing Story
   Rebecca Rodriguez Carey   43

SURVEILLANCE

3. What on Earth Am I Even Doing Here? Notes from an Impossibly Queer Academic
   Stacey Waite   49

3.1. Nonlinear Transformations: Queer Bodies in Curriculum Redesign
   Alex Gatten   59

3.2. Embodying Structures and Feelings
   Anna Rita Napoleone   65

LIMINAL SPACES

4. Embodiment in the Writing Center: Storying Our Journey to Activism
   Trixie G. Smith, with Wonderful Faison, Laura Gonzales, Elizabeth Keller, and Scotty Seacrist   71

4.1. As Time Moves Forward
   Dena Arendall   88

4.2. An Academic Career Takes Flight, or the First Year on the Tenure Track, as Seen from Above
   Jasmine Lee   91

RESILIENCE

5. Graduate Student Bodies on the Periphery
   Kelsie Walker, Morgan Gross, Paula Weinman, Hayat Bedaiwi, and Alyssa McGrath   97

5.1. Down the Rabbit Hole
   Elitza Kotzeva   110

5.2. Writing in the Body
   Janel Atlas   113

EMOTIONAL PAIN

6. "Never Make Yourself Small to Make Them Feel Big": A Black Graduate Student's Struggle to Take Up Spaces and Navigate the Rhetoric of Microaggressions in a Writing Program
   Triauna Carey   119

6.1. Bodies in Conflict: Embodied Challenges and Complex Experiences
   Nabila Hijazi   131

6.2. Out of Hand
   Jennie Young   137

CULTURE OF WHITENESS

7. Bodies, Visible
   Joshua L. Daniel and Lynn C. Lewis   143

7.1. Dancing with Our Fears: A Writing Professor's Tango
   Mary Lourdes Silva   158

7.2. "Do Not Disturb—Breastfeeding in Progress": Reflections from a Lactating WPA
Jasmine Kar Tang   163

RELATIONSHIPS

8. The Circulation of Embodied Affects in a Revision of a First-Year Writing Program
Michael J. Faris   169

8.1. More Bodies Than Heads: Handling Male Faculty as an Expectant Administrator
Jacquelyn Hoermann-Elliott   184

8.2. About a Lucky Man Who Made the Grade
Ryan Skinnell   188

TRAUMA

9. A Day in the Life: Administering from a Position of Privileged Precarization in an Age of Mass Shootings
Shannon Walters   195

9.1. When Discomfort Becomes Panic: Doing Research in Trauma as a Survivor
Lauren Brentnell   208

9.2. Embodied CV (Abridged)
Denise Comer   212

CANCER AND DEATH

10. WPAs and Embodied Labor: Mina Shaughnessy, (Inter)Personal Labor, and an Ethics of Care
Rebecca Gerdes-McClain   219

10.1. Somatophobia and Subjectivity: Or, What Cancer Taught Me about Writing and Teaching Writing
Julie Prebel   237

10.2. A Scholar Anew: How Cancer Taught Me to Rekindle
My Embodiment Research
Maureen Johnson   241

10.3. A Comp Teacher's Elegy: To Carol Edleman Warrior
Michelle LaFrance   244

10.4. Born for This
Elizabeth Boquet   248

Index   255

ACKNOWLEDGMENTS

Melissa—I would like to thank Anna for inviting me for a margarita at Disney World and for not letting me give up; our anonymous reviewers for pushing us in all the right ways; Rachael Levay at Utah State University Press for believing in us; our authors for their insightful, poignant, and brave writing; my family for understanding that "Mom has to work"; and my body—without it, none of this work would be possible.

Anna—First, I would like to thank Melissa for being not only a wonderful colleague and mentor but also a true friend throughout this process and beyond—hopefully future margaritas and projects are in store for us; Rachael Levay for believing in this project from day one; the authors of this collection for helping me learn about embodiment in ways I would not have without their stories; the reviewers for their insightful feedback; my family, friends, and colleagues who continue to support me; and last, but not least, my animals, who help me realize there is much more to life than academia.

OUR BODY OF WORK

1
INTRODUCTION
Institutional Embodiment and Our Body of Work

Melissa Nicolas and Anna Sicari

MARGARITAS AND RESEARCH

This book started, as so many wonderful collaborations do, after a long day of conferencing and a couple of margaritas at a noisy hotel bar. Anna was interviewing Melissa for a research project, but talk quickly turned to our lived experiences as female teachers, scholars, and writing program administrators.[1] Energized by our conversation (and perhaps the slight buzz from the tequila), we theorized from the everyday personal stories we were sharing. As we talked about Melissa's research and Anna's dissertation, we recognized not only our shared research interests but also the ways our bodies influenced our everyday work and informed the very conversation we were having. In increasingly animated dialogue, we acknowledged that our actual flesh-and-blood bodies, what Margaret Price (2011) calls "fleshy presences," impacted our work every bit as much as the institutional structures we worked in. Indeed, even the ebb and flow of our conversation was informed by our exhausted bodies running on caffeine, overwhelmed by the busyness of the conference.

At the time, we were surprised at the stories we were telling. While we knew the stories were true—yes, as a newly minted assistant professor, Melissa was mistaken for the administrative assistant, and, yes, as a graduate student and as an assistant professor, Anna has often been told that smiling and performing the role of "Miss Sunshine" will be important to her success—we came to realize we wanted to hear more stories like ours, stories like those told in *Women's Ways of Making It in Rhetoric and Composition* (Ballif, Davis, and Mountford 2008) or in *WPA: Writing Program Administration*'s 2016 "Symposium: Challenging Whiteness and/in Writing Program Administration and Writing Programs," because these stories take fleshy presences seriously.

A fleshy presence, as Price (2011) explains, is our material self: the blood and bones and organs and tissues that create the contours of our

https://doi.org/10.7330/9781646422340.c001

bodies. We believe in the importance of having open exchanges about embodied experiences in the academy in order to have more complicated and nuanced conversations about intersectionality and identity and how racism, sexism, colonialism, classism, and ableism (among many other isms) stem from patriarchal systems of power. Yet, too often, we do not have these conversations for fear they are too personal, not academic or professional, because of the shame associated with having certain bodies and/or the knowledge that no one will listen.

We are listening. Through discussions about the embodied work of WPAs, this collection, relying heavily on narrative and intersectional standpoint theory, participates in and extends conversations in writing center, WPA, pedagogical, composition, and feminist research and extends calls, particularly from women scholars of color (see Craig 2016 and Kynard 2015, for example), to embrace intersecting areas of study and research in order to better interrogate the body as we strive to make the academic structures we work within more inclusive and accessible.

ON EMBODIMENT

When we began this project, we used the term *embodiment* to describe the emphasis we wanted to place on fleshy presences, but as chapters started coming in and we dove deeper into the literature, we came to understand *embodiment* is not easily defined. As Abby Knoblauch (2012) explains, the terms "embodied" and "embodiment" are employed by different authors—and sometimes the same author—to mean different things at the same time (50–52). Indeed, Knoblauch identifies three categories of embodiment: *embodied language, embodied knowledge,* and *embodied rhetoric. Embodied language* refers to the "terms, metaphors, and analogies that reference . . . the body itself," while *embodied knowledge* is a "knowing through the body" and *embodied rhetoric* employs embodied knowledge, as well as "social positionalities as forms of meaning making within a text itself" (52). The delineation of these types of embodiment is a useful heuristic.

For example, composition studies is ripe with embodied language: essays have "body" paragraphs and writers give "birth" to ideas. And as has been well documented, composition itself has been rhetorically embodied as feminine, relegating it to second-class status and gendering the construction of unjust labor practices (e.g., Enos 1996; Holbrook 1991; S. Miller 1991; Schell 1997; Strickland 2011). Using embodied rhetoric, scholars have emphasized the need for reading bodies ethically (Johnson et al. 2015). As well, scholars use embodied rhetoric to describe feminist writing program administration (Barr-Ebest 1995; Goodburn and Leverenz 1998; Kazan and Gabor 2013; Miller 1996; Ratcliffe and Rickly 2010), and, increasingly, women's leadership (Cole and Hassel 2017; Detweiler, Laware, and Wojan 2017). Scholars have raised awareness of the rhetoric of whiteness in the field (Craig and Perryman-Clark 2011; García de Müeller and Ruiz 2017; Inoue 2016), as well as ableism (Nicolas 2017; Vidali 2015; Yergeau 2016) and heteronormativity (Alexander and Rhodes 2012; Denny 2013; Waite 2017).

In *Our Body*, we are most interested in Knoblauch's second category: knowing *through* the body. Knowing through the body is an epistemology of a fleshy presence, knowledge mediated through the very muscles, bones, and skin of our physical selves. This epistemology builds on Kristie Fleckenstein's (1999) case for the somatic mind. She writes, "The concept of the *somatic mind*—mind and body as permeable, intertextual territory that is continually made and remade—offers one means of embodying our discourse and our knowledge without totalizing either. *This 'view from somewhere' locates an individual within concrete spatio-temporal contexts*" (281; emphasis added). This "view from somewhere" acknowledges the body is required for meaning making. To argue otherwise—to believe the body is solely constructed through discourse—is to erase the actual physical body that exists in time and space because "embodiment is required for meaning and being" (284).

The view from somewhere is what Katherine Hayles (1993) suggests is the difference between bodies and embodiment. For Hayles, "The body points toward the normalized and abstract, whereas embodiment refers to the contextual and enacted" (156). The body is constructed and coded (inscribed) through discourse, but *embodiment* requires that discourse and materiality, time and space, individual experience, cultural assumptions, and so on be *incorporated* into and read *through* the body. For Hayles and Fleckenstein, embodiment refuses abstraction and assimilation because embodiment is necessarily about individuals' experiences in space, time, and place—what Price (2011) might call a "*kairotic*" space. Embodiment is a fleshy epistemology, a knowing through, of, and with the body.

Despite the growing scholarship on embodiment, one of the reasons conversations about fleshy presences are still happening in conference hotel bars instead of in the pages of our journals and books is that stories about our corporeal realities are still coded as too personal, too messy, or even just too anecdotal. Indeed, how many of us have been told we can't actually be experiencing what is happening to us because humans are postracism, -sexism, -ableism, -colonialism, and so on? Or because our institutions have strict policies and penalties for such isms?[2] We believe at least some of this dissonance can be attributed to what we see as the conflation of *institutional bodies* with *institutional embodiment*.

Institutional bodies are *a priori*: without bodies, institutions, classrooms, and writing programs would cease to exist (see Porter et al. 2000, for example). Like other *a priori* knowledge, we don't think much about it. For example, we don't question, debate, or negotiate the mechanics of 2 + 2 = 4; we just go about our day knowing it is so. It is the same with institutional bodies. We know a class needs students and a teacher, so we go about our days simply assuming those bodies—*any*bodies—are teaching and learning and administering. It is easy for institutional bodies to be everywhere and nowhere because their fleshy presence is assumed and beside the point; institutions need bodies but pay little attention to embodiment.

The aim of this collection, however, is to draw attention to *institutional embodiment*. Institutional embodiment is a kind of *a posteriori* knowledge gained through individuals' experience of and within the institution. Institutional embodiment is about the ways fleshy presences show up, even if they are not expected to (more on this in a moment). To be *institutionally embodied* means to be recognized as some*one* who takes up space and time and place; some*one* who has a fleshy presence. Indeed, this collection pushes back on the idea of institutional bodies, *any*bodies, as generic placeholders. Too often, *any*body, as Rosemarie Garland-Tompson (1997) explains, is "male, white, or able-bodied[, and their] superiority appears natural, undisputed, and unremarked, seemingly eclipsed by female, black, or disabled difference" (20). She calls these unremarkable bodies "normates" (8). Normates are *institutional bodies* because they are everywhere and nowhere; they are idyllic, not flesh bound; they are pervasive in our discourse yet refuse to be pinned down. The normate is an Aristotelian version of perfection against which *no*body will ever measure up. *Institutional embodiment*, however, calls attention to the ways *individual* bodies—fleshy presences—inhabit, interact with, and create institutions. Focusing on institutional embodiment allows *every*body to become visible.

An interesting thing happens when we shift our view from *any*body to *every*body; we begin to notice which bodies stand out, which bodies are marked. Marked categories are the ones we call attention to (see Ahmed 2012; Morrison 1992). So even when we do consider individual fleshy presences, cis, male, white, hetero, abled men are still considered the "norm" or baseline against which all other fleshy presences are judged (Cedillo 2018). For example, the expectation of an unmarked body is implicit in most common diversity statements at the end of job ads that encourage "women and minorities" to apply. If women, people of color, members of the LGBTQIA community, and persons with disabilities were expected to show up, there would be no need to encourage them to apply.

This fact is perhaps no more evident than in the case of graduate students and contingent faculty. Without these groups of *any*bodies, it is highly unlikely compulsory first-year composition would exist, at least in the form it takes today; there just wouldn't be enough teacher bodies to put in front of the student bodies. As the authors in our collection make clear, while institutional bodies are essential, very often institutional embodiment is at best overlooked and at worst openly disregarded. For example, in "Graduate Student Bodies on the Periphery" (chapter 5 of this collection), Kelsie Walker, Morgan Gross, Paula Weinman, Hayat Bedaiwi, and Alyssa McGrath remark,

> Whether it's about their groceries, their mental health, their physical well-being or professional support, graduate students are expected to make do, or, failing that, to do without. It is assumed such conditions are, if not ideal, at least temporary. Yet such experiences, absorbed and unspoken, inscribe themselves upon the graduate student body: as anxiety, depression, hunger, exhaustion, fear, or even illness, all of which are exacerbated by financial instability and professional precarity. (97)

What Walker et al. are describing is not only the apparent disregard institutions have for the material conditions of their graduate students but also the tacit acceptance that the way things are is the way they are supposed to be: "if not ideal, at least temporary." The role graduate students play is vital not only to our programs but also to the larger departmental and college structures they support. Nevertheless, the health and well-being of those graduate students—their fleshy presence—is less of a concern (if a concern at all) than the need for their institutional bodies to do the labor (see Strickland 2011).

Institutional disregard for (or at least ineffectiveness with) dealing with the health and safety of the bodies that live therein is not just a problem for graduate students. In chapter 9, Shannon Walters describes what it was like to be responsible for a writing program during the trauma of a mass-shooting scare on her campus. With no clear guidance coming from her university, she concluded that "the question [of how to respond] boiled down to a question of security, but it involved *every*one making their own call, managing their own anxiety, and weighing their own personal thresholds of precariousness" (203; emphasis added). While the threat of a mass shooting is an extraordinary event, institutional disregard for individuals is apparent in the everyday as well.

Lauren Brentell (chapter 9.1), Nabila Hijazi (chapter 6.1), and Ryan Skinnell (chapter 8.2), for example, discuss the emotional and personal toll research takes on our bodyminds. In chapter 10, Rebecca Gerdes-McClain tells the heartbreaking story of Mina Shaugnessy's early death from cancer as a possible result of the tremendous burden she carried as a female scholar and writing program administrator. Likewise, we also read stories from Julie Prebel (chapter 10.1) and Maureen Johnson (chapter 10.2) about the impact their own cancer diagnoses have had on their academic life, and Denise Comer (chapter 9.2) shares her "Embodied CV" that juxtaposes her personal life and physical and mental health with her academic responsibilities.

By focusing on institutional embodiment, our authors' stories highlight ways a focus on fleshy presence complicates normative understandings of institutional bodies. In particular, as Sarah Ahmed (2012) explains, "Bodies stick out when they are out of place. Think of the expression, 'stick out like a sore thumb.' To stick out can mean to become a sore point. To inhabit whiteness as a non-white body can mean trying not to appear at all" (41). For example, when there is one brown person in a "sea of whiteness," the brown person stands out (41–43); in a sea of hearing people, a Deaf person stands out; in a sea of straightness, a queer person stands out; in a sea of mental health, mental illness stands out. Who stands out is like a game of "Which one of these is not like the others?" The goal of this children's game is to choose the picture that is slightly off, that doesn't look like the other ones. The pictures that are alike are the "normal" ones, and the one that has some variation is the "wrong" or "abnormal" one. Most often, the wrong or abnormal bodies are the ones that belong to people who do not occupy places of privilege. As Isaac Wang (chapter 2) explains, his body both stands out and is erased by the colonial practices that emphasize helping students write better Standard (white, European) English. Likewise, Jacquelyn Hoermann-Elliot (chapter 8.1) describes how her pregnancy marks her as an outsider, causing her to scrutinize her "own words because [she] know[s] being with child is synonymous to being seen as having only half a brain (or less) in the academy" (185).

According to Melanie Yergeau (2016), writing studies itself is predicated on the idea of real students not measuring up to idealized students. Hyberableness and standardization play such a central role in the field that to decenter the normate might threaten its very existence. Yergeau argues, "Without inaccessibility, we would not be rigorous. Without inaccessibility, we would not have placement. Without inaccessibility, we would not have assessment. Without inaccessibility, we would not have literacy. Without inaccessibility, would we even know ourselves as a discipline?" (158–59). In other words, the standard for traditional ENG 101 is based on institutional bodies and normate educational experiences. When students who do not have these bodies and these experiences present themselves to the academy, the institution tries to erase their embodiment by measuring them against a narrow standard, with the goal of making them *unremarkable institutional bodies.*

But, as disability and queer theorists remind us, there really are no ideal bodies (see, among others, Denny 2013; Dolmage 2014; Price 2011; Vidali 2016). Christina Cedillo (2018) writes, "Individuals whose bodies are perceived as non-normative are framed as unreliable rhetors who cannot speak to more than a thin sliver of experience, even though every individual's embodied identities determine their unique experiences and navigation of academic spaces. All bodies are not identical; neither are their needs, expressions of movement, or preferred modes of reception."

In this collection, Triauna Carey (chapter 6) discusses how the microaggressions she has experienced as a Black graduate student and TA frame her as an unreliable narrator, causing her to doubt herself and her place in the academy while also making her angry with the white powers that be. Likewise, Stacey Waite (chapter 4) and Alex Gatten (chapter 4.1) illustrate how their queerness complicates their institutional identities and often causes them to question their institutional place.

Our Body captures some of the intricacies and nuances of embodiment. Whether implicitly or explicitly, our authors take a feminist standpoint, believing that who we are in relation to our research matters and that all attempts to know are socially situated (Harding 1986). Most of our authors also engage with intersectionality (Crenshaw 1993; also Craig 2016; Kynard 2015) as they draw on multiple locations and identifications of their bodies (social, cultural, racial, economic, institutional, and so on). In these ways, our authors are participating in writing and feminist studies' embrace of storytelling as valid way of creating meaning. For example, *Living Rhetoric and Composition: Stories of the Discipline* (Roen, Brown, and Enos 1999) contains nineteen stories from well-known scholars describing how they came to be teachers and scholars of writing. *Women's Ways of Making It in Rhetoric and Composition* (Ballif, Davis, and Mountford 2008) and *How Stories Teach Us: Composition, Life Writing, and Blended Scholarship* (Robillard and Combs 2019) are just two of many additional examples of how personal story is valued in our field. To date, however, there has been little attention paid to interrogating what it means to inhabit the world of writing studies from the perspective of institutional embodiment.

Recent work done by scholars Shereen Inayatulla and Heather Robinson (2019) showcases the need for this kind of fleshy epistemology. Inayatulla and Robinson draw from their own autoethnographies as they seek to render visible the "underrepresented statuses of the communities to which [they] belong and the labor [they] undertake in [their] administrative roles, both of which are rendered invisible because of the ways in which [their] intersectional identities are erased, conflated, demeaned, or hierarchically positioned" (4). Their "autotheory of administrative practice" (6) could not exist without their reflections on institutional embodiment, and they, too, discuss the need for intersectional feminist research because so much WPA work has been centered around white feminism, echoing similar calls from WPA scholars invested in antiracist work such as Genevieve García de Müeller and Iris Ruiz (2017), Collin Craig and Staci Perryman-Clark (2011), and Carmen Kynard (2015).

Our authors carefully situate their work from their own standpoints and through various critical lenses, such as critical race, queer, feminist, decolonial, and disability theory. As Vinitha Joyappa and Donna Martin (1996) write, "Feminist scholarship draws upon the wisdom of different disciplines, while simultaneously offering a critique of knowledge and methods on patriarchal understandings" (7). The various theories incorporated by our authors highlight their different bodily experiences and truly embrace the idea of "learning WITH (emphasis added) difference" (Garcia 2017) while also creating a necessary fleshy epistemology that is, at yet, underdeveloped in the field.

OUR OWN FLESHY PRESENCE

As we were working on this book, we (Anna and Melissa) kept having moments when our own bodies were getting in the way. Of course, viewing our bodies as "getting in the way" of our work is the polar opposite of the argument we are making with this collection. We bring this contradiction to readers' attention to highlight just how commonplace it is to disregard our own embodied experiences and to acknowledge how truly difficult the work we are asking readers to do is in our day-to-day reality. We got sick; we were hospitalized; we had stress-induced work stoppages and slowdowns; we dealt with hostile work environments, job searches, moves, and a host of other professional and personal life issues that demanded things from us physically, emotionally, intellectually, and spiritually. We hit points at which we decided putting this collection out was just more than we could handle. And yet. And yet we couldn't escape the fact that the reasons we wanted to quit were exactly the kinds of issues we wanted our book to discuss. We wanted a book that addressed, not elided, the realities of having a fleshy presence expected to perform in institutionalized ways. More important, we wanted a book that produced knowledge from the body, *especially* when the body got in the way.

When we were sipping margaritas, we imagined a rather small but important audience for this collection: women TAs, gWPAs, and new WPAs (both staff and faculty). Our foggy goal was to create a primer of cautionary tales and sage advice for our comrades who were learning to navigate life as women in the academy. What we did not want to do, however, was create a collection of "overcoming" narratives (Dolmage 2014), such as those in *Women's Ways of Making It in Rhetoric and Composition* (Ballif, Davis, and Mountford 2008). In the introduction to their book, Michelle Ballif, Diane Davis, and Roxanne Mountford attest that their goal is to "demonstrate how women have succeeded," to share stories of successful women in order for them to "serve as models for other women academics in a sea of gender and disciplinary bias and to have a life, as well" (3). We feel as though *Women's Ways of Making It*, in its attempt to be inspirational, does not do enough to complicate the realities of institutional embodiment. As just one example, only two of the nine "heroic" women covered are women of color. All appear to be cishet, and none identify as women with disabilities.

We were hoping to collect and share the stories we would have liked to read when we were new to the field, mostly as a way of creating solidarity: "This did not just happen to me"; "This is a larger problem than that person, that department, that university." And after our initial CFP went out, we did indeed receive many such compelling stories. But as we took our first stabs at theorizing what we had, two overlapping truths emerged.

First, the essays we originally received did indeed speak to the audiences we imagined. Graduate students and new WPAs would certainly benefit from engaging those chapters as part of their preparation and introduction to the field. The second truth, however, was that our collection was milky white, straight, and abled; there were just two voices in our first round of submissions that belonged to people who did not resemble us: cis, white women with tenure-track jobs.[3] After we processed our role in perpetuating white, and other, privilege(s), we made a concerted effort to dismantle that privilege by reaching out to authors who did work on embodiment from a multitude of intersectional perspectives. These outreach efforts resulted in the wider array of voices represented herein.

While we have tried to work through our implicit biases, we are all too aware that as the coeditors we were the decision makers regarding what voices have been given authority in this book; we are aware of our cishet whiteness, our tenure track-ness, and the privileges these bring, and we are still very much "in process" in terms of understanding how to challenge ourselves to do better. We have not made space for *every*-*body*. During the selection of essays for this collection, we were critically self-reflexive about what voices—what bodies—we were drawn to, what stories resonated with us, and then we tried to actively resist solely relying on what felt comfortable in order to include a kind of diversity we hadn't seen in print before. We invite readers to have this conversation with us: Whom were we not able to see? Whom did we not hear?

Second, opening our thinking about what "counted" as an embodied perspective was the drive for us to think more broadly about who our audience would be. While the essays in this collection speak mostly about WPA work, the topics they address are of interest to anyone concerned with intersectional identities and how those identities influence our positionality in the institution. In this latter sense, this collection can play an important role in graduate composition courses more broadly and can also aid more experienced teachers and WPAs with understanding the complexity of twenty-first-century intersectionality.

OVERVIEW

The chapters in this book are based on real people's lives; therefore, some of this work might resonate with you in uncomfortable ways as it takes up issues of harassment, exploitation, abuse, mental illness, death, and pain. We want you to know about this possible discomfort not to dissuade you from reading deeply, but as Ahmed (2015) reminds us, "so often th[e]se conversations do not happen because the difficulties people wish to talk about end up being re-enacted within discussion spaces, which is how they are not talked about." Instead of turning away from or discouraging these discussions, we and our authors gently invite you to embrace these issues in order to render the "Body, Visible" (Daniel and Lewis, chapter 7) and to create a much-needed space in the field to talk about the body.

As part of our commitment to creating space for many bodies, we invited two kinds of submissions: short, personal narratives and what most would consider academic essays. What you hold in your hands—or see on your screen, or listen to on your audio device—is organized around nine themes we saw emerging in the work. For each thematic cluster, we paired a more traditional essay with two or three shorter pieces in an effort to showcase multiple standpoints on similar topics. While the groupings represent the way we (Anna and Melissa) make sense of the work herein, we encourage you to work through the book in whatever ways makes sense to you. And, truth be told, our thematic organization belies the fact that every chapter speaks to multiple other chapters; when embodiment is the topic under discussion, there are no neat, linear, or clearly demarcated boundaries around our stories. From thinking about what embodiment looks like for students, particularly marginalized students, to understanding how their own bodies do not fit institutional expectations, the authors in *Our Body* respond to Hélène Cixous's (1975) call to "write the body."

A quick glance at the themes in this book—discomfort and pain, surveillance, liminal spaces, resilience (ah! hope!), emotional pain, the culture of whiteness, relationships, trauma and pain, cancer and death—suggests a heavy read. And, as we mention above, there are messy and painful moments in these chapters, just as embodied life is sometimes messy and painful. However, we also see this work as cautiously hopeful by participating in Jacqueline Jones Royster and Gesa Kirsch's (2012) call for transformative research. The bodily experiences our authors commit to print create an archive of embodied knowledge beyond the abstract because this knowledge stems from their material realities. Many of the scholars in this book explore the ways that, even when their bodies do not fit institutional expectations (usually unspoken, often implicit), they have found strategies of resistance and tactics to navigate the academy.

The need to "move forward," however, is something this collection also critiques, as some authors balk at the idea of making the best out of a bad situation, instead discussing the problematics with progress narratives and linear and lateral moving. Progress does not have to mean, should not mean, forgetting, ignoring, or rerendering the body invisible. We find these conversations remarkably relevant as the planet is rethinking "regular" life due to COVID-19 and learning how to revise the future so our bodies are better listened to. We find hope in the current embodied research many of the graduate students in this collection are taking up, as their work highlights how personal research can be and how important embodied research is for enacting any type of institutional change. We respect and admire how willing they are to write and study their own painful, difficult, and often traumatic experiences because institutionalized ways of being can be excruciatingly hard to notice, much less change. Individually and collectively, the authors in this collection rise to that challenge.

Theme 1: Discomfort and Pain

Isaac Wang argues for creating opportunities for decolonial alliances by locating the body through listening for whiteness because of the ways bodies of color do not fit the white racial habitus in the academy. This critical listening attunes the body (*every*body) to the negotiations and compromises WCDs and WPAs of color might need to make in order to get to where they need to be through code switching and passing. Wang writes about the discomfort of these experiences and what dwelling in these moments can look like for "incremental changes that allow the next generation of students and scholars of color more freedom to embody difference" (41). Rebecca Rodriguez Carey's "An Embodied Life: My Postpartum Writing Story" takes an entirely different approach to embodied discomfort, as Carey explores embodied writing while being pregnant and a mother, finishing her dissertation, and entering a new job. Both chapters encouraged us to rethink moments of discomfort, and pain, as potential sites of strength.

Theme 2: Surveillance

Complicating and possibly even challenging Wang's concept of embodied listening for whiteness and his use of passing, Stacey Waite's chapter discusses the importance of her visibly queer body, a body that sticks out in normate spaces. In the chapter "What on Earth Am I Even Doing Here? Notes from an Impossibly Queer Academic," Waite questions whether or not it is possible to truly queer a writing program, and she discusses the political surveillance her English department has been under for their commitment to social justice, as well as the ways she has been policed and surveilled. For Waite, institutional embodiment challenges her to question how she can reconcile the demand for an institutional body (a WPA) and her embodiment as a queer academic. She powerfully ends this chapter focusing again on her presence: "My body, my presence won't change everything, but it will not be moved out of view—no matter how many times the normative pull of institutional surveillance swallows me whole" (57). Taking on Waite's theory of queer pedagogy, Alex Gatten discusses the disruptions of their transitioning body and the new curriculum they helped develop for their writing program in the chapter "Nonlinear Transformations: Queer Bodies in Curriculum Redesign." Gatten, too, poses that the body can never be separated from the work. This grouping ends with Anna Rita Napoleone's "Embodying Structures and Feelings," a chapter that explores the laboring body of a working-class mother; she writes, "The personal and the professional mesh together. There seem to be no boundaries" (68).

Theme 3: Liminal Spaces
Trixie Smith, along with Wonderful Faison, Laura Gonzalez, Elizabeth Keller, and Scotty Seacrist, return to the writing center and tell a multivocal story of institutional embodiment from the perspective of a writing center director (Smith) and the graduate students (Faison, Gonzalez, Keller, and Seacrist) working with her. Smith complicates a linear narrative by telling her story in multiple scenes, all of which raise important questions for her about her embodied work as an administrator and a lesbian woman. Wonderful Faison questions how her writing center can make her feel safe as a lesbian woman yet, at the same time, unsafe and uncomfortable as a Black woman (echoing both Wang's and Waite's discussions). Gonzales asks why multilingual students are viewed from a deficit model when, by the logic of multilingualism, they possess sophisticated language skills. Keller tells of a tutorial wherein she and a student from the Middle East spent a significant amount of time discussing how bodies smell because the Middle Eastern student received the message that Middle Eastern bodies smell "different" than American bodies. (Keller's discussion of the "otherness" of bodies that are considered "foreign" is a theme that will emerge again in chapter 5.) Seacrist rounds out the chapter by detailing the ways his voice is perceived as "effeminate, lispy, faggoty" (78). His voice quite literally says things about his sexuality that he cannot control.

As WPAs who work closely with the graduate students in our program, we were encouraged to see work from scholars such as Trixie Smith bringing in the voices of their graduate students, as well as important work from so many graduate students who responded to our call. Graduate students live in liminal academic spaces; their bodies are constantly under surveillance from their own students, from their professors, from their mentors, and from the very discipline they are trying to join (also see Nicolas 2008). Nonnormative graduate student bodies must negotiate additional layers of complexity in trying to find a place in the institution, and, as seen in other chapters, graduate students are not any more immune to nonacademic stressors than anyone else. In "As Time Moves Forward," for example, Dena Arendall describes the traumatic experience of losing her father while working on her dissertation. In the following chapter, Jasmine Lee discusses the exhaustion of life during her first year of a tenure-track position and the embodied difficulties of this transition in "An Academic Career Takes Flight, or the First Year on the Tenure Track, as Seen from Above." We see these stories as powerful when read together because they all address the liminal spaces of finding a place in a center, program, or an institution, particularly for transitory bodies.

Theme 4: Resilience

In chapter 5, "Graduate Student Bodies on the Periphery," Kelsie Walker, Morgan Gross, Paula Weinman, Hayat Bedaiwi, and Alyssa McGrath share their experience of institutional embodiment through overlapping themes of "foreign bodies," institutional passing, and the needs of bodies not being met institutionally, echoing work done by contributing authors Wang, Waite, Smith et al., and R. Carey. This chapter also explores the exploitation of contingent institutional bodies and suggests ways senior WPAs and faculty mentors can learn from them in order to create more inclusive spaces for the next generation of graduate students. Bedaiwi describes her (mostly) white students' reactions to her as a hijab-wearing Muslim woman, while McGrath identifies the precarious position she was in as a graduate student who was pregnant at a university that did not have pregnancy leave for graduate students. Walker and Gross discuss the financial hardships and exigencies facing so many graduate students who receive no funding or not enough funding to meet basic living expenses. Weinman concludes the chapter by discussing her "model-minority" status as an East Asian woman. The authors of this chapter view their embodied narratives as necessary resources for institutional reform and hope administrators take note of these stories in order to better understand where financial support and time might be most effective, as graduate students are "the next generation of institutional leaders" (108).

Concerns about finding the time and energy to write while balancing multiple responsibilities also resonate in the narratives in this grouping. Elitza Kotzeva writes about finding time to write before more domestic duties of doing laundry and walking the dog, exploring her material exigencies and noting how the demands of her position as a tenure-track faculty member are different from her graduate students. In "Writing the Body," Janel Atlas describes her pregnancy loss and how this experience became the genesis of her dissertation.

This cluster highlights several different positionalities of resilience while navigating institutional and personal embodied experiences.

Theme 5: Emotional Pain

Picking up Bedaiwi's discussion in chapter 5, Triauna Carey explores the microaggressions she has experienced as a Black graduate student and TA, which cause her to doubt herself and her place in the academy while also making her angry with the white powers that be. In "'Never Make Yourself Small to Make Them Feel Big': A Black Graduate Student's Struggle to Take Up Space and Navigate the Rhetoric of Microaggressions in a Writing Program," Carey calls on WPAs to take a critical look at the ways microaggressions occur in their programs and, even more poignantly, calls on WPAs to be self-reflective about the ways they themselves may participate in committing microaggressions and/or promoting a programmatic culture that allows microaggressions to pass unchallenged. Similar to Waite's earlier plea and Wang's hope for institutional change, Carey urges: "As scholars, educators, and researchers of color, we must use our writing, classrooms, and research to share our experiences . . . as graduate students embodying these experiences, we must take up space, especially in spaces that were not originally intended for us" (128). While Carey highlights the emotional labor of dealing with microaggressions on a daily basis and the impact of not being the person expected to "show up," she emphasizes that the impact of people of color taking up unmarked spaces in the academy is powerful, much like Waite's claim that the mere presence of her body makes a difference.

While Carey discusses her emotional labor as a marginalized graduate student, Nabila Hijazi writes on her emotional labor as a researcher as she interviews Syrian women refugees about their experiences with language programs. Hijazi, a Syrian Muslim woman, shares her own experiences back home (in Syria) with these women as they talk, and their stories intersect and collide. We see Hijazi's embodied research as powerful and hopeful, as we believe much insight will be gained into ways we can better our writing and literacy instruction for all bodies. We end this grouping with Jennie Young's essay, "Out of Hand," which describes how emotional pain manifests physically. Emotional experiences are, in complicated and different ways, embodied experiences, and these chapters offer readers an opportunity to dwell on their own emotional and embodied institutional stories.

Theme 6: Culture of Whiteness

Chapter 7, "Bodies, Visible," stays with the idea of institutionalized marginalization by challenging the white racial habitus (Inoue 2016) of first-year writing programs. In this chapter, Josh Daniel and Lynn Lewis argue that pervasive neoliberalism is only concerned with institutional bodies, and they take up the need for graduate students to be institutionally embodied through mentoring programs and writing program outcomes. Daniel and Lewis's chapter illustrates how T. Carey's call (in chapter 6) can be taken up through intentional programmatic changes. Similar to many of our authors, Daniel and Lewis end on a note of hope, as they believe the embodied positions they occupy as administrators allow for opportunities to make marginalized bodies, both the first-year students they serve and their graduate instructors, more visible in the program through collaboration and engagement that challenges a pervasive neoliberalism. We also see a programmatic culture of whiteness problematized in both Mary Lourdes Silva's "Dancing with Our Fears: A Writing Professor's Tango" (ch. 7.1) and Jasmine Kar Tang's "Do Not Disturb—Breastfeeding in Progress: Notes from a Lactating WPA" (ch. 7.2). Silva points out the ways students are often complicit in racist assessments as she describes the consistent negative evaluations she receives and the ways she has had to revise her curriculum to read "more white." Tang discusses the intersectional components of her identity as a WPA, new mother, and woman of color and the ways she has had to navigate space as a WPA.

Theme 7: Relationships

Programmatic revision, like that discussed in chapter 7 by Daniel and Lewis, is the subject of Michael Farris's "The Circulation of Embodied Affects in a Revision of a First-Year Writing Program." In this chapter, Farris offers a brief critique of the "distributed-grading" FYW program at Texas Tech University that, he argues, erases how writing and the teaching of writing are institutionally embodied acts. Through sharing his own administrative philosophy, informed by queer and feminist thinking, Farris argues that writing and the teaching of writing are ontological endeavors, warranting attention to the bodies that make up our programs. Farris then shares revisions he made to the program and the ways he makes institutional embodiment central to the work of rhetoric and composition at TTU. Through sharing his own affective ways of being, Farris explores how teaching "happens through relationships, through bodies being thrown together in new . . . ways that can elicit new opportunities for engagement with writing and with each other, for potentially new ways of being in the world and being with each other" (179).

Jacquelyn Hoermann-Elliott also addresses how teaching happens through relationships in "More Bodies Than Heads: Handling Male Faculty as an Expectant Administrator." In this chapter, she talks about the complicated ways her exposed vulnerability as a pregnant WPA has helped build relationships with graduate students while exposing gender biases male faculty still have against women in supervisory positions. In the closing chapter of this cluster of essays, "About A Lucky Man Who Made the Grade," Ryan Skinnell writes about the relationships and people he ignored—including his relationship with his own physical body—as he was writing and revising his monograph, identifying the isolation and lack of self-care that can come with academic deadlines and pressure. This group of essays offers perspectives on embodied relationships we form as academics and WPAs and can help us, as readers, learn "new ways of being . . . with each other."

Theme 8: Trauma

Chapter 9, "A Day in the Life: Administering from a Position of Privileged Precarization in an Age of Mass Shootings," highlights what is expected of the institutional body of a WPA and then explains why the everyday labor required of WPAs is unrealistic when we take into account the institutional embodiment of those doing the work. Utilizing a disability studies perspective of precarity, Shannon Walters discusses her position of "privileged precarization" as a tenured woman WPA and mother. Complicating the "mundane precarity" of pregnancy, Walters situates her second pregnancy while she was a WPA within the context of the threat of a mass shooting on her campus. By situating the everyday and local in a larger national conversation on gun violence, Walters shows how vulnerable we all are as bodies inhabiting different spaces and argues that we must learn from precarity. Walters's call is especially poignant now, in the face of a global pandemic in which *all* bodies live with/in precarity.

Likewise, Lauren Brentnell, in her chapter "When Discomfort Becomes Panic: Doing Research in Trauma as a Survivor," discusses her need to privilege her own mental and physical health over a research-intensive academic position as she realized her research on trauma was retraumatizing her, ultimately causing her to position herself on the job market for teaching positions instead of research ones. Denise Comer's "Embodied CV (Abridged)," like Brentnell's chapter, describes how trauma and pain impact our research and cleverly illustrates what our CVs cannot and do not say about who we are as embodied beings.

These chapters highlight what we can learn from trauma and research, particularly if we pay attention to the embodied experiences associated with such work.

Theme 9: Cancer and Death

On the theme of precarious bodies and WPA work, Rebecca Gerdes-McClain offers a unique take on institutional embodiment by examining the work of Mina Shaughnessy. In "WPA and Embodied Labor: Mina Shaughnessy, (Inter)Personal Labor, and an Ethics of Care," Gerdes-McClain does not retell the common narrative of Shaughnessy's articulation of what would become basic writing. Rather, Gerdes-McClain argues that Shaughnessy's "embodied labor experiences suggest martyrdom in the form of meeting . . . unrealistic labor demands" (220). In this chapter, we are presented with a case study in institutional embodiment that demythologizes one of our heroines. The importance of this case study is that it allows us to see Shaughnessy as an embodied WPA struggling to meet the unfair and unrealistic expectations placed on institutional bodies. Gerdes-McClain offers an intervention into the normalizing practices of overwork through Virginia Held's ethics of care. While the story she tells is disheartening, it is also an apt cautionary tale, as it brings to the fore the harsh realities of the often-conflicting demands between what our institutional bodies are supposed to do and what our embodied selves can actually perform, ideas that resonate throughout this collection.

Julie Prebel's "Somatophobia and Subjectivity: Or, What Cancer Taught Me about Writing and Teaching Writing" is a poignant retelling of Shaughnessy's story through a different person's body. Prebel writes about being diagnosed with cancer and her subsequent treatments while she was working. While she tried to be an *any*body in her tenure file, she realized she could not remove her embodiment from the process because there were delays in her scholarly production. Like Comer (ch. 9.2), Prebel needed her own version of an embodied CV in order to give an accurate and truthful accounting of her embodied life on the tenure track.

Similarly, Maureen Johnson discusses her diagnosis of triple-negative breast cancer three weeks before her PhD graduation ceremony and the ways her cancer diagnosis and treatment removed her from her research on body positivity, just as Brentnell (ch. 9.1) needed to move away from trauma research.

This thematic cluster ends with chapters that explore death. Michelle LaFrance explores the death of a friend and student, and Elizabeth

Boquet writes about the death of her mother. Both of these narratives paint a loving, caring picture of the ways fleshy presences come into and out of our lives, forever changing the ways we experience our own embodiment.

As we state earlier in this introduction, without bodies, institutions would cease to exist. And yet, institutional embodiment, that is, the way real people take up the work of institutions, is a topic in much need of theorizing: let's look, really look, at the marked bodies that show up to do the work and the knowledge gained through our bodily experiences and interactions with/in the institution. We believe all the authors in this collection highlight the complexities of writing and thinking with bodies, and the possibilities of embodied writing and research make us hopeful institutional change is possible.

CONCLUSION

During a particularly stressful week when we were discussing this collection, Melissa said perhaps what we really need to do for institutional change is to just blow things up. Sadly, we are all working in a time in which explosions both actual and metaphorical are happening daily.[4] Violence is real and rampant. People are being killed or incarcerated, and children are being put in cages by a government only concerned with white (usually cishet) male bodies. Words are being used to incite, anger, bait, and threaten on a national and international level. Institutional, colonial, and patriarchal attachments to white, able-bodied straight men help perpetuate these abhorrent conditions. And our institution—the academy—is not immune. As the authors in this collection so skillfully describe, recognition of institutional embodiment is still very much an ideal, necessitating the need for institutional passing. But institutional passing is not sustainable.

If we had any doubts about the need for this collection, they have been erased as we revise this introduction under mandatory stay-at-home orders brought on by COVID-19 while protests against anti-Black racism, police brutality, and systemic racism are occurring across the nation in response to the murders of Ahmaud Arbery, Breonna Taylor, George Floyd, Tony McDade, Sean Reed, and David McAtee, among countless other institutionally sanctioned murders of Black people at the hands of the police. In a way too poignant and painful, a virus that can infect *all* bodies has brought institutions, both small and large, to a standstill because the flesh-and-blood people who make up these institutions are in real physical, psychic, spiritual, and emotional crises; at the same critical time, it is the people, the bodies, that suffer the most from this virus, the Brown and Black bodies, that are also the ones fighting another pandemic of police violence and are calling on our institutions to respond and take action.

Due to these intersectional crises, our institutions have been forced to think about embodiment in ways heretofore unimagined or actively resisted. For example, many of the things people with disabilities have been asking of universities for decades, such as flexible schedules, work-from-home options, multiple content-delivery formats, assessment choices, and the like—things we have been told were impossible just a few months ago—have suddenly become not only possible but necessary. A cynical person might say that only when there is nothing to shield privileged bodies from harm (i.e., no vaccine), no institutional walls to protect them from infection, no normal, only then do institutions take notice and take action. Somewhat similarly, institutions and the writing programs housed within them are heeding long unanswered calls by scholars of color (see College Composition and Communication 2020, for example) to look at our own mission statements, practices, and policies to better understand how exclusionary the academy is to the bodies of those who are Black, Indigenous, and people of colors (BIPOC). Only after the horror of George Floyd's brutal murder made national headlines did the same calls for antiracist resources, pedagogies, and assessments seem to get—at least in these very early moments of the current antiracist/#BlackLivesMatter moment (late spring 2020)—white people's attention. A cynical person might say it takes protesting during a pandemic for institutions to take notice and take action. A cynical person might even say this response, too, will slowly fade as we carry on in a "back-to-business" fashion once the media and white people lose interest in combating structural racism. The cynics are not wrong, and we find much can be gained from cynicism.

But we consciously choose not to be cynical.[5] Like our authors, we want to hope. We want to believe these pandemics will open conversations about fleshy presences, about institutional bodies and institutional embodiment. We hope our current crises change institutional DNA to the point at which a collection like this one is redundant. We want to believe institutions can, in fact, change (see Porter et al. 2000) and be better spaces for BIPOC's bodies, disabled bodies, queer bodies, women's bodies, *all* bodies. The only way such change can happen is if we listen to these bodies and learn from fleshy presences.

We hope the words in this book, the words grown from a fleshy epistemology, challenge readers to do better. Some readers may be angered by some of the essays or feel drained, tired, and exhausted; some readers may find chapters that resonate with their own experiences. No matter the reaction, we believe the field must rethink and rework our practices if we wish to create a more ethical discipline. Like Stacey Alaimo (2008), we agree that "ethical practices do not seek to extend themselves over and above material realities, but instead emerge from them, taking into account multiple material consequences" (238). Our authors explore what it means to take into account the multiple material consequences of bodies that remain on the margins in order to transform our practices and make our work more ethical and therefore more livable. To say it another way, we hope the questions this book invites become part of our body of work.

NOTES

1. We use the terms *writing programs* and *writing program administrators* (*WPAs*) to denote a wide range of writing programs from first-year composition to writing centers to writing-across-the-curriculum programs, as well as other writing-based programs.
2. For a compelling account of how nonwhite bodies are surveilled, discounted, disregarded, insulted, and otherwise traumatized in the academy, see #BlackintheIvory on Twitter (Davis and Woods 2020).
3. It is important to pause here and ask, What about our original call was not inviting, inclusive, or trustworthy? In what ways did our call signal, to the very authors we wanted to hear from, that this collection might not be a place where their work was appreciated? While we can never know for sure—so much time has passed it is doubtful people will remember the original call—one possibility is that the voices we wanted to hear from were wary about sharing their experiences because all too often those voices are relegated to the margins, tokenized, or ignored completely. As editors, we should have done more in the call to acknowledge this warranted w(e)ariness and commit to respecting the work that would be shared with us. Our future CFPs will reflect this realization.
4. During the process of putting this collection together (about three years), there have been more than two dozen mass shootings. During the week this footnote was written, there were two mass shootings: one in El Paso, Texas, and the other in Dayton, Ohio. A third active shooter in Virginia was stopped before he could hurt anyone and bring the total for the *week* to three events.
5. Is the freedom to make a choice about whether or not to be cynical part of our (Anna and Melissa's) white privilege?

REFERENCES

Ahmed, Sara. 2012. *On Being Included: Racism and Diversity in Institutional Life*. Durham, NC: Duke University Press.

Ahmed, Sara. 2015. "Against Students." *The New Inquiry*. https://thenewinquiry.com/against-students/.

Alaimo, Stacy. 2008. "Trans-Corporeal Feminisms and the Ethical Space of Nature." In *Material Feminisms*, edited by Stacy Alaimo and Susan Heckman, 237–64. Bloomington: Indiana University Press.

Alexander, Jonathan, and Jacqueline Rhodes. 2012. "Queer Rhetoric and the Pleasures of the Archive." *enculturation*, January 6. https://enculturation.net/queer-rhetoric-and-the-pleasures-of-the-archive.

Ballif, Michelle, Diane Davis, and Roxanne Mountford, eds. 2008. *Women's Ways of Making It in Rhetoric and Composition*. New York: Routledge.

Barr-Ebest, Sally. 1995. "Gender Differences in Writing Program Administration." *WPA: Writing Program Administration* 18 (3): 53–72.

Cedillo, Christina. 2018. "What Does It Mean to Move? Race, Disability, and Critical Embodiment Pedagogy." *Composition Forum* 39 (1). https://compositionforum.com/issue/39/tomove.php.

Cixous, Hélène. 1975. "The Laugh of the Medusa." *Signs* 1 (4): 875–93.

Cole, Kirsti, and Holly Hassel, eds. 2017. *Surviving Sexism in Academia: Strategies for Feminist Leadership*. New York: Routledge.

College Composition and Communication. 2020. "This Ain't Another Statement! This is a DEMAND for Black Linguistic Justice." https://cccc.ncte.org/cccc/demand-for-black-linguistic-justice.

Craig, Collin, and Staci Perryman-Clark. 2011. "Troubling the Boundaries: (De)Constructing Identities at the Intersections of Race and Gender." *WPA: Writing Program Administration* 34 (2): 37–58.

Craig, Sherri. 2016. "A Story-less Generation: Emergent WPAs of Color and the Loss of Identity through Absent Narratives." *WPA: Writing Program Administration* 39 (2): 16–20.

Crenshaw, Kimberlé. 1993. "Mapping the Margins: Intersectionality, Identity Politics, and Violence Against Women of Color." *Stanford Law Review* 43 (6): 1241–99.

Davis, Shardé, and Joy Melody Woods (#BlackinTheIvory). 2020. "No place is safe." Twitter, June 7, 2020. https://twitter.com/smileitsjoy/status/1269764740005482497?ref_src=twsrc%5Etfw%7Ctwcam%5Etweetembed%7Ctwterm%5E1269764740005482497%7Ctwgr%5E%7Ctwcon%5Es1_&ref_url=https%3A%2F%2Fwww.opencampusmedia.org%2F2020%2F06%2F12%2Fno-place-is-safe-not-a-one%2F.

Denny, Harry. 2013. "A Queer Eye for the WPA." *WPA: Writing Program Administration* 37 (1): 186–98.

Detweiler, Jane, Margaret LaWare, and Patti Wojhan. 2017. "Academic Leadership and Advocacy: On Not Leaning In." *College English* 79 (5): 451–65.

Dolmage, Jay. 2014. *Disability Rhetoric*. Syracuse, NY: Syracuse University Press.

Enos, Theresa. 1996. *Gender Roles and Faculty Lives in Rhetoric and Composition*. Carbondale: Southern Illinois University Press.

Fleckenstein, Kristie. 1999. "Writing Bodies: Somatic Mind in Composition Studies." *College English* 61 (3): 281–306. https://www.jstor.org/stable/379070.

Garcia, Romeo. 2017. "Unmaking Gringo Centers." *Writing Center Journal* 36 (1): 29–60.

García de Müeller, Genevieve, and Iris Ruiz. 2017. "Race, Silence, and Writing Program Administration: A Qualitative Study of US College Writing Programs." *WPA: Writing Program Administration* 40 (2):19–39.

Garland-Thompson, Rosemarie. 2017. *Extraordinary Bodies: Figuring Physical Disability in American Culture and Literature*. 20th anniversary ed. New York: Columbia University Press.

Goodburn, Amy, and Carrie Leverenz. 1998. "Feminist Writing Program Administration: Resisting the Bureaucrat Within." In *Feminism and Composition Studies: In Other Words*, edited by Susan Jarratt and Lynn Worsham, 276–90. New York: MLA.

Harding, Sandra. 1986. *The Science Question in Feminism*. Ithaca, NY: Cornell University Press.

Hayles, Katherine. 1993. "The Materiality of Informatics." *Configurations* 1 (1): 147–70. https://doi:10.1353/con.1993.0003.

Holbrook, Sue Ellen. 1991. "Women's Work: The Feminizing of Composition." *Rhetoric Review* 9 (2): 201–29. https://www.jstor.org/stable/465908.

Inayatulla, Shereen, and Heather Robinson. 2019. "'Backwards and in High Heels': The Invisibility and Underrepresentation of Femme(inist) Administrative Labor in Academia." *Administrative Theory & Praxis* 42 (2): 212–32. https://doi.org/10.1080/10841806.2019.1659045.

Inoue, Asao. 2016. "Friday Plenary Address: Racism in Writing Programs and the CWPA." *WPA: Writing Program Administration* 40 (1): 134–54.

Johnson, Maureen, Daisy Levy, Katie Manthey, and Maria Novotny. 2015. "Embodiment: Embodying Feminist Rhetorics." *Peitho* 18 (1): 39–44.

Joyappa, Vinitha, and Donna Martin. 1996. "Exploring Alternative Research Epistemologies for Adult Education: Participatory Research, Feminist Research, and Feminist Participatory Research." *Adult Education Quarterly* 47 (1): 1–14.

Kazan, Tina, and Cathy Gabor. 2013. "Magic, Agency, and Power: Mapping Embodied Leadership Roles." *WPA: Writing Program Administration* 37 (1): 134–60.

Knoblauch, A. Abby. 2012. "Bodies of Knowledge: Definitions, Delineations, and Implications of Embodied Writing in the Academy." *Composition Studies* 40 (2): 50–65.

Kynard, Carmen. 2015. "Teaching While Black: Witnessing and Countering Disciplinary Whiteness, Racial Violence, and University Race-Management." *Literacy in Composition Studies* 3 (1): 1–20.

Miller, Hildy. 1996. "Postmasculinist Directions in Writing Program Administration." *WPA: Writing Program Administration* 20 (1): 49–61.

Miller, Susan. 1991. *Textual Carnivals: The Politics of Composition*. Carbondale: Southern Illinois University Press.

Morrison, Toni. 1992. *Playing in the Dark: Whiteness and the Literary Imagination*. Cambridge, MA: Harvard University Press.

Nicolas, Melissa, ed. 2008. *(E)Merging Identities: Graduate Students in the Writing Center*. Southlake, TX: Fountainhead.

Nicolas, Melissa. 2017. "Ma(r)king a Difference: Challenging Ableist Assumptions in Writing Program Policies." *WPA: Writing Program Administration* 40 (3): 10–22.

Porter, James, Patricia Sullivan, Stuart Blythe, Jeffrey T. Grabill, and Elizabeth Miles. 2000. "Institutional Critique: A Rhetorical Methodology for Change." *College Composition and Communication* 51 (4): 610–42.

Price, Margaret. 2011. *Mad at School: Rhetorics of Mental Disability and Academic Life*. Ann Arbor: University of Michigan Press. https://doi.org/10.3998/mpub.1612837.

Ratcliffe, Krista, and Rebecca Rickly. 2010. *Performing Feminism and Administration in Rhetoric and Composition*. New York: Hampton.

Robillard, Amy, and D. Shane Combs, eds. 2019. *How Stories Teach Us: Composition, Life Writing, and Blended Scholarship*. New York: Peter Lang.

Roen, Duane, Stuart Brown, and Theresa Enos, eds. 1999. *Living Rhetoric and Composition: Stories from the Discipline*. Mahwah, NJ: Lawrence Erlbaum.

Royster, Jacqueline Jones, and Gesa Kirsch. 2012. *Feminist Rhetorical Practices: New Horizons for Rhetoric, Composition, and Literacy Studies*. Carbondale: Southern Illinois University Press.

Schell, Eileen. 1997. *Gypsy Academics and Mother-Teachers*. Portsmouth, NH: Heinemann.

Strickland, Donna. 2011. *The Managerial Unconscious in the History of Composition Studies*. Carbondale: Southern Illinois University Press.

"Symposium: Challenging Whiteness and/in Writing Program Administration and Writing Programs." 2016. *WPA: Writing Program Administration* 39 (2): 9–52.

Vidali, Amy. 2015. "Disabling Writing Program Administration." *WPA: Writing Program Administration* 38 (2): 32–55.

Waite, Stacey. 2017. *Teaching Queer*. Pittsburgh: University of Pittsburgh Press.

Yergeau, Melanie. 2016. "Saturday Plenary Address: Creating a Culture of Access in Writing Program Administration." *WPA: Writing Program Administration* 40 (1): 155–65.

1.1
PAINTING

Rita Malenczyk

In 2016 I became a painter. It happened in a strangely sudden way. I'd been president of the Council of Writing Program Administrators for two years, a stint preceded by two years as vice president and two as past president, and before that by three years on the executive board. Being president was a wonderful gig: I organized and chaired two conferences, worked with some amazing people (because WPAs are, as a group, pretty terrific), and was able to initiate some changes in the organization: a stronger diversity task force, a rejuvenated consultant-evaluator service.

After my term ended, though, I found myself exhausted, with little time or energy to administer my own program or to write. It wasn't the service to CWPA that had tired me out: it was, rather, my WPA job, which I'd been doing for over twenty years and was unable to leave for a variety of reasons. The work I'd been doing for CWPA was a welcome and interesting contrast to my day job. Though I found (and still find) excitement in teaching and supervising peer tutors, the rest of my position carries with it responsibilities (e.g., placement and assessment) that, frankly, I'm no longer challenged by or interested in after all these years, even as I recognize the importance of that work. I found myself not wanting to get up in the morning, arriving at the office later in the day than usual, going through the motions of my work, unable to find that spark that would ignite my interest once again. (I was—and still am—a runner, but despite the joys of crossing the finish line at the end of a race, running wasn't enough to keep me motivated to work, to make me get up in the morning seeing a day full of possibilities rather than a day full of dreaded chores.)

Because looking for a new position wasn't, for various reasons, an option for me, I began looking for other activities that would add new dimensions to my life without draining more energy from an already-depleted source. I decided I wanted to do something creative that wasn't verbal, so on a whim I picked up a copy of Betty Edwards's *Drawing on the*

https://doi.org/10.7330/9781646422340.c001.1

Right Side of the Brain. Drawing seemed like the easiest route into nonverbal creativity for me because all you needed was pencil and paper, even though the book's instructions also called for things like a viewfinder and a mirror and some complicated pencils, all of which I think I used once and then got tired of because there were more interesting things to be had from drawing.

One of those is just the simple act of seeing—or, as Edwards puts it, seeing and drawing what's in front of you. One might argue that, well, we see all the time; and that's obviously true. But in drawing it's a question of paying attention to the edges and hollows of the things we see, the lines and shadows they are comprised of; and to do that you must (paradoxically) make strange whatever it is you're seeing. One of the first exercises in the book was to copy, in pencil, a drawing turned upside down. So I did it. And that was when I figured out I could draw—I mean, the drawings looked like what they were meant to look like, my left hand (another drawing exercise) looked like my left hand.

But there was no color, and I've always loved color. So I decided to paint.

My first foray was into acrylics because they cleaned up easily, dried quickly, and were more controllable—and therefore less scary—than watercolor. I bought some books with titles like *Acrylic Painting for Beginners* and taught myself color and value. I painted still lifes, I painted portraits, I painted animals. I painted my dog several times in the same pose—lying on the couch—because I wanted to get a sense of the lines of his canine body, the muscles that propelled him while moving and contained him while at rest. Searching online, I found a couple of free photos of cats with contemplative expressions and painted them. I painted portraits of my sons Sam and Pete, my friend Lauren, and my friend Theresa's brother the chef.

They were pretty good, those paintings. Yet acrylics left me feeling as if something was missing. When I was about nine years old, I had a set of oil paints, but I only painted a couple of pictures before I gave it up, maybe because I didn't have any outside encouragement. I remembered, though, loving the texture and linseed smell of the paints, the—well, the oiliness of them. So I bought more books and amassed a collection of oil paints and continued with my explorations in color and value, getting used to the texture of the medium, painting more portraits (of my husband and of my son Nick), more still lifes, and even cityscapes and landscapes. Eventually I began to paint on black surfaces, which is what I usually do now because I've forgotten how to paint on white.

I also got hold of some watercolors and, finding they weren't as scary as I'd thought, produced ink and watercolor sketches: at Christmastime, a sleeping reindeer; at moments of leisure, kitchen implements (yes, a potato masher); for Father's Day, a set of my husband's fishing lures. More and more often, in both oil and watercolor—I've pretty much abandoned acrylic—I paint snippets of things, caught from various angles: a part of a white picket fence, a portion of a brick wall. A pile of lemon slices. The beautiful blue stare of my son Sam's Siberian husky.

Painting and drawing have changed the way I think and feel. I see the outdoors differently: I pay attention to the colors of the sky at various times of day, not to memorize them so I can paint them but just because, when you paint, you notice things like that. I notice tree trunks are not, generally speaking, brown, but different shades of gray. I can see pinks and yellows in snow at times of day when the sky isn't pink and yellow. And I see colors I just want to capture in art because with paints (as opposed to pencils), I can. While there are rules, I've learned to bend them because painting is in large part about emotion. In 1908, Henri Matisse (2008) wrote, "The very theory of complementary colours is not absolute. In studying the paintings of artists whose knowledge of colours depends upon instinct and feeling, and on a constant analogy with their sensations, one could define certain laws of colour and so broaden the limits of colour theory as it is now defined."

Because of the instinct and feeling I've come to pay attention to, life is different now—but not in the ways I'd thought it would be when I took up painting. I thought I'd be reenergized to do the work I'd been doing, but that's not the case. I still write, present at conferences, and publish, but not necessarily on WPA topics—and, quite honestly, I don't miss writing about WPA work as much as I thought I would. I've also taken on fewer administrative problems to solve, focusing more on classroom teaching and writing center tutor education. I'm not sure why I haven't jumped back into my day-to-day WPA work with renewed vigor, as I'd expected; maybe because I don't want to burn out again. And I simply have a new interest, have found a new source of challenge and joy. I've sold a few paintings, which is gratifying but not essential; for me what's essential is the calm painting and drawing bring to me, the focus I get while in the painting zone, the use of a different side of my brain—and I won't give that up.

REFERENCES

Matisse, Henri. 2008. "Notes of a Painter." In *Colour*, edited by David Batchelor, 53. Documents of Contemporary Art. Whitechapel Gallery, London. MIT Press.

Discomfort and Pain

2
EMBRACING DISCOMFORT
Embodiment and Decolonial Writing Center Praxis

Isaac Wang

One of the strangest things about coming to the continental United States is that I no longer know what my body signifies. When I moved institutions from the comfort of my home in Hawai'i to the barren whiteness of Indiana, though I didn't notice it at first, what my body meant changed. In Hawai'i, mixed-ethnicity people like me are more common than anywhere else in the United States. According to the most recent US Census Bureau information, 23.8 percent of the population of Hawai'i checked the box for "Two or more races" (United States Census Bureau 2018a); by contrast, that number for the rest of the United States is 2.7 percent (United States Census Bureau 2018b). Both the visual signifiers (how my body presents as a mixed-ethnicity man) and what it means when I lay out my ethnic heritage like a hand of cards have vastly different implications in the Midwest than they do in Hawai'i. In the Midwest, people can definitely tell I'm not white, but they don't really know what to make of me. The fact that I don't speak English with much of an accent means I'm not a recent immigrant and am not marked for the blatant racism many first-generation Asians and Asian Americans in my community face. But because I'm obviously not white, my body does not pass smoothly through a predominantly white community either. In a dimly lit bar, I'll see someone—usually white, male, and over forty—squinting at me over a half-finished beer before asking me in a slurred drawl, "So, where are you from?"

As I was sitting in a coffee shop a few months ago, I overheard someone say behind me, "Asians are just the cutest babies—but then they grow up into joyless adults" (this was in reference to an Asian mother who was sitting with her baby a few feet from me). I turned around to the man in his midtwenties (you already know he was white), wearing a band T-shirt and skinny jeans, and without thinking or skipping a beat told him, "Fuck you!" In the extremely awkward ensuing conversation,

https://doi.org/10.7330/9781646422340.c002

he told me in a conciliatory tone, "I wouldn't have even guessed you were Asian." That comment stuck with me as I turned the interaction over in my head later that evening. Abby Knoblauch (2012) talks about embodied knowledge as "very clearly connected to the body. Embodied knowledge often begins with a bodily response—or what we might call 'gut reactions'" (54). We all know this kind of knowledge, the pit of the stomach, tensing of shoulders response to a word, a gesture, a red MAGA cap on the burly man walking behind you. In this interaction, my body itself pulled words out of my mouth. But for the first time in my life, I also had the discomforting realization that my body posed a question I could not hear nor answer.

In Hawai'i, I don't have to typically identify myself as Asian. When I talk to people in Hawai'i, the question "What ethnicity are you?" comes up frequently as a friendly interrogation. Because Hawai'i is so ethnically diverse, this question does not have the same racist undertones as it does on the continental United States. It isn't a veiled way of asking, "Where are you really from?" Instead, people in Hawai'i usually ask this question to ascertain relationships; the most common question is, "What high school you grad?" Back home, I can tell people I am Chinese, Uchinanchu, German, English, and Scots-Irish—but on the continent, that identity is compressed down into Asian.

Because I am a scholar of color who has worked in writing centers for nearly all his academic life, issues of race, identity, and language in the context of writing center administration are not abstract for me but are part of the day-to-day negotiation of how I do my work. In this chapter, I draw on Asao Inoue's (2015) theory of white racial habitus, Sara Ahmed's (2017) discussion of "being in question," and Christina Cedillo's (2018) critical embodiment pedagogy to explore how our bodies as writing center administrators of color simultaneously prevent us from "passing" while creating opportunities for decolonial alliances. In calling for a renewed examination of our pedagogy, Cedillo states, "We must draw attention to how we create and hold space" (para. 23).

Through this project, I work through a central question of my experiences in shifting from a writing center in Hawai'i to a writing center on the continental United States: How can I inhabit my embodied difference in a way that resists colonialism and creates opportunities for alliances among Indigenous peoples, settlers of color, and white folk? I believe that as writing program administrators, our disabled, queer, Brown, and Black bodies—contested though they are—allow us to attune ourselves to the subtle workings of white racial habitus and begin movement towards decolonial futures.

In his book *Antiracist Writing Assessment Ecologies,* Asao Inoue (2015) introduces the term "white racial habitus" to describe the ways whiteness and racism have become entangled in writing and writing assessment. In defining racial habitus, Inoue draws on Pierre Bourdieu's concept of habitus to explore how educational settings are racialized. Bourdieu (1973) defines habitus as "systems of durable *dispositions,* structured structures predisposed to function as structuring structures, i.e., as the principle of the generation and structuration of practices and representations" (64). For Bourdieu, habitus does not refer to conscious behaviors but instead to a set of embodied dispositions and tastes shaped by and through lived experience rooted in culture. According to Inoue (2015), racial habitus is "one way one might think of race as a set of structuring structures, some marked on the body, some in language practices, some in the ways we interact or work, write, and read, some in the way we behave or dress, some in the processes and differential opportunities we have to live where we do (or get to live where we can), or where we hang out, work, go to school, etc." (43).

Using the framework of habitus, it becomes evident race is not an abstract concept but is embodied in practice—it is tied to space, ways of being, and performance. White racial habitus, then, is the structuring structures of whiteness that pass unnoticed, unmarked as racialized. Race in the classroom, Inoue (2015) argues, functions alongside and in a similar way to the Foucauldian concept of power, "hiding behind power relationships set up by the judgment of student writing by teachers who use a dominant discourse. To put this another way, power is hidden more effectively because a set of white racial dispositions is already hidden in the assessment in various places, assumed as the standard" (28). In educational settings, students are expected to act in ways that conform to white language practice and ways of being; they are expected to conform to the unspoken expectations of whiteness that lie tacit beneath the surface of grading rubrics, classroom discussion, and syllabi. In the writing center, this pressure to conform to the standards of whiteness often plays out as student discomfort. For students of color, both their bodies and their language (which is ideologically bound to their bodies as a marker of deficit) prevent them from feeling at home in the writing center.

One of the ways this plays out in practice is through the racialization of bodies and the connection of nonwhite bodies to language varieties that have been historically deemed as inferior or "broken" versions of English. In Hawai'i, for instance, Hawaiian Creole English, or Pidgin, is a marginalized language that often uses Hawaiian grammatical structures and borrows words from 'Ōlelo Hawai'i, Japanese, Chinese, Portuguese, and Filipino. Although Pidgin is recognized as one of the state languages of Hawaiʻi, it is still linked to racialized deficiency, and students are made to believe from a young age that their language broken (Drager 2012, 62). In a study published in 2000 that looked at language attitudes among university students, the researchers found that speaking Standard English was correlated to superiority traits and perceived as a higher quality of speech (Ohama et al. 2000, 370). In the writing center where I worked, I lost count of the number of local students who revealed to me in tutorial sessions that they had been told they "spoke broken English" and felt their writing was not very good as a result.

I started tutoring in a writing center in Hawaiʻi in my junior year of undergraduate study. That writing center was the first space I had been in during my time as an English undergraduate that there was a deliberate privileging of Indigenous epistemologies and where we were given support to language in ways that drew on our home knowledges. In our weekly meetings, we talked through tutoring in languages other than English and were encouraged to tutor using the languages most natural for us and our clients. At any moment the center was open, it was normal for Japanese, Spanish, Mandarin, or Pidgin to be spoken in different sessions all around the room. The fact that tutors and writers felt freed to use languages other than academic English (or an approximation of it) to talk about writing was a result of ongoing pedagogical discussions in our center but was also connected to how the design and construction of our space decentered Western knowledges in a way that invited embodied decolonial practice.

Whereas most locations in universities (and even in my university in Hawaiʻi) are decontextualized, and material space is disconnected from place, the design of our center deliberately drew on Kanaka Maoli culture and knowledge. The first thing a writer coming into our center was greeted with was a poster on the door that read, "*I kū ka makemake e hele mai, hele nō me ka mālo'elo'e*," which is translated as "If you wish to come, do not be hesitant, for you are welcome." This *ʻōlelo noʻeau* provided protocol for how our center welcomed people in but also signaled that the welcome into our center was rooted in Kanaka Maoli knowledge. Our center was also decorated with bright floral *pareo*, as well as posters and pictures from Kanaka Maoli artists, putting the connection between our center and the community prominently on our walls.

These design choices provided more than a surface-level nod to Hawaiian culture but also affected how we inhabited that space. As a tutor in Hawaiʻi, I felt comfortable using Hawaiian words and concepts to explain writing—but more than just enjoying the linguistic freedom, I felt I was able to be in the space in a way that was comfortable. In writing this chapter, I talked to Maile, another tutor who worked at the writing center with me. Maile told me of working with a Kanaka Maoli student from Hawaiian studies, whom she greeted with a *honi*. Mary Kawena Pukui, one of the founders of Hawaiian studies, describes the *honi* as "placing the nostril gently beside that of the person greeted. Kissing the cheek or gently touching lips to lips is recent" (Craighill and Pukui 1972, 171). In contemporary culture in Hawai'i, it still is considered common courtesy to greet with a *honi*. This is how I grew up—whenever I went to a party, the first thing I did was go around and *honi* everyone. Within the academic context, however, the *honi* is usually replaced with a handshake. Despite the white racial habitus of the school environment, Maile told me, she knew a *honi* was the appropriate greeting for that particular student: "It would have been awkward if I didn't *honi*, and our session probably wouldn't have gone as well." Because the pedagogy in our center emphasized decolonial practice, and because the physical space of the center emphasized connection to the Hawaiian community, Maile was able work with writers in a way that drew on Kanaka Maoli practices.

How does white racial habitus infect the writing center? And how does white racial habitus constrain people of color, choking our lungs and compressing our bodies? To answer this question, it is helpful to turn to Sara Ahmed's (2017) discussion of passing in her book *Living a Feminist Life*. For Ahmed, passing is related to how we move and are prevented from moving through space. People of color cannot just "pass through" spaces frictionlessly—we are challenged, delayed, and sometimes prevented from moving through at all. Our bodies do not fit: Ahmed states, "If you do not inhabit existing norms, it can be uncomfortable. . . . Comfort is about the fit between body and object: my comfortable chair might be awkward for you with your differently shaped body. Comfort is about an encounter between more than one body; the promise of a sinking feeling" (123).

The issue of comfort and creating comfortable come up in writing center scholarship: Jackie Grutsch McKinney (2005) has problematized the way writing center practitioners use the shorthands of coffee makers, plants, and comfy couches to create a space that is "home," pointing out that the homes we are creating are primarily comfortable for white, middle-class tutors and writing center directors (16). In her keynote at the International Writing Centers Association conference, Neisha-Anne Green (2017) gave powerful voice to this problem, stating, "In writing centers . . . we've gotten bold and considered ourselves 'Home.' As I attend conferences and summer institutes, I'm acutely aware of the lack of people who look like me. How the hell can this space be home if I'm always alone?" For people of color, comfort is often out of the question. The writing center is comfortable only as long as we conform to the expectations of whiteness—but even then, our bodies always remind us the spaces we inhabit were not made for us. We cannot sink into an unknowing, unaware comfort. The friction we feel when we do not pass through easily—the tension in our shoulders and twisting in our guts—always pulls us up to the surface.

The shift from working in my old center in Hawai'i to my new center in Indiana was dramatic departure—but one that manifested itself in the details I only noticed as I began to feel my way through the space. In my Indiana center, instead of being greeted by an *'ōlelo no'eau*, the first sign visitors to the center see reads, "Please show your ID at the front desk." Whereas the *'ōlelo no'eau* in my old center signaled anyone was welcome and the conditions of welcome were grounded in Kanaka Maoli rather than Western academic knowledge, this new welcome foregrounds monitoring, control, and the regulation of bodies. To work with a tutor, my body must match with my photo ID. The first thing I must do upon coming into the center is prove, through official identification, that I belong. My old center's *'ōlelo no'eau* reminded me of the place I was—reminded me of the history of Hawai'i and the need to resist every day the pernicious influence of colonialism. My new center's sign reminds me I am monitored and part of a system that monitors and regulates bodies of color.

In this experience of discomfort, this lack of passing, the writing center practitioner of color has two options: either attempt to conform to the expectations of whiteness and take up the privileges that come along with a performance of whiteness, or resist the expectations of white racial habitus and embrace discomfort. I can understand choosing the first path. Those of us who have made it into the academy have had to endure the pressing weight of being marked as Other, of often being the only not-white person in a room, of being all too aware of just how little we fit in. It is an attractive option to try to tame our tongues, to try to manage our bodies so they blend in as seamlessly as possible against the painfully white, fluorescent-lit halls of our institutions. I do not judge those who take this route; often, it may be a necessary tactic for survival. But in doing so, we eschew opportunities to initiate change.

Krista Ratcliffe's (1999) concept of "rhetorical listening" provides one way to think through how I can begin to attune myself to some of the ways white racial habitus is at work in my center, with the ultimate goal of working against it. Rhetorical listening, as Ratcliffe describes it, is "standing under discourses that surround us and others, while consciously acknowledging all our particular and fluid standpoints. Standing under discourse means letting discourses wash over, through, and around us and then letting them lie there to inform our politics and ethics" (205). In speaking of the process of rhetorically listening while standing under another's discourse, Ratcliffe states, "This process both invites the desires of others into our consciousness and accords these desires a place in which to be heard" (207). For Ratcliffe, the desire for mastery of another's discourse is replaced by a desire for an understanding, a "receptivity." With rhetorical listening, Ratcliffe moves away from the aggressive, colonizing politics of dialectic and towards a more dialogic approach to engagement; she places the emphasis on a mutual hearing, multiple voices laid alongside one another without negation or forced synthesis.

Rhetorical listening has been applied to the writing center in Romeo García's 2017 "Unmaking Gringo-Centers," which draws on Ratcliffe's theory in calling for scholarship and praxis that moves beyond a Black/white racial binary and trains tutors to act as "decolonial agents."[1] The focus on the Black Other as a proxy for all colonization in the writing center, García argues, has meant the struggles of other students of color—particularly Mexican Americans—have been hidden under a well-intentioned but insufficient paradigm that has reproduced itself through the good intentions of a "progressive" writing center community (38).

In order to initiate a shift towards writing centers that truly embrace diversity, tutors must work as "theorists of race." For García (2017), this begins "with listening, both in the sense that Krista Ratcliffe discusses it—as a code for cross-cultural communication—and as I conceive of listening—as a form of actional and decolonial work" (33). In moving towards practice, García imagines combining rhetorical listening and thick description to help tutors begin to reflexively work towards understanding the myriad of ways race and power play out in a session.

Of course, the limitation of even this kind of rhetorical listening is that the process must work differently for people of color. Inviting the discourses and desires of others into one's consciousness does not work equally well for everyone. For the privileged members of the white majority, who face no existential threat, standing under the discourses of others is fine; however, a person of color in the academy, sometimes surrounded by people desiring their nonexistence, cannot rhetorically listen in the way Ratcliffe describes. Listening for the primary purpose of understanding is a privilege of whiteness. I think, however, that there can be a kind of tactical listening deployed in order to disrupt whiteness from more marginalized positions.

The process for persons of color listening for the workings of whiteness is different. In the academy, white desires are constantly washing over us, and white speech is always in our ears. In order to survive, we often must either ignore or shut out those discourses and desires. We often must choose to ignore the ways we are being pushed to the margins, even though our lack of passing makes it often impossible to ignore. To listen for whiteness is to attune ourselves to the ways we are being excluded, to listen for and feel the ways our bodies do not fit. It is to observe and feel the discomfort of being the only person of color in a room full of white people. It's feeling my shoulders knot and my tongue stumble over words because I'm having to choose white words and not just say, "I'm pau." However, as I listen and attune myself to my own body, I can begin to see some of the ways whiteness is working and begin to move towards resistance.

In her essay "What Does It Mean to Move?: Race, Disability, and Critical Embodiment Pedagogy," Cedillo (2017) points out how embodied and situated knowledge has often been discounted in composition and that othered ways of knowing, being, and composing are also neglected. In order to move forward, Cedillo states compositionists must "understand the embodied I/me as a strategic site of invention that moves in and about the world, destabilizing notions of space . . . that are normative, ableist, and racist. And we must deliberately set about creating and holding space for others to let them know that they are recognized and welcome" (para. 31). I believe one way of locating the body as a site of invention is through the kind of listening I describe, not shying away from discomfort but instead sitting in it and listening for the ways our bodies do not fit. As we become able to more clearly articulate the conditions of our marginalization, we are also able to more directly counteract the ways whiteness is acting on us in our specific locations.

Through listening and allowing the whiteness that presses down on us to move to the front of our consciousness, we may begin to start to strategize ways practices in our centers—as well as the spaces themselves—may be changed in order to decenter whiteness. As a writing center practitioner, I can strategize with tutors, working with them to think through aspects of our space, practice, or interactions that discomfort them. Instead of allowing ourselves to become acclimatized to the discomfort, through embracing discomfort we can come together to identify problem areas and begin creating strategies that work in our specific spaces and for the tutors and writers who come through our centers. Even though whiteness discomforts in different ways, the material aspects of whiteness that discomfort us may often be the same, and through collaborating and listening to one another, we can begin to see the ways our centers must change in order to address the embodied needs of people of color.

How does one begin to do this kind of work? Dae-Joon Kim and Bobbi Olson (2017) draw on their experiences in the classroom to explore how the naturalization of whiteness means some students and instructors who are Other often end up seeking to gain power in ways that reinforce racist structure (124). In writing centers, which have a long history of marginalization within English departments, the pressure to take up the mantle of whiteness is felt strongly. Writing center directors must interact with faculty members and school administrators, often from a position of limited authority and power. To act in ways that actively resist white racial habitus is to risk losing funding for new desks and computers; to not fit smoothly into white departmental culture is to become "a problem" in your institution and anger the allies you desperately need. Resistance must be strategic. In order to get what we need, there sometimes must be temporary compromises. At least, that's what I used to tell myself.

But here are the facts. You can try not to be a problem all you want, you can control how you move through space, how you dress, how you greet people. You can wear the cloak of whiteness until it chokes your voice and inflames your soul. But here are the facts. You can still die in a traffic stop. Making temporary compromises in a system that's been built to crush us doesn't make sense. I know that for some, survival means the moment of discomfort, the moment when the body feels the atmospheric pressure of generational oppression and whiteness, is a moment that must be passed through quickly. To dwell in the moment carries the threat of centuries of violence crushing any promise of life. If I rush to pass through the discomfort, I survive. But I miss the potentialities hidden in the moment, the possibilities unlocked through feeling my way and letting my body lead. It is like any embodied experience: once you are out of it, you lose all possibility of understanding it. Failing to pass opens an opportunity for my body to lead me towards formulating strategies of resistance—and if this discomfort means I can begin to claw towards incremental changes that allow the next generation of students and scholars of color more freedom to embody difference in the center, I'll take it.

NOTE

1. Though this is beyond the scope of this paper, I want to note one problem I have with García: although García attempts to move beyond a Black/white binary, whiteness is still the oppositional force in his model. As people of color, we must start thinking about our relationships to one another, not just to white people

REFERENCES

Ahmed, Sarah. 2017. *Living a Feminist Life*. Durham, NC: Duke University Press.
Bourdieu, Pierre. 1973. "The Three Forms of Theoretical Knowledge." *Social Science Information* 12 (1): 53–80.
Cedillo, Christina. 2018. "What Does It Mean to Move?: Race, Disability, and Critical Embodiment Pedagogy." *Composition Forum* 39. http://compositionforum.com/issue/39/to-move.php.
Craighill, E. S., and Mary Kawena Pukui. 1972. *The Polynesian Family System in Ka-'u, Hawai'i*. Rutland: Charles E. Tuttle.
Drager, Katie. 2012. "Pidgin and Hawai'i English: An Overview." *International Journal of Language, Translation, and Intercultural Communication* 1 (1): 61–73.
García, Romeo. 2017. "Unmaking Gringo-Centers." *Writing Center Journal* 36 (1): 29–60.
Green, Neisha-Anne. 2017. "Moving Beyond Alright." Paper presented at the Annual International Writing Centers Association Conference, Chicago, IL, November.
Grutsch McKinney, Jackie. 2005. "Leaving Home Sweet Home: Towards Critical Readings of Writing Center Spaces." *Writing Center Journal* 25 (2): 6–20.
Haraway, Donna. 1988. "Situated Knowledges: The Science Question in Feminism and the Privilege of Partial Perspective." *Feminist Studies* Vol 14, No. 3., pp. 575–599. https://www.jstor.org/stable/3178066.
Inoue, Asao. 2015. *Antiracist Writing Assessment Ecologies: Teaching and Assessing Writing for a Socially Just Future*. Fort Collins, CO: Parlor.
Kim, Dae-Joon, and Bobbi Olson. 2017. "Deconstructing Whiteliness in the Globalized Classroom." In *Performing Antiracist Pedagogy in Rhetoric, Writing, and Communication*, edited by Frankie Condon and Vershawn Ashanti Young, 123–58. Fort Collins, CO: WAC Clearinghouse.
Knoblauch, A. Abby. 2012. "Bodies of Knowledge: Definitions, Delineations, and Implications of Embodied Writing in the Academy." *Composition Studies* 40 (2): 50–65.
Ohama, Mary Lynn Fiore, Carolyn C. Gotay, Ian S. Pagano, Larry Boles, and Dorothy D. Craven. 2000. "Evaluations of Hawai'i Creole English and Standard English." *Journal of Language and Social Psychology* 19 (3): 357–77.
Ratcliffe, Krista. 1999. "Rhetorical Listening: A Trope for Interpretive Invention and a 'Code of Cross-Cultural Conduct.'" *College Composition and Communication* 51 (2:) 195–224.
United States Census Bureau. 2018a. "QuickFacts: Hawai'i." https://www.census.gov/quickfacts/hi.
United States Census Bureau. 2018b. "QuickFacts: United States." https://www.census.gov/quickfacts/fact/table/US/.

2.1

AN EMBODIED LIFE
My Postpartum Writing Story

Rebecca Rodriguez Carey

Life. They say it's what happens when you are busy making other plans. And while I was in college, I had only one plan: get in, get out. As quickly as possible, of course. I had a laser-like focus on my studies. Eyes on the prize. No time for anything else. Graduate school was no different. At least the early years. As a student interested in the social effects of mass incarceration, I was anxious to learn more about the relationship between families and incarceration. I took a tour of the county jail for one of my classes and saw several visibly pregnant incarcerated women. While it struck me as odd at first, as the weeks went by, I couldn't help but think about the women I saw.

What would happen to them? What would happen to their babies? And what were the societal implications of incarcerating pregnant women? I didn't know it at the time, but the tour was the beginning of my dissertation writing journey. Fast forward a couple years, and I was in the thick of interviewing pregnant and incarcerated women for my dissertation in the hopes of shedding some light on those early research questions of mine. However, near the end of my graduate school journey, I would learn my (disembodied) plan of finishing graduate school with the same laser-like focus would be significantly altered.

Having been together since high school, my husband and I were eager to become parents.

Being "all but dissertation," or all but done, as I like to call it, I reasoned that graduate school would be the perfect time to become pregnant and raise a baby. I could work from home, and my baby would sleep all day long, allowing me plenty of time to write and finish my dissertation.

But, as I would later find out, the act of writing cannot be separated from our (postpartum) bodies—rather, they are intricately connected.

Because I had an unplanned cesarean section, the recovery was more difficult than I had imagined. The pain of being cut open and having my organs shifted around and then stitched back together was real. The middle-of-the-night feedings were real. And the exhaustion was real. Oh, how that exhaustion was (is) real. And certainly, learning how to take care of a tiny human while recovering from major surgery all while dissertating was real. Because I'd had another major abdominal surgery the year before my c-section, it would be months before my body would be fully recovered. Regardless of the pain, I was in complete heaven. I devoured every possible minute with my tiny human. I memorized her long eyelashes and chubby cheeks and took in that intoxicating newborn smell. I was so enthralled with my newborn that writing was the furthest thing from my mind. But, in academia, the deadlines don't wait for expectant and new mamas.

As much as I was loving taking in my tiny human, the voice in the back of my head whispered, "You should be writing; you should be writing. This dissertation isn't going to finish itself." But, as much as I tried to get back on the writing track, the "before-you-know-it" narratives filled my head. Babies don't keep. They grow up so fast. Don't blink. They're only little once. So, I loved on my baby some more, never quite calming the voice that said I needed to write if I had any desire to finish my dissertation and degree. It was then that I had to reconcile what it means to write before I was ready and before my body was fully recovered. I had to learn a new normal.

I soon discovered that writing during the "fourth trimester" was anything but easy. No longer could I set aside an entire day, or night for that matter, for writing. Nope, my writing would be crunched into ten-minute chunks here and there between clustered nursing sessions. Logging just fifteen minutes of writing a day would be considered a success. My writing sessions more closely resembled chicken pecking, as I'd tap the computer keys with one hand while trying to balance my daughter with the other hand. My lower back would grow stiffer by the minute, but when your baby's *finally* asleep on your lap, allowing you some time to write, you stay put in the chair and power through the soreness. You suppress the need to get up to pee and eat because you don't know when your next writing session will be nor how long it will be. As much as you would love to sleep while your tiny human is sleeping, because you're so mentally and physically exhausted, you can't. Because you can't quite calm the voice that says you should be writing. Remember? The deadlines don't wait for expectant and new mamas in academia.

I didn't realize until later how much being pregnant and having my daughter would influence my writing. It's true, a simple sentence that once took five minutes to write now seemed to take an hour. But in other ways, writing with a newborn made me a stronger writer.

No longer could I wait until the very last possible day to begin writing before a deadline, as those long writing blocks of time weren't guaranteed anymore. Daily writing would become a necessity, as I'd string together ten-minute chunks of writing here and there until my dissertation was complete.

This postpartum period influenced not only *how* I wrote but *what* I wrote about. Had I not struggled to climb into bed after having a baby, it's unlikely I would have thought to ask my participants about their own postpartum experiences and the struggles that come with climbing into bed after just giving birth. Had I not suffered from painful clogged milk ducts, I probably wouldn't have thought to ask my participants about how incarceration influenced their own lactation experiences behind bars.

And I learned being pregnant and having my daughter affected my own responses to the women I was writing about. While their stories of being shackled to a hospital bed during childbirth or the near-immediate separation from their babies at birth evoked feelings of sadness in me before I was pregnant, once I became a mother, it wasn't uncommon for a tear to fall onto my laptop as I wrote about their harrowing experiences. I couldn't help but look down at my daughter and hold her a little tighter as I thought about the irony of the situation and how very different my birth experience was from my participants'. Unlike my participants, I was able to give birth outside the confines of prison. I was privileged to be *writing* about their experiences as pregnant prisoners rather than to be *living* them.

If it wasn't clear to the young college student in me before, it's crystal clear to me now that life cannot be separated from our writing. Life informs our writing. Life is the reason we write. Fast forward a couple years, and I have just finished my first year on the tenure clock. As I'm writing this very piece, I sit with yet another newborn daughter on my lap. Just like with her sister, I find myself chicken pecking away at the computer keys and suppressing the need to get up to pee and eat because I don't know when my next writing session will be nor how long it will be, and of course, the deadline is in a few days. Remember? Deadlines don't wait for expectant and new mamas in academia.

Milk begins to leak from my breasts, which is my cue to start wrapping up the sentence I'm on, as I know it's only a matter of time until my newest tiny human needs me again, thus effectively ending my writing session (yet again). I have more to write. I always do. But for now, I'll say this: *Cheers*. Cheers to all the thoughts in my head that won't ever find their way onto paper because of well, life, an embodied life. After all, that's what happens when you're busy making other plans.

Surveillance

3
WHAT ON EARTH AM I EVEN DOING HERE?
Notes from an Impossibly Queer Academic

Stacey Waite

What on earth am I even doing here? This question occurs to me when I am at the important meeting with the important people and notice, again, that I am the only queer body in the room. And that the women look like women (whatever that means) and the men look like men (whatever that means). And one might say I look like those men; but one might more accurately say I look like a sixteen-year-old boy, my jeans marking me as younger than their jeans mark them, even though we are the same age and wearing the same "dad" jeans. I suddenly feel that the black sweatshirt I've worn to work today looks different on me than it looks on the chemistry professor or the dean. My body sinks into itself. All my life, I've been inappropriate—my clothes, my voice, my choice of partners, my refusal to behave in the ways outlined for me by very important people like these. Yet here I am, in the room with the important people deciding how other people (my students, my colleagues) should behave, whether they win the award, whether the conditions of the assessment have been met. It is antithetical to everything queer, to everything I am and believe.

I must confess that as a visibly genderqueer administrator and professor, I think these thoughts more than I'd like to. I come back, again and again, to the question of what I am even doing in the academy, inside an institution, working to transform structures I am not even sure can *be* transformed. This question is both theoretical and practical; it is a question about both ideas and embodiment. The question of whether any institutional space can even be queered, the question of how (or whether) queer pedagogy or queer(er) administration is possible, the question of whether my queerness can survive inside a large institution in a deeply red state—these questions live in/on my body. It is exhausting to be a queer body in normative space, to ask yourself to return to work the next day to do it again—to use the bathroom in an academic building, to order your lunch in the student union, to meet a new group of students who will, undoubtedly, move their eyes up and down your body with, at best, curiosity, waiting for you to explain your gender, to sum it up for them so they can stop looking for it.

In her 2015 video essay from *The Writing Instructor*'s special issue entitled "Queer and Now," Jacqueline Rhodes reflects on the impossibility of queer pedagogy: "I struggle with the melding of queer and pedagogy. Can such a thing as queer pedagogy even exist? For pedagogy is about disciplining the subject. Pedagogy is a heterosexed political indoctrination in service of a heterosexed institutional imperative. The queer challenges such disciplining, such assimilation, and resists the demarcation of acceptable and unacceptable, appropriate and inappropriate."

If this is true of pedagogy, and it is, then it is undeniably true when it comes to administrative work, which is always in *direct* "service of a heterosexed institutional imperative." Do I *do* anything to that imperative by the presence of my body in the room? Does my queer body *do* anything at all to "resist the demarcation of acceptable and unacceptable"? Or am I just the university's version of Ellen DeGeneres—here to make people comfortable with my good sense of humor about the whole thing, here to check the box that one of "us" (whatever that means) was here in the room when this decision was made.

Of course, Rhodes's (2015) idea that one cannot truly queer an institution, something that exists to discipline and regulate, is not an idea particular to our current moment. Audre Lorde (1984) told us decades ago that "the master's tools will never dismantle the master's house. They may allow us temporarily to beat him at his own game, but they will never enable us to bring about genuine change" because systems cannot necessarily be transformed from the inside, though they can give us the illusion that we have the power to change them (112).

Take for example the fact that in 2013 the Supreme Court repealed the Defense of Marriage Act. For me, a parent who works in the state of Nebraska, this ruling had meaning. It meant, for example, that my partner and our about-to-be-born child could now be part of the "family-plan" insurance my university offers. In this way the ruling changed an individual life, but of course it did not transform marriage; it did not bring marriage out of its sexist, heterosexist, and oppressive history. Nevertheless, I headed right into our Human Resources office with our now valid New York marriage license to make the change to my insurance. The woman at the front desk was nice. I won't tell you her name. She is telling me what information I need to put down for my insurance plan, and she says, "Your wife and your wife's son." "Oh," I laugh nervously, "he's *our* son, like, he's my son, too." She shifts in her chair: "Of course," she says and repeats, "Of course." We continue talking, and in the course of our conversation she says it two more times: "Your wife and *her* son." On my way back to the English building, I stop in my calm-down spot. I have a calm-down spot on campus, a small alcove between the building I work in and the natural-history museum. I sit there when the exhaustion kicks in. I've sat there after a meeting about a numerical, data-driven assessment program was handed down from the dean's office, after a meeting in which I was told a graduate student instructor who slept with at least one of his students would continue to teach in our department, after a staff member in another department asked me what my gender was in the elevator (like, just in the elevator, for no reason), and after an undergraduate student got herself "moved" to an independent study of a course so she didn't have to read *Fun Home*, the dirty award-winning graphic novel her queer graduate instructor had assigned. I won't go on, but the point is, I could.

The way my body tries to contain its outrage and grief reminds me of my own sophomore year in college when I signed up for an ethics course in the philosophy department, a course in which we read arguments for and against gay marriage for three weeks. Every Tuesday and Thursday, I got to listen to my peers make arguments for and against my humanity—whether I was fit to have children, or go to the courthouse and file for a marriage license, or step foot in a church or other holy place. My professor, whom I liked and respected, took the neutral route, asked questions of all the students, and I never could tell what she actually thought. I think she thought this was pedagogy—but we can never consider something pedagogy (a truly theorized practice) when our students or colleagues sit in a room with us and we have done nothing to indicate to them that their very bodies, their very being, are not up for debate in the room.

In November 2017, the University of Nebraska was in the national spotlight. I won't bore you with the details, but the point is that conservatives in our state went after our English department. A group of state senators (I won't tell you their names) penned an opinion piece for the local paper in which they voiced their outrage that our Department of English "advertises its core values as pursuing social justice, affirming diversity, engaging with a broad array of real and imagined communities based on empathetic understanding, fostering a sense of belonging and instilling a desire for civic engagement" (Brewer, Erdman, and Halloran, *Lincoln Journal Star*, Nov. 1, 2017). Sounds terrifying, doesn't it? They asked, quite seriously in tone, whether the English department actually teaches English anymore. They worried about conservative students not getting a fair shake in our classrooms. They indicated that classrooms should be places of free speech. Our institution and department remain under political surveillance, and the University of Nebraska remains under censure by the AAUP.

Surveillance, as Michel Foucault articulated, is the key component to institutional social control. A person must only *feel* the possibility of being watched in order to be compelled to control their behavior in the normative direction. I'm always nervous when I'm teaching, especially before meeting a new group of students. I usually feel sick. I usually sit in my calm-down spot before the first class. I try not to think of who is watching, or the ways my students will be watching. I imagine my body is something impossible to destroy: a mountain, a military tank, air. But it will not stop me from knowing I am watched, from knowing a photograph of me would be a really great way to show how the English department has lost its liberal mind, to show its radical queer agenda.

I think of who is watching when, in my first-year writing course, a student touts her religious tolerance of queer lives by saying she thinks the "hate-the-sin-love-the-sinner" approach allows her to love both her church and her gay friends. To my knowledge at this moment, there is one other queer person in the room besides me. This student's jaw drops, and they look at me in disbelief. I can see in their eyes they don't want to have to be the one who takes this on. Because teaching is an embodied and affective experience, the discomfort in the room is palpable, some bodies leaning forward in agreement, some taken aback, waiting for their professor's response. My mouth is suddenly dry. My hands are trembling a bit because I know I am indirectly being watched. I know my institution would want (yes, institutions have ravenous desires) me to make sure this student feels their contributions are valued and that differences of "opinion" are welcome in all our classes. And I know my own body is telling me I cannot let this circulate as just one of many perspectives on queer lives. I think of queer and trans youth who cannot go home, who decide not to live because they cannot go home. I don't need to tell you what I did or said. It wasn't perfect or that interesting. I can tell you I lay down on my office floor when class was over.

I think of who is watching when the students in my Rhetoric, Society and Argument course discuss the public rhetoric surrounding #BlackLivesMatter. I listen to some of the white students say we should give "equal time to *both sides*." I am thinking of that every Tuesday and Thursday I listened to my peers in college make arguments for and against my humanity. I am thinking of "hate the sin, love the sinner." I am wondering what both sides of debate on a person's humanity means. I am thinking that the conservative state senators are watching me. I feel my white queer body in the room. I feel the shifting tension in the body of my *one* Black student. I tell the white students "No." I refuse the moment of debate. I give a soapbox lecture on the significance of positionality in the context of making arguments. I lean on the fact that I am here teaching this course; I am the "expert" in argument making. I show them the flaws in making arguments about the lives and stories of people who are *not* you. My *one* Black student seems bored—probably not the first or last time he has had to witness white people being led, gradually and carefully, through logics he has known and felt in his body his whole life. And in a sense, this moment is no different than the moment that could have been, the moment in which white students would "debate" his humanity. The moment is more of the same in that white bodies are front and center—the purpose of the lesson is them—their ignorance, their shame, their perceived objectivity on race in America. It is also me—my white body, my perceived objectivity on race in America, my decisions about how to position my own whiteness being surveilled by the regulatory power of whiteness on a local and global scale.

In a recent essay in the *Guardian*, Ijeoma Oluo (March 28, 2019) describes this problem: "Once again, what might have been a discussion about the real, quantifiable harm being done to people of color had been subsumed by a discussion about the feelings of white people, the expectations of white people, the needs of white people." To be clear, I am not exempt from the harm of whiteness, nor I am suggesting race, gender, and sexuality are the same kinds of oppression, or that the one Black student in my course felt exactly the same as I did in my own undergraduate course. But I am saying that the overlaps and excesses of our bodily experience are connected, that systems of oppression are designed to keep those of us on the margins thinking only about our differences from one another and not about the ways our interlocking experience gives us power. Lorde (1984) puts it this way: "In a world of possibility for us all, our personal visions help lay the groundwork for political action. The failure of academic feminists to recognize difference as a crucial strength is a failure to reach beyond the first patriarchal lesson. In our world, divide and conquer must become define and empower" (112).

My university doesn't want to be in the public-opinion section, doesn't want its budget cut by a conservative governor, doesn't want to be perceived as being biased against *any* student, even the biggest, most sexist, most racist, most homophobic asshole you can imagine. The university wants that student to be welcome too. Everyone welcome. Every opinion. Every idea. Voiced. Respected. *What on earth am I even doing here?* I think again in the classroom that day. I remember that no matter how many resistant and nonnormative essays I teach in my courses, no matter how many productive conversations I have with students, I work within the confines of the institution; I work for a state that believes this very institution should have the right to fire me for my queerness if they so choose.

And yet, the university has sometimes been my haven—the place my queerness was celebrated or welcome, the place I thought carefully about whether, as a queer person, I even wanted the right to the institution of marriage in the first place. Can marriage, after all, be saved from its history? Can any institution be saved? Can queers getting married intervene in the sexist and heterosexist fabric or normative marriage? Should we want to? Can institutions be changed, or saved, or a force of the positive kind?

My body, my life is, in this way, quite the paradox—to be a queer body inside the academy, to be queer and married, to be queer with children. After all, so much of the scholarship I read and teach in queer theory might suggest to me that my "normative" choices (working for a large public institution, getting married, having kids) are the trap, the very thing that distracts me and makes it impossible for me to enact true resistance in the actual world. Most queers in the academy remember their delight, for example, at that moment Lee Edelman (2004) told us, in *No Future: Queer Theory and the Death Drive*, "Fuck the social order and the Child in whose name we're collectively terrorized; fuck Annie; fuck the waif from Les Mis; fuck the poor, innocent kid on the Net; fuck Laws both with capital ls and small; fuck the whole network of Symbolic relations and the future that serves as its prop" (29).

And on the one hand, yes. Fuck all of this. Fuck the right clothes, fuck appropriateness, fuck assessment, fuck the institutions in which we work. On the other hand, I don't see myself as having the luxury of truly living this idea, and I am not sure I would want the life in which I did have that luxury. Edelman's (and others') embrace of antirelationality and his critique of how the future has been wielded against queer people can feel, at least momentarily, empowering and liberating—the fresh air of not giving a fuck. However, José Esteban Muñoz (2009) offers this critique: "The here and now is a prison house. We must strive, in the face of the here and now's totalising rendering of reality, to think and feel a then and there. Some will say that all we have are the pleasures of this moment, but we must never settle for that minimal transport; we must dream and enact new and better pleasures, other ways of being in the world, and ultimately new worlds" (1).

Muñoz (2009) has characterized the "anti-relational" turn as a product of the complex privileged position of the gay white male, and he has posited that an "educated hope" is the imperative stance for queers of color and other marginalized queer communities. Muñoz calls us to imagine "other ways of being in the world" as a way of making new (future) worlds. If Muñoz is right, and I suspect he is, it is never as simple as abandoning hope, as refusing to care about or work inside any institution. It is never as simple as the death drive, the *theoretical* positioning of not caring about life itself as it is posited by the culture in which you live. There was a moment in my life when I thought a man who held me by the queer throat would actually kill me, and that moment lives in my body; it lives in every moment I want to "fuck the whole network of Symbolic relations and the future" because I want to live. I want others like me to live. I want (and must have hope) that the symbolic relations can be changed to make the world more possible for those of us on its margins.

Deborah Kuzawa (2019) articulates "the primary purpose and benefit of a queer method" as "exposing the dominant sociocultural binaries and discourses and providing openings to questions that reshape those binaries, discourses, and the broader culture in the process" (154). I have to believe my presence *does* matter, that the binaries can be reshaped or reimagined. I think of the institutions (of higher learning, of marriage, of gender) as things not likely to just go away, so the question remains: What can we do with what's here, even in the face of its failures and violence?

In her book *Repurposing Composition*, Shari J. Stenberg (2015) begins an opening chapter of the book with a quote from Adrienne Rich about the position of women in higher education. Stenberg views Rich as making a call for "repurposing the institution, for locating possibilities, complexities and contradictions and then for finding ways to *remake* it into something else, as something else that is more spacious, expansive, and reflexive for all of its inhabitants" (15). It is the difference between trying to make changes to existing structures through their own channels and trying to actually transform the structures through innovative and perhaps even disobedient means. This is why Stenberg sees such value in feminist repurposing, in the idea that an institution, while often not able to be destroyed entirely, can be made into something else—can be a thing used in entirely different ways and for different purposes.

Lauren Bruning, an undergraduate student in one of my composition classes, enacted a very interesting moment of this "repurposing" in her response to Foucault's elaboration of the panopticon. In her reflection on the #MeToo movement, Bruning writes:

> I hypothesize the #MeToo movement has gained stature because of the way it exposes individuals, similarly to the way Foucault's Panopticon functions. Men who used to say inappropriate comments to women, or catcall, or grope, or rape, are forced to consider the possibility that these actions will be publicized and affect them negatively. Women who feel attacked or abused can expose their abuser publicly. The possibility of surveillance influences the way one acts privately.

I loved this moment in Bruning's essay—how she repurposed the culture of surveillance, which, in class discussions, had been definitely positioned as the enemy, the prison, the ultimately institutional enactment of social control to operate as a panopticon directed at the prison guards, as a culture of surveillance that watches the watchers. I think of Bruning's analysis as I think about how to imagine what a queer academic might be or do to transform our surroundings, to protect queer students, to "remake" the academy into "something else that is more spacious, expansive, and reflexive for all of its inhabitants."

But the doubt always creeps back in, and maybe it should. Can we really queer institutions? Can we be queer administrators or professors within these institutions? This is a question of both theory and body. Having been a director of composition, graduate chair of my department, and a professor, I am often in the position to advise and teach new teachers (both high school and college instructors), to help them see the work before them in their institutional context. We talk all the time about how to deal with teaching in a culture of assessment, about how to both work within *and* resist the norms that surround us about teachers, about students, about education itself. But I don't always share with them what it feels like on the days my body grows tired of creating the well-worded question to nudge a homophobic comment in a student paper; when it grows tired of saying the sentence "That's not always possible for queer instructors or instructors of color"; when it grows tired of colleagues suggesting simple solutions to complex teaching problems; and when it grows tired of feeling "less adult" than my colleagues, as the queer academic is never quite the adult in the room, never quite the fully arrived scholar. The truth is that how I feel on the days my body grows tired of resistance, that how I sometimes deal with the dissonance is: I hate myself. I ask, *What on earth am I even doing here?* It is the body that leads to this question. It is the disciplining of the body done in the name of professional composure and behavior. In "Queer: An Impossible Subject for Composition," Jonathan Alexander and Jacqueline Rhodes (2011) remind us that "queerness pushes hard at composition. It insists that we look at what is *not* composed—but more importantly it insists that we heed what *refuses* to be composed" (183). The question I am always left with, as a queer administrator especially, is, What if the cost of refusing to be composed is too great? If the institution cannot truly be queered, as Rhodes suggests, then I will never be truly valued or safe inside it. But sadly, how does that fact make the institution any different from any other place on earth I might be at any given moment?

The truth is I am here because without the work of the visible troublemakers (my English teachers in high school who taught off the curriculum, the few visibly queer figures of authority I knew of as a teenager and college student) inside their various institutional locations, I might not have known my life was possible. I might not have imagined someone who looks like me could work in a "professional" context, could talk to a dean or chancellor. I might have thought impossibility was already and always the only option. Instead, I know now that I am mostly impossible but momentarily possible in fleeting openings for queer repurposing and queer visibility.

What on earth am I even doing here? I am uncomfortable. I am making everyone else uncomfortable. I am saying the right thing, the wrong thing, nothing. I am here so the meeting of the committee is, in that small interval, queerer than it was before I arrived. I am here being watched. I am here so others feel watched by the radical queer agenda. I am here to give a student an A on a disorganized but brilliant essay. I am here to value queerness where I see it, to resist bigotry where I see it. To make queer life and queer vision more possible for myself and for the students I teach. I am here to be exhausted, to sit in my calm-down spot, to lie down on my office floor. I am here to be a queer body that is also a mountain. My body, my presence, won't change everything, but it will not be moved out of view—no matter how many times the normative pull of institutional surveillance swallows me whole. I will still live queer in its belly. I have no other choice, no other hope.

REFERENCES

Alexander, Jonathan, and Jacqueline Rhodes. 2011. "Queer: An Impossible Subject for Composition." *JAC* 31 (1): 177–206.

Bruning, Lauren. "Power in Numbers—Changing the Culture through Social Media." Unpublished essay, last modified March 2019. Microsoft Word file.

Edelman, Lee. 2004. *No Future: Queer Theory and the Death Drive.* Durham, NC: Duke University Press.

Kuzawa, Deborah. 2019. "Queer/ing Composition, the Digital Archive of Literacy Narratives, and Ways of Knowing." In *Re/Orienting Writing Studies: Queer Methods, Queer Projects*, edited by William P. Banks, Matthew B. Cox, and Caroline Dadas, 150–68. Logan: Utah State University Press.

Lorde, Audre. 1984. *Sister Outsider.* New York: Crossing.

Muñoz, José Esteban. 2009. *Cruising Utopia: The Then and There of Queer Futurity.* New York: New York University Press.

Rhodes, Jacqueline. 2015. "The Failure of Queer Pedagogy." *Writing Instructor*, March. http://parlormultimedia.com/twitest/rhodes-2015-03.

Stenberg, Shari J. 2015. *Repurposing Composition: Feminist Interventions for a Neoliberal Age.* Logan: Utah State University Press.

3.1

NONLINEAR TRANSFORMATIONS
Queer Bodies in Curriculum Redesign

Alex Gatten

When I began my first term as a writing program administrator,[1] I was one and a half years on testosterone, nearly two years post-op from top surgery, and, as is necessary for any queer body or person, half in and half out of the closet. (As for many queer people, my daily interactions often involve continual comings out, the "closet," if it exists, really more of a permeable membrane than a fixed structure.) I'd posted in the graduate students' Facebook group one year before when I'd changed my license, and my public request to use he/him pronouns filtered from them up to faculty. That same summer, I had met with my advisor and told him my progress was delayed on my first dissertation chapter by depression, brought on by the struggle to make myself and my body legible to state and federal bureaucracies. A year later, I applied for and accepted a position as a graduate writing program administrator in our first-year writing program, which was (and is) undergoing a massive program redesign to become an active and multimodal curriculum.

This brief introductory narrative might be somewhat difficult to follow, moving back and forth among some major milestones in my life, my transition, and my embodiment. On first drafting, the form wasn't necessarily intentional, but as a queer person, I feel most comfortable with the nonlinear, the complicated, and the difficult. In *Teaching Queer: Radical Possibilities for Writing and Knowing* (2017), Stacey Waite's exploration into queer pedagogies refuses "like my body . . . linear formations . . . the category of discipline . . . I do not believe the story of my scholarship is separate from the story of my life or the body I live" (16). Like my body, the curriculum has shifted and transformed in nonlinear ways and does not engage with the disciplinary conventions instructors expect (since it is housed in an English department at an R1 institution). More than that, the curriculum is not merely "like" my body—the two have intertwined in their simultaneous transitions. It is

https://doi.org/10.7330/9781646422340.c003.1

common to attempt to fit gender transition into linear narratives of the body: first the discovery/realization, then hormones, then surgery, and then a triumphant emergence into legibility and acceptability. But the realities of transition are often much messier and nonlinear. Thousands of moments define transition beyond purely the physical: the first time I asked someone to start using different pronouns than those assigned to me at birth, the first tentative engagements with online communities, and changing understandings of my gender identity. I'm not sure I will ever want to be simply recognized as a man; some days I feel I walk beside my younger self as I walk the hallways of my department. I had surgery before I had really decided to commit to hormones, having felt more hurried by the health issues resulting from chest binding, and by the then-recent 2016 presidential election, than by a desire to be perceived consistently as a (cisgender) man. Hormones continue to transform me, too; my face looks different today than even four months ago (when I had already been on testosterone more than a year and a half). I've vacillated back and forth between pastel, typically feminine-coded clothing and more masculine clothing, the division between the two having become essentially meaningless past fears about others' reactions to my presentation—but at many moments these old fears persist, still appearing over my shoulder, a lingering shadow of the hurt and fear my younger self experienced.

The summer I began my tenure as a graduate writing program administrator, we had just won a grant to develop an Active Learning Center (ALC) in our department in conjunction with our new multimodal curriculum.[2] An old computer lab was restructured and rebuilt to instead become a collaborative learning environment, with tables on wheels, mobile and individual whiteboards, a smartboard, a large blackboard, and a variety of seating options. It's a space students generally find stimulating and enjoyable and instructors find intimidating—the possibilities of the space are exciting, messy, and scary, all ideal for students to engage in the active, collaborative, and multimodal composition at the heart of our new curriculum. Its purpose is to encourage flexible and collaborative studio work. Throughout the summer, the room was under construction; I saw only illustrated maps anticipating what it would look like. During that time, I had to help construct a new studio-centered curriculum paradoxically featuring a room that did not yet exist and that I didn't yet know how to engage with myself. I was simultaneously learning how to navigate a body that newly "passed" as male with more frequency even as that body, and its location in the world, continued to change without a discernible "finishing" point. My body, like the new curriculum and the new classroom, existed and exists in hybrid spaces, refusing to adhere concretely to others' expectations.

My hybrid status as both a graduate student and writing program administrator has made the hybridity and nonlinearity of the curriculum and my body apparent. While I have received overt messages of support, any time of transition also makes clear the linearity and binaries that undergird both our social and academic institutions and the difficulties that implicit, Western, normative linearity imposes, particularly for those of marginalized embodiments. That summer, I attended a social gathering of graduate students in a T-shirt and shorts and chatted with one or two graduate students who were men about baseball (although I can't remember the exact details). Another graduate student asked a friend, I would find out later, if I was "becoming a bro" now based on my presentation and conversation (I've been a fan of baseball since my teens). Simultaneously, several months later, I went to a different social gathering of graduate students that was crowded enough that we naturally divided into groups in two spaces. I stayed with my closer friends, and the room happened to be primarily women except for myself; someone commented that "all the women stayed upstairs" while the men had gone downstairs. Both attempted to fit me into preset binaries, and both responded to my transition as if it either hadn't happened (although I had been openly gender nonconforming for some time) or was inevitably leading to a certain kind of male performance (despite my explicit efforts to avoid upholding strict gender binaries in presentation or in my interests).

The transition of a writing program, and people's response to it, is similar. Transition is, regardless of the kind, always messy, disordered, disorganized—and, of course, exciting, but perhaps all the more terrifying for its excitement. Many want to know what the final product will be (and indeed, many do seem to see bodies of all kinds, including the embodied space of a classroom, as a kind of product), even as they hope for more time to adjust. It reminds me sometimes of the popularity of before-and-after "transformation" picture collages of transgender people, which necessarily emphasize the "after" as a kind of linear product, a stable identity in binary opposition to what came before. By necessity, pieces of the new curriculum have been put in play one at a time and out of order as we seek to think through them, with them—we can't, after all, write a curriculum without also simultaneously performing it, the identity of the program "moving beneath our feet as we teach, as we write about teaching" (Waite 2017, 13). As a graduate student at the time of this writing, I'm often more privy to some of the chatter around our writing program compared to our faculty directors. I have heard varieties of excitement about all the new possibilities intermingled with anxiety, a desire to know how "exactly" the new curriculum will work, as well as outright belief that it either simply won't "work" at all (as if a curriculum is a machine one simply presses "go" on) or that our emphasis on active learning and multimodality means the course isn't actually a writing course anymore. Similarly, I can't compose or decompose my gender, in all the various ways one composes and identifies a gender or genders, without also performing it, incomplete and messy and always-already failing.

My identification with nonlinearity and messiness has, I think, complemented my work on our program's redesign, but that identification, and my status as a graduate student, has also made me vulnerable to critiques against and anxieties toward it. I became attached quickly to the messiness and multiple possibilities presented by the new classroom—like my body, it underwent an extensive sort of surgery via construction. It, like my body, pushes boundaries of what feels comfortable, makes visible what we might want to keep invisible. I can feel the boundaries of my body "pushing up against what is possible" (Waite 2017, 13). I can feel the width of my shoulders, the space I take up (which always feels small, subversive), the brush of the "undercommons of the university," in Susan Stryker and Aren Z. Airua's words, and beyond, the murky boundary between me and the possible and the legible. You can feel yourself more acutely in the active-learning classroom. Due to immovable furniture in the middle of the room, we can't (consciously or unconsciously) put the room into rows. This configuration consequently prevents the instructor from having a "safe," separated place to stand and necessarily calls attention to our bodies and their movement in ways that have become invisible in more traditional classrooms. The consequently circular arrangement of the room mirrors a circular, nonlinear approach to pedagogy that deemphasizes linear "progress," individual exceptionalism, or top-down hierarchies of pedagogy.

Due to several outside factors (such as time and contract constraints), we were limited to specific and less-than-ideal circumstances under which we could unveil the new room to instructors. I was tired from preparing for the upcoming, end-of-summer workshops, partially due to a lack of support from upper administration at the time—I'd stayed on campus, along with one of our directors and another graduate student assistant director, until 8 p.m. the night before setting up the program's computers and copier because the program wasn't given temporary extra workers to help us after construction in the building. Nonetheless, I was excited to unveil the room. It had become emblematic of the new curriculum and would, I was soon to find out, also become a sort of symbol for all of the excitement and anxieties about the program changes to come because it is a physical space, a material embodiment of the new and the uncertain of our curriculum design. The session with graduate instructors did not go as I had anticipated; despite the room also being new to me, it had become an integral part of my imaginary of the program. For others, however, its newness was shocking. Graduate instructors' immediate responses to the room centered on anxiety and panic that they might "have" to teach in there, concern about how whole-group discussion would work in the room if the students would be facing different directions, concern that the room was too "immature"/preschool-esque, and a general sense of being overwhelmed. Like my embodiment, the embodiment of the room caused stress and a desire (and inability) to place the room into two categories: a room that would function like a traditional classroom with more technological options (with an emphasis, for example, on instruction and whole-class discussion) or a room that would do something too messy or disorganized to facilitate the "rigorous" and "disciplinary" work our students "should" do. I became aware, for the first time in my new position, how invisible much of the labor of a WPA transitioning a program is, and how invisible, similarly, much of my own transition has been.

Between my exhaustion from working so hard preparing for the room and that moment and a summer fraught with navigating newly concretized gendered assumptions due to my changing embodiment, I became somewhat irrationally and suddenly frustrated. Although my peers' responses were understandable given the circumstances, I nonetheless felt their responses personally and keenly because of the many varied intersections and hybridities I was navigating as transgender, as a graduate student, and as a WPA. I left the room for some time, wanting and needing to be out of the body of the room, out of my own body, to forget the feeling of invisibility, of unacceptability and immaturity, but unable as always to forget or escape.

My body and my transition have disrupted binaries, my body still hybrid, although it "passes" often to strangers. But both my body and the active-learning classroom "disrupt binaries in some very specific, embodied, sexed, and gendered ways—ways that cut right to the heart of who we think we are, or who we think others are" (Waite 2017, 10). I have been developing the curriculum on the assumption that it would allow for, if not necessitate, the kind of queer pedagogy Waite sets forward, a queer pedagogy my body has taught me. In the vein of queer pedagogy, I have offered, then, not a linear narrative of my transition and its impact on my work as a WPA but rather a nonlinear, disordered account of the messy intersection between my transition and the transition of our writing program, complicated always by the limits, boundaries, and possibilities of the narrative space of this document. But this narrative, in its messiness and brevity, has hopefully made visible the intersections of WPA work, fluid embodiment, and space.

NOTES

1. At the time of this writing, the first-year writing program is run by two faculty directors (one with split duties and one contingent) and two graduate assistant directors.
2. For pictures and videos of, and information about, our Active Learning Center, please visit the University of Connecticut First-Year Writing website: https://fyw.uconn.edu/resources-for-instructors/writing-across-technology/active-learning-center/.

REFERENCES

Stryker, Susan, and Aren Aizura, eds. 2013. *The Transgender Studies Reader 2*. New York: Routledge.

Waite, Stacey. 2017. *Teaching Queer: Radical Possibilities for Writing and Knowing*. Pittsburgh: University of Pittsburgh Press.

3.2
EMBODYING STRUCTURES AND FEELINGS

Anna Rita Napoleone

My working-class background taught me I needed to hustle in order to make ends meet. I often was working in a couple of different places and going to school at the same time, moving from place to place—from work to school to work again—on any given day. I see the juggling and moving about from place to place as a normative way of being: always thinking about what the next steps will be and what hurdles might there be. In doing so, I have always calculated my time, as it never felt it was mine to use up but was rather imposed on me.

Calculating where I needed to be, what I could get done and what I couldn't, and finding ways to get done what absolutely needed to be done—it was all a normal way of being. I thought of myself as resourceful. After all, how well I made use of time was tied to my material reality and well-being. Such understandings and feelings of myself as resourceful, juggling, hustling (and lucky) became characteristics/values/ways of being I have come to embody. Yet, upon closer inspection, they reveal the way power is felt and circulates on and through the body.

When I recently got hired as a writing center director and as site director of a National Writing Project (an NWP director must be NTT faculty in an R-1 institution), I believed this job to be ideal for me, as it required being in multiple places during the day and did not require that I publish. I knew I would have to hustle but I knew how to do that. Also, there were multiple facets of the job I really enjoyed, such as working with tutor-interns, teaching a class on tutoring and writing, working with graduate students and faculty, and working with K–12 teachers. The administrative work (keeping budgets, etc.) was something I knew was necessary and something I didn't mind, as I was often good at it. I felt lucky to have the position, as it was also a unionized position. The lecturer job description stated I needed to keep up with scholarship, not produce it. Yet, I now feel this urgency to produce, as it seems to be a sign of my relevance and credibility. Such feelings (of luck and urgency) are produced and enfleshed by being in spaces where what is valued and relevant isn't the laboring body doing the work but rather the work of publications one produces. What I realize is that being NTT faculty at an R-1 university brings about feelings not solely my own but rather produced in relationship to the institutional structures.

The R-1 university is a place that privileges research and publication, which is demonstrated in its dispensation of benefits, titles, and money, and also in its allocation of respect. I need to publish in order to be heard and to be relevant. If I don't publish, if I merely "keep up with the scholarship," I fear my "luck" will run out. Even if I keep my job, a lack of publications might push me down the faculty pecking order. In many ways, most of them informal and subtle, lecturers are from the start behind the eight ball compared to tenure-track faculty.

In my office I find myself calculating what needs to get done and when. My office is also a place where I try to write but find myself feeling unsure of writing, in part because of my own insecurities about belonging in the academy. Also, publishing is not part of my work, so the time I spend writing is time I am not really doing my job. Both my director positions require that I be present in the space, as that is important for the morale and the regular functioning of the two academic units I direct. In the writing center it is important to be present for tutors, students, and assistant directors, as well as for meetings with faculty and for workshops. In the Writing Project space, it is important to collaborate with codirectors. Therefore, on any given day, I am in the writing center, in the Writing Project office, and also in my office, which is located in the writing program, as I need to be visible there, too. Having to be on campus in these spaces for most of the day means I must be available and visible for support in its multiple forms (administrative, emotional, institutional, etc.). As NTT faculty with administrative duties, I am positioned as a laboring body that must be seen in order to be working. Most of my day is dedicated to being on campus, being visible, being present. My writing must be done elsewhere, on personal time, as there is no designated time to write. I have been told that, of course, I can find time to write, but I have a dual position and three offices, and I must work alongside others in two of those, so there's little time left for writing. I often find myself calculating hours, and often minutes, and trying to be resourceful and innovative by combining different aspects of my job. If I work more hours in a position that is only 20 percent of my job, I note the additional hours I have worked. That way, when I do write, I can claim that time as my time.

For example, I recall trying to write both an article I was hoping to submit and a proposal for a conference when a tutor-intern visited me in my office. It was not during office hours. She told me she too was a first-gen student, and she said she was happy to see a fellow first gen who was successful. I recall being surprised, and I had a flashback to a conversation earlier on in the semester with a tenured professor, who, when I spoke to her about my new position, said, "I am happy you are working for us. I mean with us. With us." I don't think *successful* is how NTT faculty are typically viewed by the institution. I was very excited to talk with the tutor-intern, as I had started to feel I was connecting with tutors and this talk seemed to confirm those feelings. And, talking with students about their experiences as first gens is important work and is something I have done in the past and will continue to do. Talking with this tutor-intern was an important moment for me, yet I found my anxiety rising while we were talking. My thoughts drifted to the writing I should be doing. I attempted to refocus my energy on what she was saying, but my mind wandered as I thought of the limited time I had. I needed to pick up my daughter from her after-school program, and I still had to get to the writing center to finish discussing with one of the assistant directors a workshop presentation we were planning. As the tutor-intern left, I noted the time. It had been almost an hour. I called down to the writing center and told the assistant director I couldn't make it downstairs and to please call if she needed me. I hung up and found myself feeling guilty, unable to write, as I thought my work should be downstairs. I shut my computer, took my coat and bag, and headed down to the writing center. Writing time would have to be found elsewhere.

My first-gen student sees me as doing well, and I think, "Yep, lucky me," and yet I want to tell her, "Nope, it's not what you think." The façade of keeping it together when oftentimes I can barely keep up and performing a positive outlook when I am frustrated and anxious speak to how we not only work within structures but also embody them. I feel I am being hustled. I try to claim that time back, only to be more overwhelmed, and realize feelings of luck and resourcefulness are not traits and values but defense/survival mechanisms for trying to function in institutions that privilege a rigid hierarchical system in which the production of texts holds value over the very bodies interacting in the space.

Finding time to write means finding it elsewhere, which oftentimes means at home, on my personal time. I find myself telling my daughter that she can watch yet another episode of Mickey Mouse, or that she needs to learn how to play by herself so I can give myself the allotted forty-five minutes of writing two to three times a week, as I promised myself. Forty-five minutes turns into two hours, as writing isn't all I am doing—I am also answering emails so I am not bombarded the next day. After some time, my daughter steps in front of me as I am immersed in writing a paragraph on class affect and says, "Mommy, I don't like that you are always typing." Feelings of guilt and aggravation for not being a good mom and for not being a very good scholar are combined in that moment, the personal and professional mesh together. There seem to be no boundaries. I feel I am everywhere and nowhere.

Liminal Spaces

4
EMBODIMENT IN THE WRITING CENTER
Storying Our Journey to Activism

Trixie G. Smith, with Wonderful Faison, Laura Gonzales, Elizabeth Keller, and Scotty Seacrist

I wanted to tell you a story because stories are powerful, living things. In fact, Native scholar and novelist Thomas King (2008) tells us "the truth about stories is that that's all we are" (2). I took all my stories and laid them out side by side trying to discover which story was most important, most illustrative of where I want us to go. But I discovered a few things in this process. Most of these stories were not mine, or at least not mine alone, so I needed to pay some respects and build some relationships before I could hand you other people's stories. I also discovered I couldn't rank the stories. They all had their own values, ways of knowing and being, and their own importance for understanding and constellating what we mean, what I mean, when I talk about embodiment in the writing center. And that is what I'm here[1] to interrogate; it's a journey I've been on for the past few years, at least in dedicated, named ways. I think I've really been on this journey for thirty years.

TAKE 2

I want to tell you a story because stories are powerful, living things. I think I must start with my own story, my own body in the writing center, so you'll know you can trust me and perhaps relate to me. I have been working in writing centers since 1986. I started as an undergraduate peer tutor, the first at my school's new WC, untrained except for my education courses and mostly alone. I was questioning, however, why the opening of our writing center coincided with the development of our sports program and our first athletes on scholarships, including several nonnative speakers of English recruited to play tennis and soccer. Why were these the main bodies we were seeing in the WC? What did it mean that we brought people in to win at sports for us but knew up front they

https://doi.org/10.7330/9781646422340.c004

would need extra help with their academics? Why weren't we already helping students with their academics, the non-sports players? I knew plenty of folks who had come to me for help or who had bemoaned their grades and the hard times they were having as they struggled to write. At the same time, I was a budding feminist, having encountered and embraced feminist literary theory in several classes, but I was still clueless about my own queerness. It's hard to tell a story of queerness in the Deep South, in the Southern Baptist church where I spent all my time, in the Southern Baptist liberal arts college that concentrated more on the arts than the liberal end of things. It's hard to tell such a queer feminist story, even if it's your own.

Fast forward ten years. I'm working in my third WC now as a graduate student. I am much more confident in my feminist storytelling and am learning to tell my own story of lesbian/queer existence. And I'm constantly wondering about how my lesbian identity fits into my work, my teaching, my research. I find myself negotiating when and how to mark my body for others to read and questioning when it's important and when it isn't. Exactly why might my 3 p.m. Monday client need to know I'm a lesbian? Does it matter when a student is analyzing a poem by Robert Frost? What about Emily Dickinson? Does it matter when I'm helping a student argue for or against marriage equality in her women's studies class? Do I have to out myself in order to speak as an authority about how much money it has cost me because my partner of ten years now is not my legally recognized spouse? Can I just wear my rainbow jewelry? Will that be enough? Should I dress a certain way? Will that help me say things I want to say without actually having to say them? Will it put people at ease if they know where I'm coming from and which box to put me in?

Fast forward another twenty years. I'm directing my own center now, and for years I've been collaborating with others to conduct workshops about awareness and creating "safe-enough" spaces in classes and writing centers for those who identify as Other.[2] I've asked folks to think about the power of words and labels and how it can change in a heartbeat depending on context; to talk through scenarios of misogyny and homophobia and ableism; to dig deep and really consider race, class, gender, sexuality, ethnicity, age, ability, languages, and how all of these intersect, collide even, in students' writing, in the writing center, in our larger institutions; and to consider what this means for the work we do, as well as HOW we do it. I've asked my consultants to be activists on our campus, and many have taken up this call. But I'm never quite satisfied with the answers and solutions I've found on my own or in the books I've read, even the changes I've implemented in my own center. It seems like there's more: more to be considered, more to be understood, more to be done.

I've worked hard to make our writing center inviting and homey, for example. But then folks like Nancy Grimm (1999) and Jackie Grutsch McKinney (2013) challenge me and ask, Whose home are you modeling this after? Does everyone actually feel good or comfortable at home? Is there a different metaphor, a different story we want to tell? A different way of thinking about our bodies in time and space? Similarly, Harry Denny (2010) challenges me, challenges us, to interrogate the complex, diverse, and ever-changing face of the center. Scholars focused on students' right to their own language, code meshing, and translingualism challenge us to consider the voice, accent, and rhetorical styles of various cultures, including both clients and consultants in the WC (Perryman-Clark, Kirkland, and Jackson 2014; Young 2012). Anne Ellen Geller, Michele Eodice, Frankie Condon, Meg Carroll, and Elizabeth Boquet (2007) challenge us to be tricksters, flexible shape shifters, morphing from animal to animal or shape to shape in order to take advantage of the opportunities before us for engaging with each other and with our clients. They also encourage us to remember, in our bodies, what it feels like to be learners encountering new material or developing new skills. They ask us to remember the discomfort and the struggle, and perhaps the victory, of meeting a new challenge. It's important to experience this, to remember what this process feels like *in your body*, not just your head.

TAKE 3

I want to tell you a story because stories are powerful, living things. They are theories and methodologies, pedagogical guides and heuristics. The stories I want to tell, however, are not mine alone, so I want to say thank you to all those who share in these stories, whether purposely or not. These include folks I've talked to either in person or through their texts (see the references list at the end of this chapter).

One of the privileges of directing a large writing center and teaching at a large research university is encountering a rich diversity of colleagues, including smart and exciting undergraduate and graduate students. Their research inside and outside of class, their projects in the center, the questions they ask me and each other, often serve as impetuses for my own questioning and research. I want to share some stories that have been shared with me by the storytellers themselves so you can understand how they have shaped my thinking, research, and actions about embodiment in the writing center. You will also come to understand how they call us all to action, to embodied acts of activism.

LIKE A FLY IN MILK
Wonderful Faison

Writing centers are neither havens for togetherness nor islands of intimacy insulated from political and social relations.

I do not write this piece easily, as my mentor, chair, and future colleague runs the writing center in which I work. I do not write this piece easily because I want the writing center where I work to be perfect: free from racism, sexism, classism, heterosexism, and all the ills of this world. I want a writing center oasis. But when I was asked to write this piece, I chose to write a truth; not the Truth but *my* truth about writing centers.

When discussing race, more specifically Blackness, in writing center spaces, I often feel an identity clash. How can a writing center that makes me feel "safe" to express my lesbian identity, flaunt pictures of my girlfriend, and ask different consultants their opinions on engagement rings, make me feel "unsafe" as a Black body? Could it be the writing center's "lesbian" color schemes of lavenders and cool blues that warm this lesbian body? Is it the blinding whiteness (of people), the navigating of microaggressions, or the putting on of linguistic airs (speaking Standard English instead of Black English to clients and consultants) that cause this identity conflict? Why do I feel like a fly in milk? Why must I ask clients, "What do you mean by 'those people'?" and why must I remind them that "real" Americans aren't just white people? Why can't I just call them undercover racists? Why and how does the academy stop me from calling a spade a spade? How does the academy shut the mouth of Blackness? Furthermore, why do people think that because I am a person of color, I know how to deal with racism in writing any better than a white consultant? Why pick the fly to discuss the milk?

Navigating whiteness is a struggle for people of color. In fact, we navigate whiteness—its norms, beliefs, and cultures—every day. However, this navigation is burdensome and leaves one feeling bent—bent to standards created with others in mind, standards that relegate Black bodies to invisible spaces and places. One such place and space is the writing center. As a Black person, quite frankly, I am inherently fearful of white people, and as a Black consultant, I am fearful and feel "unsafe" in writing center spaces, which are historically white. Truthfully, my fear comes in one color: white. When I stand in the Bessey Writing Center at Michigan State, a deep sense of foreboding fills my body. I am surrounded. I feel like a fly in milk.

However, there is one safe zone, if any zone can be safe, where Black consultants often feel safe [in their bodies] in the writing center space—the social area. In this social area, the Black consultants come together to laugh, joke, make a mockery of the astounding whiteness in the center, and just be our normal complex selves, talking about our lives, our loves, Our Struggle. We protect ourselves from the Other because we feel safer, stronger, better, and better equipped to face whatever bigotry we may encounter—we feel less like flies in milk.

WHAT IS IT WE "NEED HELP" WITH? FLIPPING THE DEFICIT MODEL TOWARD MULTILINGUALISM IN ACADEMIA
Laura Gonzales

I was a pretty stubborn eight-year-old when I moved with my family from Santa Cruz, Bolivia, to Orlando, Florida. While I was mainly concerned about the prospect of moving to Disney World, I also knew moving to a new country and learning a new language would pose some challenges. However, being the determined overthinker I was and continue to be, I thought I had it all figured out.

"Papi," I said as my dad pushed my swing and my legs hung loosely, intermittently hitting the ground. "I think I figured out how to get the gringos to like me."

"Oh yeah baby? How?" he questioned.

"Well, I think as long as I stay quiet it'll be okay. I mean, I kind of look like a gringa, so as long as I stay really quiet and blend in nobody will know I'm different."

Mi papi didn't spare my eight-year-old feelings as he replied, "Well baby, I think the gringos will always find a reason to not like you. Your last name is Gonzales, and that's not a gringo last name, so they'll still know you're different from them, even if you don't say anything and even if you look like them."

Needless to say, he was right.

I spent the next few years fervently trying to fit in as I moved between missing my friends and family in Bolivia and simultaneously trying to forget about them so I could start a new life in Florida. From the start, I was flooded with and confused by people trying to "help" me:

I was offered (and I rejected) the opportunity to enroll in a bilingual school that would help me integrate into English-dominant classrooms.

I was given a "special" chair up front in my third-grade classroom because I was the "special" classmate from Bolivia who needed "help" listening to instructions and understanding English.

I was pulled out of my fourth-grade classroom and missed a spelling test each day so I could attend English-as-a-second-language classes because I needed "help" reading in English.

I was taught I was "special" and I needed "help."

I decided I wanted to go to college and major in English when I was in fifth grade.

Two years after moving to Florida, after spending countless nights in front of the mirror mouthing words so I could diminish my accent and pass my ESOL test, I asked my fifth-grade teacher if she would recommend me for advanced language arts in middle school, mostly so I could be with my friends. "I can't recommend you for advanced classes in middle school, Laura," said Miss Weiss. "English is not your first language, right? You're special, and advanced classes are not for special people like you who speak more than one language."

Though I did hold onto that grudge and did go on to major in English and eventually teach writing years later, I'm still trying to figure out what exactly they mean by *special* and what exactly it is multilinguals need *help* with. Doesn't the fact that we speak two (or more) languages inherently mean we know more words than our monolingual peers?

Break

While efforts to support students who speak English as a second (or third or fourth or fifth) language have certainly increased and improved over the last twenty years, the rhetoric surrounding these efforts often upholds deficit models that position multilingual students as less capable or proficient in educational settings. At my current institution, I recently attended a workshop that promised to help writing instructors "deal with" international students in their classrooms. Despite their rich linguistic histories and communicative abilities, these multilingual students are more often than not placed in a "preparation-for-college writing class" before being able to enroll in first-year writing courses, further contributing to a deficit perception of multilinguals by implying these students need additional preparation to help them integrate into first-year writing. In our writing centers, the deficit model for multilinguals is often taken up from the moment we see an appointment for a student whose last name we can't pronounce. We take up and uphold these ideologies because deficit-based discourses are all around us, because we are taught and trained to "help" multilinguals rather than being taught to stop and acknowledge what multilinguals can teach us.

I'm not by any means suggesting efforts intended to facilitate linguistic and cultural transitions in the United States are irrelevant or unnecessary. However, as we continue building infrastructures and programs to support linguistic and cultural diversity in writing centers and other educational spaces, it's important we remain conscious of how the language we use to describe these efforts shapes the experiences (in reality, the very bodies) of students who do indeed bring a rich set of assets to our communities and classrooms.

FOOD CHOICES, LIFE CHOICES
Elizabeth J. Keller

I was a PhD student at MSU, and I was working one of many shifts at the MSU Writing Center. I had been a writing consultant for several years, as both an undergraduate and graduate student, and I thought I had experienced many, if not all, situations while working with student writers. As a PhD student and writing consultant, I worked with many other doctoral students who were writing for their exams, dissertation proposals, and dissertations. Some of the student writers I'd worked with were "regulars," while others made one appointment with me and never returned. Such was the case when I consulted with Kim, an international graduate student from the Middle East working toward her PhD in natural science. She was writing her dissertation and also preparing some of her written job-market materials. I had never worked with Kim before, but I had worked with several international students in my career as a consultant. Before we began our session together, I reviewed what Kim wanted to work on: organization of one section of her dissertation, a few parts of her job-market materials, and grammar and general sense making in her job-market letter. Since I considered myself an experienced writing consultant, and for all intents and purposes I was, I viewed the upcoming consultation as routine and pretty standard for what I was used to.

Our session went off without a hitch, and we made a lot of progress on the different pieces of writing Kim had brought to work on. However, toward the end of our session, with about twenty minutes left, she asked me a question I was not prepared for: "Do I smell funny or different to you? And be honest!" You can imagine my surprise at her question, especially since everything we had discussed in the previous hour and a half revolved around paragraphs, sentences, word choice, and surviving graduate school. I paused for a minute, which felt like an hour, and I looked into her eyes and said, "No, Kim, I don't think you smell funny. Why?" She quickly responded to my question by telling me she had been made acutely aware of how the foods she and her family regularly cooked and ate at home were often not part of the standard American diet. She went on to tell me that since she was applying for jobs in the United States, she didn't want her food choices, which for her represented a large part of her culture and heritage, to prevent her from securing a job. We spent the remaining fifteen minutes of our writing consultation talking about ways she could comfortably and safely navigate the job market without ignoring her culture, the food she loves to eat, and ultimately a significant part of her identity. At the end of our time together, Kim told me I not only helped her with her writing but, more important, I helped her feel comfortable in being who she is (being in her own body) and finding balance in two different worlds. My session with Kim changed me as a writing consultant, teacher, and person. I had studied embodiment at MSU in several different classes, but I hadn't really let myself experience it, feel it, or sit with it. And in Kim, here it was, staring me straight in the eyes. Kim said she was concerned about the smell of her body, but I think what she was really concerned about was fitting in with a new workplace community; ultimately, Kim was worried the smell of her body would be one more excuse not to hire her.

QUEERING THE STRAIGHTENING INSTITUTION
Scotty Seacrist

As I write this, I am hearing a voice in my head. My voice. One no one else can actually hear. It is the voice I hear when I speak, when I think, when I read, and when I dream. But for some reason, it is not the voice everyone else hears when I speak. You know that strange thing that happens when you hear your own voice on a recording and you have no idea you sounded like that? For me, my voice on a recording does not just sound different, it sounds *different*. It sounds odd, strange, faggy, queer. I have come to realize that every time I speak, I hear what I consider to be a normal voice, when in reality everyone else hears an effeminate, lispy, faggoty voice. For a long time, that queer, faggoty voice everyone else heard was not my voice. I would not accept it. It was a defect of my body. My vocal chords could not produce the tone that matched my relatively normal body, so I was constantly outed. One of my good friends used to joke that when I speak, rainbow-colored chiffon and a unicorn spill out of my mouth. At certain points in my life, I would have been mortified by such a joke.

But I have been thinking extensively about the mismatch of the voice in my head, the voice everyone else hears, and my body. Why am I so shocked my audible voice and the voice inside my head do not match? I think my shock comes from what I have been taught. I have been taught, both explicitly and implicitly, to act in a way others will read as the behavior of a cisgender straight man. That is not what people hear when I talk, and there is no getting around that.

Now I do not see my faggy voice as such a bad thing. Rather, I see the rainbow chiffon and unicorns as an extension of my body, and of me. My voice is part of who I am, and it communicates something more than my words can. My voice emits and radiates a queerness. That queerness has shaped my every experience, and all those queered experiences have shaped my body that produces my fagtacular voice.

In my spare time, I am a higher education scholar and administrator. I often feel the straightening college campuses and institutions of higher education inflict on queer bodies. In such spaces, I experience flashbacks of my insecurities, especially when speaking to rooms full of presumably straight folks. But then, I remember that joke about rainbow-colored chiffon and unicorns spilling out of my mouth, and I feel empowered. Just by being me, I queer the straightening institutions that surround me, leaving the most fabulous rainbow-colored chiffon and prancing unicorns in my wake, and this is how I embody my queerness.

TAKE FOUR

All these, now former, consultants first shared their stories with me because of the very real, visceral effects of these encounters on their bodies in the center, as well as on the bodies of their clients and students in the center. Telling these stories here has helped each of us think about how bodies move through time and space, particularly the space and place of the writing center. These embodied experiences urge us to consider both the affordances and costs to/on the body of visiting a writing center, sharing composing practices and projects, and interacting with often unknown entities. As our bodies move into and through the center, we have an opportunity to name our worries and articulate our experiences, but we might also choose to leave our needs unnamed and perhaps even silence our own strengths and literacies because we're not always (ever?) sure whether they fit in this time and space. These stories ask, Does the smell of my body, affected by diet, habits, physical resources, health, affect my acceptability? Affect my writing? Does the tone and timbre of my voice, the accent of my voice, the volume of my voice, the language I voice, determine what you think about me, about my writing? I think what Wonderful, Laura, Beth, and Scotty have shown us is that yes, our bodies matter. Our bodies affect the space of the writing center, just as the space of the center affects our bodies. It's a recursive relationship that can be both helpful and harmful—sometimes simultaneously.

These stories and many more shared with me over the years—stories about butch bodies, femme bodies, disabled bodies, autistic bodies, Brown bodies, immigrant bodies, Native bodies, accented bodies, tattooed bodies, violent and violated bodies, sexually harassed and harassing bodies—have been circling in my mind for some time, just as the many stories shared in this collection should be circling in yours. These shared stories, as well as the dozens that have gone unvoiced, have led me to ask some really big questions I would put out to writing centers across the globe.

What would it mean for the work and membership of our writing center community if we were fully aware of the bodies that occupy the spaces of our centers? What does it mean that we tutor human to human, body to body, whether in person or online? What could it mean for our programs if we truly thought about the bodies who are writing/talking/sharing in our sessions: fat bodies, queer bodies, professional bodies, casual bodies, variously abled bodies, gendered bodies, old bodies, young bodies, minority bodies, privileged bodies, emotional bodies, accented bodies, bodies dressed and styled to present particular rhetorical messages? Bodies that carry cultural meanings, past experiences, trauma, and other social and ideological commitments. Bodies that carry lived stories that can affect not only what we write but how we write, how we think, how we organize and make sense of information, how we view or talk about writing, how we view school and schooling in general, how we interact with each other and how we "fit" into physical spaces. What would/does this awareness call us/challenge us to do in our centers, on our campuses, around our communities, through our fields?

TAKE 5

At this point, I've now hosted a half dozen or more different roundtable discussions with a variety of colleagues utilizing some form of these questions. These experiences have all been very different and have felt different in my body, some leaving me excited about the possibilities for change in the center—changes in tutor recruitment and tutor training, changes in the operations of our centers, changes in the stories we tell about our center. Other discussions have left me frustrated with the difficulty of such ideological shifts (see Waite in this collection for more about the im/possibilities of institutional change). All have left me thinking about what comes next and remembering that bodies come in all shapes, sizes, and hues and that they all carry their own individual and collective stories.

Scene 1: At an East Central Writing Centers Association conference roundtable session, a blond-haired, blue-eyed young man in blue suit and tie sprawls across the chair in the front row: "We bring our bodies to the center. So what?"

White-boy privilege, taking up literal space. "Do you mind if I use you as an example?" He sits up a little straighter and answers a bit nervously, "Okay."

I ask the others, "What do his bodily presentations say? What do his blond hair and blue eyes make us think? What does his blue suit tell you? What does the challenge in his voice say? What is speaking here besides his voice?"

A lively conversation ensues.

Scene 2: At another roundtable, participants were given generic gingerbread persons and markers and asked to partner up and write descriptions of their partners simply by looking at them. What did people see? What did they write? One participant said she tried to stick to clothing because it seemed innocent enough until she started doing it and realized how she judged T-shirts versus ties and holey jeans versus dress pants. Another got caught up on hair, natural or not, and what this choice says about a person; another was concerned with how much cleavage is allowed in the professional realm and how much cleavage pushes it over the edge? There were observations about hair color and style, about makeup or not, about height and weight, about facial hair and glasses, about smiles and frowns. About how we notice and judge so many of these physical characteristics. How we might measure or judge a writer before we ever encounter their writing. We then asked these partners to talk to each other. What was missing from this description because it was based on sight alone or individual, first-time encounters with others' bodies? We then heard stories of bad days, not enough sleep the night before, a need for coffee or lunch. We also heard about distrust of institutions, including the WC, and distrust of peers who are really experts or peers who don't know one's field or research. We heard about misreadings of sexuality and gender, as well as race, age, and ability. We heard about issues of class that aren't apparent in appearance but that quickly come through in the writing.

Scene 3: I come home from one of these conferences to hear from a colleague that a community college near him was on lockdown after the shooting of an employee, the print-shop manager. News reports identified a suspect, a former student worker who didn't graduate. What these mainstream news reports didn't reveal was the open gayness of the victim or the white-supremacist ties of the suspected killer. My colleague says to me, "It's sad, it's scary, and it hits close to home." And I wonder how it's affecting the work of several openly gay consultants in the writing center at his institution. Or perhaps the undecided queer student who needs help with her writing as she struggles through life decisions and political stances. How can we remember these incidents, these bodies, in our own writing center work?

NEXT STEPS

Earlier I told a story of wanting and needing more in my center, in all centers. My journey has illuminated a few steps for me, for us, to enact change in the stories of our centers. These steps are presented in an order that belies the need for all of them to be happening simultaneously and for realizing one feeds the other in an ongoing, recursive nature that adds layers to the stories we tell and enact. Step 1: we must center bodies—our bodies, our consultants' bodies, our clients' bodies—and how these bodies tell or carry stories in our sessions, in our workshops, in our research. I ask us to think about what bodies are present and what bodies are missing? What bodies do potential clients see when they walk past our centers or read our PR materials, when they check out our websites or social media platforms? What messages are we presenting about who is welcome, and in what ways, in our centers? This might include discussions of dress, how we take up space, how/where/when we talk (or not), what we talk about. It also includes consideration of how we present the writing center to others. In our PR materials, for example, especially things like bookmarks given out at intro-to-the-WC workshops, it is important to me that the language talks about what we, consultants and clients, can do together, not just what consultants will do for clients; I want a story of bodies working together, not remediation, not service.

Centering bodies also includes thoughtful consideration of our clients as humans with bodies and lives outside our center. How often do we judge them, even subconsciously, by their appearance? What conclusions about their bodies and abilities do we draw when we see their names on our scheduling forms? How are we affected by the strong smell of cologne or cigarette smoke or body odor? Can we see signs of stress or fatigue on/in their bodies? What do we do with someone's tendency to cry or another's quiet demeanor that makes it hard to relate?

A client came to visit me. I had been "warned" by the satellite coordinator that this would happen because of an incident the night before. The coordinator saw it as a complete misunderstanding but also acknowledged the client was genuinely upset and needed to vent. This client was sure the other consultants, including the graduate coordinator, those not working with her directly, were laughing at her. In my conversation with this client, I discovered she was quite lonely since moving to the United States from Iran. She had experienced some harassment and mockery on campus and about town because she chose to wear her hijab. And she felt all alone. Her body was carrying the weight of a war not of her making; the weight of a prejudice founded in stereotypes and media hype; the weight of past experiences with small-minded individuals who were actually making fun of her. She needed a listening ear and some understanding, and she needed this before she could concentrate on her paper for her first-year writing course.

But how do we prepare ourselves and our staff members to center the body? We must consider our training programs and ongoing professional development. We must have difficult conversations on a regular basis to help us be aware of our own bodies, as well as those of our clients. If we don't acknowledge what we are bringing into the center on our bodies, how can we be attuned to what our clients are bringing with them? We must check in with each other, continually, and hold each other accountable when we forget or don't practice what we preach. We must talk about race, and gender, and sexuality, and age, and ability, and class, and ethnicity, and experience. We must talk about the social constructedness of writing and the expectations placed on students through genre, class assignments, instructor comments, peers both on campus and off, and perhaps even parents or significant others or kids. Likewise, we must think about the limits placed on our bodies by what's going on in the world around us and how news flashes make us feel or respond.

I direct a large center at Michigan State University. It's no secret our school went through massive trauma as the Larry Nasser case unfolded in front of us on the national news and in the halls of our buildings on campus. We could walk across campus and see the teal bows wrapped around trees by mourning families, bows meant to remind us of the bodies sexually assaulted and abused by this one man who was left unchecked and in charge. This wound opened up numerous other wounds of sexual assault and harassment, gendered and raced bullying that had not been officially addressed by the university. Likewise, this constant bombardment of abuse stories triggered numerous past memories and experiences for people across campus, many of whom worked in our centers and sought (writing) help in our centers. It became imperative that every consultant know/have at hand the list of resources available on our campus to help students, to help each other, move through these struggles and take care of their mental and physical bodies. It also meant taking a stance that allowed our consultants to miss work and go to campus rallies; it meant helping folks make protest signs, even supplying the materials for these actions.

Step 2: We must think about space. What are the spaces we've provided for the bodies of our clients and consultants? Is the space of our writing center comfortable for those who use it? Is it conducive to the types of work (and play) that happen in the center? Does it look like and feel like a space bodies want to spend time in? Centers often don't have a say in where they're located on campus, but when we do or can, we must advocate for spaces consultants and clients can easily access and inhabit.

For me this has meant thinking about the setup of the reception desk in regards to the front door and the pathway through to the communal areas for sessions and meetings. Are the pathways wide enough for bodies with different modes of ambulation—canes, crutches, wheelchairs, and so forth? It has also meant thinking about the furniture in our center. I learned, for example, through our Resource Center for Persons with Disabilities (RCPD), that many persons on our campus who are neuroatypical need chairs that don't roll for reasons of both balance and distraction. When talking about this change in our center, I also learned from consultants that some of them desired chairs without arms so their bodies didn't feel corralled or pinned in. We continued to work with RCPD in order to get an adjustable-height desk to host one of our communal computers and software on one of our communal computers for the visually impaired. We saved up and bought new varied chairs. We're still struggling with room temperature and communal versus private spaces, often interpreted as loud versus quiet spaces.

A few years ago we had a consultant who struggled with extreme ADHD, among other neuroatypical diagnoses. His frankness about what he needed and what would help his body succeed in our writing center space led to what is now a hallmark of our center: a wide range of toys and manipulatives. We soon discovered numerous students, faculty, and staff enjoyed manipulating toys, creating with pipe cleaners, playing with the Play-Doh during sessions/committee meetings/classes. In fact, we've seen this phenomenon grow in offices across campus as folks have come to the center and taken this idea back with them. We also discovered through this consultant the importance of being able to walk and talk during a session, or plop down on the floor to hash out an assignment. He helped us expand what we saw as space for consultations, as well as furniture types and arrangements in our official space. It is impossible to be all things to all people, but how do we create space for those who most need us?

In a different effort to make bodies feel welcome in our space, we've always had water, coffee and tea, but a recent request had me thinking about the 40 percent of the client base who are nonnative speakers of English and mostly of Asian descent on our campus—either Chinese or Korean—and who have asked for different kinds/brands of tea. When providing snacks and food for client open houses and staff training, we've tried to move towards healthier options: more salad with our pizza, fruit with our bagels, granola bars with our chips. When we have fruit next to the candy bowl, we see fruit and candy go at equal rates. Unfortunately our budget hasn't yet allowed us to provide healthy fruit on a weekly basis. We keep the candy bowl because both clients and consultants have told us that sometimes this is all they get a chance to eat during the day (prompting workshops on self-care, including nutrition and time management, but also prompting handouts and training about resources on campus, including the student food bank).

Step 3: As mentioned previously, this paper began a few years ago as the keynote for the Northeastern Writing Centers Association Conference. Through Q&A, conference sessions, and a closing conversation about the theme of embodiment in the writing center, we came to the conclusion that is now step 3. As writing center professionals, whether administrators, consultants, faculty, staff, or students, we must be activists fighting for systemic change.

While acknowledging bodies in the center is the start, it can't be the end. We must actively work to change oppression and the systemic problems of racism, (hetero)sexism, classism, ableism, and so forth. And we must actively fight against the toll this takes on people's bodies (and consequently their writing).

In our center we've been thinking about language usage for several years and working incrementally to effect change on our campus. One of the starting points was teaching consultants about language theories and practices such as students' rights to their own language, contrastive rhetoric, code meshing, translanguaging, and others. We know from our own consultants and clients that having language denied is having our bodies denied (see Faison and Gonzales earlier in this chapter). Likewise, I've learned from other consultants and clients that having pronouns and chosen names denied is having identity denied, so we talk about this in training as well. Then, to facilitate correct naming, we changed our intake forms, inviting clients to identify their chosen pronouns and names. We also had consultants move towards making these identifications for themselves as well so we weren't asking those who don't fall into some hetero-cisgender-sexuality norm to "out" themselves, creating the space for them to opt in.

Another entry point for change is through faculty development and training. In our annual faculty workshop focused on teaching (with) writing, we address many of these same theories and practices for working with multilingual writers, for identifying students in the ways they present themselves, and for having open, neutral language in our assignments. But this just wasn't/isn't enough. Several students began working on something more, what is now known as the Writing Center Language Statement Policy. This policy went through several discussions, drafts, and approvals, including our Center Advisory Committee, and we are now in the process of enlisting support from programs and departments across campus as we roll it out. This statement makes clear our commitments to help students (and faculty and staff) move towards more inclusive language practices and to create spaces for the members of our community(ies) to use their most authentic voices (and bodies, I argue). As the statement says, "We respect writers' agency to express themselves in ways most comfortable to them, including their choice of Englishes, languages, pronouns, stories, and perspectives."

I see this language statement as the start of what will be an ongoing activist movement designed to create room for all the bodies who (may) enter our writing center spaces and places. I know there will be pushback from some areas of the university and maybe even from some students themselves, especially those colonized to fall in line with the status quo, but we will continue to educate and support students no matter their personal choices. And we will continue to look for other areas of engagement as we fight for systemic change through our center, on our campus, in our world(s).

I return to Thomas King (2008) with this paraphrase: You have heard our stories now. Do with them what you will. But don't say in the years to come that you would have lived your life differently if only you had heard these stories.

NOTES

1. This essay began as a keynote talk for a NEWCA conference, "Embodiment in the Writing Center." I am extremely grateful to the officers of NEWCA who invited me and to those in attendance who presented thought-provoking sessions and asked smart questions that helped push my thinking.
2. Actually, over the years I've moved from a focus on safe spaces, to safe-enough spaces, to brave/r spaces. I would highly recommend the special issue of *Peer Review* (2017, vol. 1, issue 2), "Writing Centers as Brave/r Spaces" (http://thepeerreview-iwca.org/issues/braver-spaces/).

REFERENCES

Denny, Harry. 2010. *Facing the Center: Toward an Identity Politics of One-to-One Mentoring.* Logan: Utah State University Press.

Grimm, Nancy. 1999. *Good Intentions: Writing Center Work for Postmodern Times.* Portsmouth, NH: Heinemann.

Grutsch McKinney, Jackie. 2013. *Peripheral Visions for Writing Centers.* Logan: Utah State University Press.

King, Thomas. 2008. *The Truth about Stories: A Native Narrative.* Minneapolis: University of Minnesota Press.

Perryman-Clark, Staci, David E. Kirkland, and Austin Jackson, eds. 2014. *Students' Right to Their Own Language: A Critical Sourcebook.* Boston: Bedford/St. Martin's.

Young, Vershawn A. 2012. "Should Writers Use They Own English?" In *Writing Centers and the New Racism,* edited by Karen Rowan and Laura Greenfield, 61–74. Logan: Utah State University Press.

4.1
AS TIME MOVES FORWARD

Dena Arendall

Fall 2017. The world was spinning, perfectly aligned on its axis. It was my last semester of coursework, and I had finally and officially settled on a topic for my dissertation. I began teaching first-year composition that semester as well, and I felt alive in the classroom, felt right at home. My father was so proud I was following in his footsteps. He had been in academia for thirty-five years. We spoke often that semester, and his pride beamed from the other end of the phone and during our weekly lunches. He gave me tips, motivated me, and told me how he bragged to anyone who would listen about his daughter, the PhD student. I called him, that first week of September, to arrange our weekly get-together, but he didn't answer. He called back, though, and left me a message: "Hey sweetie, it's your dad. My schedule is tied up for the foreseeable future. Let's not plan anything right now. Love you. We'll talk later." His voice was crackling; something was not right. On the evening of September 11, we spoke, and he was not feeling well, had been suffering from anxiety attacks. My father was the most confident, self-assured person I have ever known, so this made no sense. "But life," he said, "goes on."

He was struggling, but he assured me he was "smart enough to know it will get better, smart enough to know that it will change." I remember being exhausted that night but felt reassured by his words of positivity.

"Call me immediately!" The text came from my stepmother at 5 p.m. two days later.

Fall 2017. The world stopped spinning. I was sitting in class that Wednesday afternoon discussing the differences between top-down and bottom-up language policies of different countries. While I was engrossed in note-taking, my father was making notes as well: passwords, codes, websites, bank information. He was meticulous to the core. As I was walked to my car from class that afternoon, at 4:05 p.m., my father, the most optimistic man I had ever known, chose to end his own life.

https://doi.org/10.7330/9781646422340.c004.1

Move forward with a purpose. These are the words we found written on the first page of his planner. This was his mantra, his point of wisdom he saw every day.

Suicide. I hate that word. It hurts in my gut to write it. It does not bring shame; I am no less proud of my father than I was before. Instead, it brings sadness and fury. Here was a man who had his retirement ahead of him and hundreds of accomplishments behind him reduced to a single moment in time, a single point of a gun. He tried to get help in his last days, begged for it even. He was trying to move forward, but he was turned away, told to "sleep it off," told to "come back tomorrow."

I somehow managed to survive that semester. I finished teaching, graded papers, and submitted end-of-semester paperwork. I completed presentations in classes and wrote final abstracts, proposals, and papers. I received an incomplete in one class, but I pulled it all together over the winter break and walked away maintaining my GPA. That semester, I later realized, what I had dealt with was stress and shock, but not necessarily grief. Life around me has gone on, but sometimes, I feel I am standing still and stuck in the afternoon of September 13, 2017.

Comprehensive exams. They were scheduled to begin in January 2018, but they did not happen. My reading list seemed immensely long, though it really was not, and each reading took hours to accomplish. After completing an entire article, I had zero comprehension of any words on the paper. I began to recognize a "pre-Dad brain" and a "post-Dad brain," terms I coined to better explain this phenomenon to myself. Retention and recall did not come as easily to me as they once did, and any moments of quiet immediately sent me to thoughts of my father. The first half of the semester raced by, with me stuck in the same dark place. No matter how hard I tried, I could not shake the feelings, the thoughts, the tears. In March, my committee director finally convinced me that I was ready, that I should take the first exam. In a couple of weeks, I found out I had passed and immediately picked up the phone to call my father. He was not going to answer. This realization hit me like a ton of bricks, like I was just finding out for the first time. This happened after Test 2 and after Test 3. It continues to happen. Without fail, each time I reach a goal or gain another step, I pick up the phone to text or call. And without fail, the ton of bricks hits again, and my mind travels a few steps backward.

Move forward with a purpose. The words he left with me. Empowering, yes, but how do I move forward when every gain takes my heart, soul, and mind backward?

Prospectus. It took eight months to write this document. Eight months. My "post-Dad brain" did not cooperate in the least. For every sentence I wrote, there were three or four drifts of the brain back to that day. September 13, 2017. Living after someone you love has committed suicide is difficult and painful, almost impossible on some days. There are constant questions:

> "Why didn't I realize he was having such a difficult time?"
> "What were his last thoughts?"
> "How painful it must have been for him to see this as his only way out."

These thoughts never leave my mind. I am brought to tears nearly every day. There is always something I want to tell him, especially about school, about accomplishments, about goals, and about dreams in academia. There are always tips I need for the classroom, for motivation, or for statistical analysis. There is always a song, a reminder, a person, or an event that triggers my mind.

I finally submitted a finalized and edited prospectus in January 2019. I was not pleased with the content in the least, but it was submitted. I am not happy with any of my work anymore and feel like my motivation is gone. Someone said to me, "But you aren't doing this for him, you're doing it for you." True. But my intrinsic motivation left that day. A piece of my soul left with him that day. It is unbearably difficult to explain. In every assignment I complete, every paper I write, something is always missing. My confidence is inexplicably nonexistent. My prospectus was approved; I passed my oral exams and successfully defended my prospectus in March 2019. Immediately, I picked up the phone to call Dad. He would not be on the other end of the line.

Move forward with a purpose. These five words. Time listens. I try, but my brain does not always cooperate.

Dissertation. Twenty months later. I recently submitted a draft of my methodology chapter. I was not pleased with it. I wonder, Will there *ever* come a time when I will be satisfied with my work? The methods section I was able to focus on at least. Just a step-by-step process of how I will collect my data and answer my research questions—that, at least, I know. I am writing my chapters out of order. I tried to write my introduction, tried to write my literature review. I simply could not focus; too many unknowns, too many times my brain would go blank. And a blank thought leads me back to September 13, 2017. I know I will finish. I have come so far, and it is too late to turn back now; there are too many people I will let down. I will not be pleased with the finished product. Still, I know I will finish. Eventually. When I do, will I still instinctively pick up the phone to call Dad? Most likely. But I hope that, by then, I will have become better at moving forward with a purpose.

4.2

AN ACADEMIC CAREER TAKES FLIGHT, OR THE FIRST YEAR ON THE TENURE TRACK, AS SEEN FROM ABOVE

Jasmine Lee

A chime sounds over the intercom, followed by a brief message: "We have now reached ten thousand feet, and the captain has turned off the seatbelt sign. You may use your larger portable devices at this time so long as they remain in airplane mode. In a few moments, your flight crew will come through the cabin to serve complimentary juice, soft drinks, and water . . ."

I look at the tiny, fold-down tray in front of me. Can I fit my laptop on it? Would there be enough room for me to type? Sometime after takeoff, the passenger in front of me leans his seat back as far as it will go, and functional space in this economy seat is already hard to come by. I've been awake for four and a half hours, just enough time to finish packing, get ready, arrive at the airport, move through security, and wait to board. I'm exhausted. I stayed up late as it was to prep a new lesson, knowing I wouldn't have the energy to do much more than make copies and respond to emails in the two-hour gap between when I land and when I teach. I glance out at the cloud cover and suddenly remember I didn't start the dishwasher before I left. I'm mildly annoyed with myself. I run through a mental checklist of other things I may have forgotten: Did I feed the cat? Did I lock the door? Did I put my toothbrush in my bag this morning? I resign myself to the fact that there is nothing I can do about any of that from up here and try to focus on my writing. Even if I can't write, I tell myself, thinking about the project counts. But before long, the pressure at altitude beckons me toward sleep. The flight is only fifty minutes long, and we're nearly halfway through. I ask for a black coffee, a weak substitute for a nap, and let my mind wander. Shortly before we land, I skim my notes for the readings we'll cover today in class. On the ground, I gather my suitcase and my carry-on and hope the

https://doi.org/10.7330/9781646422340.c004.2

Park and Fly shuttle will be at the curb. If I can beat the morning traffic, I might get a parking spot.

This scenario was not what I had in mind when I devised this commute. About a year before, I applied for many dozens of jobs and flew back and forth across the country for interviews, becoming surer and surer as the months passed that I would have to do it again the following job cycle. My partner, fresh out of a computer science program, was also looking for work, with what seemed like much better odds. Near the end of the academic-job season, as my prospects thinned, he landed a position that could support both of us financially for the year. I focused my search on more temporary gigs near his new employer. We signed a below-market lease we couldn't pass up on a small place in an overpriced San Francisco Bay Area city and put all our savings into the down payment, first month's rent, and move. We began settling down. Four weeks later, through a door I had thought closed months before, I received an offer for a tenure-line faculty position at a university I had dreamed of working at. I signed on the dotted line, and I began scheduling flights.

The productivity fantasies I entertained before I began traveling went something like this: After a personally fulfilling and restful weekend at home with my partner and cat, I would spend Monday mornings finalizing my lesson plans, taking care of grading and emails, laying out my research goals for the week, doing laundry, packing, and finding time for a brief yoga practice somewhere between tasks. I would spend the short plane ride on Tuesday mornings plugging away on a book project. I would teach and hold office hours Tuesdays and Thursdays. Wednesdays I would hole up in my office and devote the day entirely to research. On Fridays, I would catch my flight back (writing in the air, of course), and once home, I'd take care of any loose ends before putting my work away for the weekend.

I felt confident that, in that ideal version of my life, I would make substantial progress on my book. I was optimistic, especially because the book will someday be, rather appropriately, about movement. More specifically, it will be about learning and openness; displacement and place making and presence; transitions and circulation and flow. Tentatively titled *Moving Writing*, the book will attempt to capture the experience of this early-career transition and put it into conversation with my literal travel to and from work. It will recount my experiences getting unstuck from my attachments to mastery and give me space to theorize the epistemological, ethical, and pedagogical potential of letting go. Informed by affect theory, the book will consider and enact alternative modes of research and teaching, ones that engage in critical and political work through opening up, showing up, and being present. In the book, I will think about what writing does—for people, for communities—and how we might teach writing in a way that honors its energy, intensity, and potentiality more fully. The book will be a record of my seeking out and imagining how to do this work I have chosen in ways that feel ethical and sustainable and sustaining for myself and my students.

By the end of my first actual year on the tenure track, though, I will have traveled 31,418 miles by plane and written a measly number of words toward the book. I will have learned academic jobs make weird demands on bodies, families, calendars, and budgets. While I will be immensely thankful each day for the security of this job and for the opportunity to do work I love and find meaningful, I will be tired and stretched thin and worn down. At some point in the year, I will learn that the humidity in airplanes is lower than 20 percent and that frequent flying can reawaken childhood eczema and cause weeks of itchy, miserable, and sleepless nights as one tries to get the flare-up under control. As I try to play cognitively with the concept of movement, I will learn the lived consequences of motion and all of the balancing, stretching, and reorienting that goes along with it. I will lose a lot of potential writing time and energy to mundane, practical life concerns I hadn't factored into my fictional schedule. I will realize, for example, how complicated it is to dress myself for travel. (What is the weather like near work? How many teaching days are there this trip? Do I have any major meetings or presentations? Will my gym shoes fit in this bag?) I will figure out it is quite difficult to feed myself affordable and healthy fuel while always on the go. (If my flight gets in at 10 a.m., and I teach at 1 p.m., will I have time to grab lunch? How much is a cup of coffee at the airport again? Will a frozen meal stay frozen between now and the time I get to the office? Has the produce I bought last week gone bad by now? Will my leftovers from Sunday be any good by Friday night?) I will stop unpacking between trips and get accustomed to living out of suitcase. I will crash hard in the middle of a travel day, curling up in my office chair for a brief rest, and then not sleep at all later that night. I will be exposed to way too many germs. I will try in vain to adjust to bouncing regularly between two quite different climates. I will try not to show any of these struggles to my students or my new colleagues, lest they think I'm not fitting in or am not committed to rooting myself in the department.

The year will not have been a complete loss. Throughout it, I will have met many wonderful students and built partnerships with fabulous colleagues. I will have learned and grown and practiced becoming the kind of person, scholar, and teacher who can observe, go with the flow, and move. In other words, I will have started becoming the kind of person who can write the book I dream of writing. Instead of composing, though, I will have spent most of the year trying to stay composed: in my office, in the guest room of a family member's house, at home on weekends, in airports while waiting out delays, on shuttles, in my car. When it's over, I will spend the first few weeks of summer trying to feel normal again and the next few trying not to be too hard on myself about the lack of progress I seem to be making. I will try not to think about starting the travel circuit all over again in a few months. I will hold out hope for the book. And I will hope, too, that when it eventually comes out, however far off in the future that may be, you will consider reading it; it will have been on quite a journey making its way to rest on your shelf.

Resilience

5

GRADUATE STUDENT BODIES ON THE PERIPHERY

Kelsie Walker, Morgan Gross, Paula Weinman, Hayat Bedaiwi, and Alyssa McGrath

Though it is often played for laughs (sometimes by graduate students themselves), graduate student life is marked by habitual scarcity. Whether it's about their groceries, their mental health, their physical well-being, or professional support, graduate students are expected to make do, or, failing that, to do without. It is assumed such conditions are, if not ideal, at least temporary. Yet such experiences, absorbed and unspoken, inscribe themselves upon the graduate student body: as anxiety, depression, hunger, exhaustion, fear, or even illness, all of which are exacerbated by financial instability and professional precarity. Whether or not graduate students choose to speak about these conditions, their bodies carry memories and markers of exploitative labor conditions, professional "in-betweenness," and injustice related to race, ethnicity, gender, dis/ability, age, and so on when they take on the role of teacher, tutor, or administrator. And since those in power consider graduate school hardships to be a "rite of passage," the hardships are subsequently silenced and normalized. As many of the chapters in this collection demonstrate, the work we produce as academics often exhausts and strains our bodies in ways that cannot necessarily be measured but will always be felt. Research, travel, teaching, and service work form but the surface of the emotional, physical, and mental labor academics do, but such things—inscribed as they are upon our bodies, not our CVs—will not always be recognized. When they are raised as concerns, invisible or unrecognized reasons for our exhaustion are—through denial or lack of concern—treated as expected, peripheral, or immaterial. And as Triauna Carey illustrates in a chapter of this collection, for Black scholars, Indigenous scholars, and other scholars of color, this unrecognized labor can take the form of processing, naming, and confronting the structural racism of academic spaces, expectations, and biases. The invisibility of this labor acquits institutions and programs of their complicity in creating and maintaining an oppressive system that relegates graduate students' status to the periphery, makes inaccurate assumptions about their bodies and needs, and exploits and undercompensates them.

Current research on graduate student experiences focuses primarily on aspects of the graduate students' professionalization and academic life, such as education and training, scholarly and teacher preparation, and navigating graduate school (Anson and Rutz 1999; Blair 2014; Long, Holberg, and Taylor 1996; Restaino 2012; Skinnell, Holiday, and Vassett 2015). Moreover, several scholars have shared stories, strategies, and approaches aligned with feminist and antiracist teaching, tutoring, and administration (Freedman and Holmes 2003; Greenfield and Rowan 2011; Grimm 1999; Inoue 2015; Kopelson 2003; Ratcliffe and Rickly 2010; Royster 1996; Villaneuva 2006). While this research is important and necessary, few publications fully account for the lived, material experiences of graduate students. Though some scholars have written at the convergence of these topics—graduate students' embodied experiences (Craig and Perryman-Clark 2011; IWCA 2001; Macrorie 1964; Mountford 2002; Taylor and Holberg 1999; Willard-Traub 2002), the very conditions of being a graduate student contribute to the drought of *firsthand* published accounts, thus decentering those experiences.

Speaking out about being a graduate student can be risky, especially if the account will be published prior to leaving one's institution or before transitioning to further study or employment at another institution. Perhaps for many, the emotional energy it takes to testify would be better spent on self-care, different research projects, or paid work.[1] As the recent controversies surrounding the WPA listserv illustrate—and the subsequent formation of the nextGEN listserv underscores—graduate students (as well as adjuncts and contingent faculty) do not have enough "safe space[s] . . . to contribute . . . in our field" (Matudela 2018). Those graduate students who do speak out are often met with skepticism, silence, or alienation, with their lack of professional experience or academic credentials as justification—despite the fact that graduate students are frequently expected to function as practicing professionals in teaching, research, and administration while earning degrees.

Aware of the risks, we came together to share our intersectional, embodied experiences as graduate student women. Our collective criticisms address deeply rooted institutional and programmatic oppression, which was exacerbated by the Trump administration's rhetoric and policies. Each author engages in autoethnographic storytelling, reflecting on the ways her body has been invisible, excluded, and exploited as she's occupied various roles in the temporary position of graduate student/

graduate assistant. If embodiment is, at least in part, a way of knowing through the body, each piece in this article is an attempt to *name* what it is we know as specifically as possible. In enumerating and examining the particularities of our institutional embodiment—the ways our bodies are read, pressured, dismissed, or exploited in the day-to-day work of the academy—we hope to encourage people in positions of authority, as well as those who will one day have authority, to advocate for progressive changes to benefit graduate students, who, to borrow from nextGEN, "are the future of our field" (Matudela 2018).

AUTOETHNOGRAPHIC METHODOLOGY

According to A. Suresh Canagarajah (2012) in his chapter in *Writing Studies Research in Practice*, autoethnography "enables marginalized communities to publish their own culture and experiences in their own voices, resisting the knowledge constructed about them" (115). Fundamentally, autoethnography is research from "the point of view of the self," usually relying heavily on the narrative, demonstrating how "culture shapes and is shaped by the personal" (113). In sharing our own "insider perspective" about a few of the most telling of our personal experiences as graduate student women and junior faculty administrators, we intend to disrupt more typical and oppressive perceptions of graduate students (114). Like other scholars who argue for and with an autoethnographic methodology (Damron and Brooks 2017; Parke 2018; Young 2007), we are socially motivated and action oriented.

The authors of this article met several times as a whole group and in pairs to discuss our embodied experiences. Writing together prompted us to consider our work more thoughtfully and critically than we might have done individually. Canagarajah (2012) concedes that one of the limitations of autoethnography is its lack of generalizability (123). We agree: our experiences are not the experiences of all other graduate students, on whose behalf we could not possibly speak. However, by working together to decide which of our stories to share and telling them from the perspectives of five graduate students with different experiences, we believe we've provided enough coverage and depth about the phenomenon of being a graduate student for our study to have value.

HAYAT

The English composition class I taught in spring 2018 was about humor and its role in breaking or reinforcing stereotypes. I wanted to teach students that everyone has a sense of humor (because some incorrectly assume Arabs do not laugh) and discover with them what humor looks like when it is used as a social justice tool. A month in, the students showed signs of resistance to the diversity in course material. The comedians they wrote about were mostly white, like Bo Burnham or the cast of *Friends*. Because my examples were nonwhite or non-English-speaking comedians, I found the students disregarded them or disliked the content. In mini-assignments, for example, they told me it was difficult to understand them or their kind of humor. Still determined, I continued to show the students comedians from different minority groups, such as Native Americans, African Americans, and even Saudis. When I referenced Arabic comedy, some students seemed to take this as an invitation to question me about my culture, where I come from, and why I wear the hijab. I saw their questions as a chance for me to get to know them and allow them to know me. Some of them told me the class was their first time seeing a real Muslim. I always feel self-conscious about my body in the academy, being the only hijabi in the writing center and the only one who teaches first-year writing composition, and this fact has greatly informed and impacted my bodily experience in the classroom.

Despite their curiosity, it seemed evident to me that the way I looked also gave students a reason to resist me as their instructor. The way I looked affected the way students received material in class. They asked me repeatedly to read the assignment sheet again. One student even asked another student, "What did she just say?," calling attention to my accent. Even when I went around in class to monitor activities, I saw students who moved out of the way, giving me much more space than needed for a teacher's body. I kept thinking to myself, Is it respect they want to show or are they afraid of me because I am different, because I represent the Arab/Muslim they have heard a lot of negative things about in the news? My student surveys at the end of the year were no different than the daily interactions in my classroom. They either highlighted how kind and understanding I was, how my assignments were easy, or how *foreign I am*. One student commented that I "needed to broaden my horizon" because I was talking a lot about the Arab world!

As a Muslim woman from Saudi Arabia, I am dedicated to wearing the hijab and dressing modestly. This commitment made me afraid the students would judge me and look at me as a *foreigner*. Furthermore, I never feel safe praying in public, especially in a time when discrimination against Muslims has escalated because of the actions and words of a past US president. I wait until I get home to pray, and I spend most of the day feeling guilty I did not pray on time because I was hiding the fact that I pray five times a day. The fear of being watched, stared at, and examined all the time by passersby or by the students themselves in class is only a small part of the daily burdens Muslim GAs must live with. Faculty often expressed sympathy for my experience, but I needed more support. It was great to hear "we stand with you," but never enough. It did not alter the reality that I was embarrassed or felt sad sometimes because of certain classroom interactions.

I suggest that administrators in the institution can better support international/Muslim GAs, as well as instructors who prioritize cultural studies agendas in their composition classrooms, by encouraging them to utilize their own cultural knowledge. I utilized cultural knowledge as a way to learn with and from difference in the classroom and in the institution I taught in. My intention for making cultural diversity in comedy a feature of my composition course was to create opportunities for the students and me to learn about each other's cultures and step out of our comfort zones. Like Simone Alexander (2003) in "Walking on Thin Ice," my difference is visible to students, and I choose not to hide from that truth. Writing programs can support international GAs and their bodies by showcasing their contributions and providing opportunities in which they can highlight their experiences as international bodies.

International GAs, too, have something valuable to teach students and other writing professionals.

ALYSSA

I sat across from the department chair (a man I had never met) to discuss possible options for me to meet my assistantship requirements the following semester. I had dreaded this meeting all weekend, as the email from the chair was vague and I was almost certain I would be asked to take a leave of absence due to my "looming medical condition," as he called it. Fortunately, the department administration offered their support and worked with me to find a solution; however, I never felt secure in my position as a graduate student, instructor, and administrator while pregnant. Instead, I saw myself as a complication to my advisors' workload as they scrambled to try to find a way for me to keep my assistantship and administrative position within the writing program.

Often students who begin graduate school with families are deemed incredible multitaskers with impressive time-management skills. But there seems to exist an unspoken assumption that graduate students will put on hold their desires to start or expand their family unit while working towards their degree. Nothing reinforces this assumption more than many institutions' lack of policies regarding students' pregnancies. My own institution's graduate school had no policy to protect my teaching assistantship when I went into labor. In fact, the department could have argued that I could not meet assistantship requirements and rescinded my funding. I was fortunate enough to have advisors and faculty who supported my decision to start a family and helped make arrangements to have my classes covered temporarily. However, my ability to remain a part of the program was entirely at the administrators' discretion.

Not only was my assistantship left vulnerable by my pregnancy, but my health and physical well-being were unprotected and exposed due to a lack of health insurance. As Kelsie points out in her section of this chapter, financial hardship is normalized by the academy. This financial insecurity extends well beyond being unable to afford costly dinners. My husband's job did not offer health insurance, we made too much for state assistance, and we could not afford the premium for private insurance. Medical expenses throughout a pregnancy add up quickly and, without insurance, I would have been forced to choose between accumulating a significant amount of debt or foregoing routine check-ups, which would leave my body and my child's development unprotected. Left with no real choice but to take on a full-time job outside the academy that offered benefits, I taught as part of my assistantship, worked an administrative position in the writing program, studied for comprehensive exams, and worked full time in retail. My body felt exhausted from the literal movement it endured running from location to location to fulfill my duties at work, at school, and at home. My growing stomach was a visual reminder of the vulnerable position I was in. I simultaneously felt joy and guilt about my pregnancy when I stepped into my roles at the university. Thus, the labor conditions for graduate students, even those working in administrative positions, and the lack of health-insurance coverage renders some of us unprotected in ways many full-time faculty and administrators don't recognize.

The instability of my position within the department represents the inadequacy of many institutions to promote a healthy work/life balance for graduate students. Instead of developing policies that protect pregnant students' physical, emotional, and mental well-being, departments make exceptions regarding assistantships or attendance policies for courses. And though I am thankful for the support I received from my advisors, not all graduate students have been as lucky. This lack of institutional support reinforces the expectation that students postpone any personal plans while in graduate school. Pregnancy then becomes scandalized: it seems unfathomable that someone might plan a pregnancy while in graduate school. Upon hearing the news that my husband and I were going to have a baby, a fellow graduate student and friend texted me, "Have you dropped out of grad school yet?" Though meant as a joke, his question demonstrates the expectation that we can develop either our personal lives or our professional lives, but not both. My growing stomach reminded everyone I passed in the hallway that I was perhaps foolishly attempting both.

I recognize I was fortunate to have the support of family and faculty members as I entered the world of parenthood. But not everyone is so lucky. Institutions must develop policies that promote a healthy work/life balance for students who want to spend time on their personal goals as well as their professional ones. Until such policies are in place and labor conditions are improved for graduate students, we are left exposed, vulnerable, and literally uninsured.

KELSIE

The money I earned from my graduate assistantship was inadequate, to phrase it with teeth gritted. After four years of PhD coursework, I had borrowed 62 percent of my federal student loan lending limit. Even with the loan money, I constantly worried and stressed not only about having enough money each month but also about all the unexpected expenses that might pop up, such as paying for medical bills and prescriptions due to no health insurance or inadequate insurance.[2] Or paying for new brake pads and tires.[3] Or paying for tree-removal services when a tree nearly falls on a house after being struck by lightning.[4] This worry and stress, internalized in my mind, affected my physical body, compounding the daily anxiety I felt as a both a woman and a graduate student. In particular, my anxiety affected my sleep. For the majority of my time in graduate school, I lived alone, so I lay awake at night contemplating escape routes if my house got burgled, the number of days until payday (and the bills in between), and the implications of writing programs/centers as academic gatekeepers. I was exhausted most of the time, so I caught up on sleep during weekends but never got enough classwork, grading, or administrative tasks done. It was a nasty, weary cycle.

Furthermore, it was expected in graduate school that I embody a professional, that is, that I should behave, perform, and appear as a professional in my field. To do this, I attended conferences to present my research, but any travel funding I received typically covered only one-third of my travel/conference expenses. And when I attended conferences during graduate school, I usually felt some insecurity about my student status. I left conferences with credit-card debt and jaded self-doubt. In my daily work at the university, I also felt obligated to dress in ways associated with corporate or industry professionalism, putting my personal style aside, to resist ageist and sexist readings of my body. I carried toxic guilt when I spent money on new clothes for teaching, yet I also carried frustrated understandings that my body and clothing choices affected my classroom authority, credibility, and collegiate relationships.

Finances and sexism aside, my graduate student status was further made clear to me in several hostile and belittling encounters I had with staff and faculty. In my fourth year as a PhD student, I was yelled at and publicly belittled by members of the writing program administrative staff while coordinating filming for a promotional video for the writing center. Shortly thereafter, I was told by office staff I could not write my job cover letters on department letterhead because letterhead was for faculty only. Early in my program, when an open search for an assistant director in the writing program was advertised, I was told by the WPA in an email not to apply because he had already selected someone for the position (someone who had not submitted an application either). And once, I was notified, without any prior warning, the day before campus closed for an extended holiday, that an upper-level class I was given the opportunity to teach was being cancelled because of insufficient enrollment. I was not made aware of the timeline for cancellation decisions nor was I given a warning prior to this email to allow me to boost my recruitment for the course. I also had no opportunity to contest this decision.

In isolation, these experiences are unsavory; one hopes they don't encounter such folks and such moments. But in sequence and by repetition, they wear a graduate student down; they scar. They erode confidence, curiosity, risk taking, and fervor. I have examined the capacity for anxiety and self-doubt I have carved out within my body, and I wonder if I'll ever be able to reclaim some bodily peace.

PAULA

As a transracially adopted Korean American, the feeling of occupying an in-between territory is not unfamiliar to me. Yet when I step into the classroom, the feeling sharpens to a point. I feel a responsibility to account for the apparent gulf between my physicality and experiences: I assume, usually, that I won't be immediately legible to my students. I'm walking a tightrope between various parts of my identity—my body often feels like a walking, talking contradiction, which always requires an explanation.

Such emotions—even passions—feel like luxuries I cannot afford, particularly when I am leading discussions about topics in which my various identities are directly implicated, such as discussions about race, gender, or adoption. As a woman of color—and particularly as a graduate student of color—I often feel I must earn the assumption of expertise and objectivity that others, because of their privileges or their positions in the university, are given by default. On the other hand, I'm also aware that, due to the relative whiteness of the academy, I may be one of the few Asian American instructors my students have ever worked with. Consequently, I often feel particularly responsible for being frank about the particularities of my own experiences as a transracial adoptee, which should never be understood as representative of all Asian Americans.

In other words, I feel as though I often function as both teacher and object lesson, and this emotional triangulation—on top of the usual stresses of teaching, studying, and professionalization—drains much of my emotional and physical energy. It means being minutely aware of not only what I present but also what I *represent*: an experience that, even with the support of my colleagues and advisors, can be as exhausting as it is lonely.

MORGAN

All graduate students face challenges as a result of their position, but those challenges are exacerbated to varying degrees, as the narratives in this article demonstrate, by intersectionality and context. I want to be up front about the fact that I was a grad student with a lot of bodily privilege: I'm white, able-bodied, neurotypical, and cisgender, and I grew up in a middle-class family with two parents who went to college. While I certainly experienced sexism and age- and income-based discrimination as a graduate student, I want to focus here on an issue of *disembodiment*: in my time developing programming for the Graduate School, I witnessed upper administrators, over and over, viewing grad students' bodies simply as placeholders, with minimal regard for how institutional policies, at best, did little to support those bodies and, at worst, harmed them.

As one example of this, I was in a meeting in which the Graduate School team was making plans for what to do with their share of university centennial celebration funds. One person floated the idea to throw a big party. Getting grad students to show up to events can be difficult considering their busy schedules and, for many, distance from campus, and event organizers tend to use food as a comical (and effective) incentive to garner attendance. They recognize many grad students are too poor (and busy and tired) to feed themselves properly, but they don't have real empathy for this or else they would fight for fair compensation of graduate students doing teaching, research, and administration.

Knowing that much of what the Graduate School was doing at this time wasn't based on any kind of systematic input from the students, I questioned, "How could we use funds in a way that would support the needs of grad students?" If Graduate School administrators had asked, they might have known grad students like Kelsie and Alyssa need more financial support, including healthcare benefits, for the important work they do for the university. Graduate students like Hayat and Paula need more support for the university's diversity initiative because just bringing international students and students of color to campus isn't enough, especially in a time when police will gun down a Black man without just cause or repercussion. If they had asked, they might have known we were afraid of what it would mean for us when Mike Pence brought his discriminatory agenda against women and the LGBTQ community to the federal level, of what it would mean for us if the 2017 Republican tax bill passed with its taxation of GAs' waived tuition, and of what it would mean for us when DACA got rescinded.

They would have known we were angry that top university administrators on our campus hesitated or neglected to reassure students at these moments because, I assume, they had to first consider what the board of trustees' responses would be. Had they asked, they would have also known we need more psychological support because, related to all these other issues, according to a study in *Nature Biotechnology*, "graduate students are more than six times as likely to experience depression and anxiety as compared to the general population" (Flaherty 2018).

By sharing this insight, I intend not to blame individuals at my alma mater but to encourage current and future academic administrators nationwide to reflect on the assumptions they make about graduate students and take action to better value them and treat them ethically.

DISCUSSION/CONCLUSION

Our narratives illuminate some of the difficult experiences of GAs and graduate students working and studying in higher education. The temporariness of these positions allows many administrators and faculty members to ease their guilt and/or complicity in exploitation and injustice. This temporariness itself, though, has lasting emotional and even professional effects—scars on our bodies and our being. As Kristie

Fleckenstein (1999) argues in "Writing Bodies," the "fluid and permeable boundaries" of "the somatic mind . . . are (re)constituted through the mutual play of discursive and corporeal coding." Graduate students literally cannot afford to "sacrifice the certainty of [our] bodies, [to lose] faith in [our] own experiences" because doing so renders us "helpless to change the system that enables [our] victimization" (286). It is impossible for graduate students to ignore the context in which we exist and its effects on our bodies, a context that can be rife with troubling labor conditions, lack of emotional and intellectual support, racial discrimination, and sexualization from students and colleagues. We share what we know from our bodily experiences in the hope that those who have power over our bodies while they exist in graduate school might stop viewing and treating graduate students as disembodied. We take some hope for our cause from Shannon Madden's (2016) introduction to a special issue of *Praxis*, as she points out that although there is a growing number of international, multilingual, and underrepresented minority students seeking graduate degrees, this population of students has a disproportionately high attrition rate, especially during the dissertation phase. The issue's focus is on building writing support for those students, but Madden takes care to address the systems in place that contribute to graduate student harm. She stresses, "It is crucial that we resist normalizing discourses which cover over identity differences and thus obscure the barriers to access that exist for students with disabilities, students of color, and students who don't occupy the assumed subject-position as privileged, white, and able-bodied" (par. 9). Our narratives collectively reveal the barriers we've endured, barriers we've all confronted and from which we've sustained some level of harm. Thus, we call upon institutions to examine how they ignore and dismiss identity differences, enabling embodied harms and scars.

We also stress the need to center actual graduate student voices in both future research regarding the experiences and needs of this special population and the creation and revision of institutional policies that impact them. "Only by understanding experiences," argues Madden (2016), "can we begin to understand the issues which impact student writers from underprivileged groups and from there, begin to design solutions" (par. 14). Graduate students' angst and outspokenness about their lived experiences in graduate school shouldn't be interpreted as naïveté and temporary frustration. Our concerns are real, and they matter. Institutions shouldn't be resistant or surprised when graduate students (or even contingent faculty) don't hedge, rationalize, or mute their complaints about the labor conditions and embodied harms they experience.

We recognize that inquiry and reform is daunting, but, as our stories indicate, graduate student bodies bear the high cost of complacency. Thus, reform is necessary for the ethical treatment of graduate students. In order for such reforms to be effective, substantial, and long lasting, however, they must address the particular, embodied needs of their graduate students, needs not always clearly visible for those most often present in board meetings or administrative negotiations. Rather than viewing critique as an obstacle to institutional effectiveness, then, we suggest narratives such as ours might be seen as a resource, which might assist the academy in understanding where its time, attention, and financial support might be most transformative. Though reform is rarely an easy process, we suggest it will likely be most effective when it accounts for and listens to those for whom reform is of real and material importance. We expect institutions engaging in reform will find eager partners in their graduate students, the next generation of institutional leaders.

NOTES

1. One of our original coauthors removed herself from this project for these reasons.
2. True story.
3. True story.
4. True story.

REFERENCES

Alexander, Simone. 2003. "Walking on Thin Ice." In *The Teacher's Body: Embodiment, Identity, and Authority in the Academy*, edited by Diane P. Freedman and Martha Stoddard Holmes, 105–18. Albany: SUNY Press.

Anson, Chris M., and Carol Rutz. 1998. "Graduate Students, Writing Programs, and Consensus-based Management: Collaboration in the Face of Disciplinary Ideology." *Writing Program Administration* 21 (2–3): 106–20.

Blair, Kristine. 2014. "[Where We Are] Composing Change: The Role of Graduate Education in Sustaining a Digital Scholarly Future." *Composition Studies* 42 (1): 103–6.

Canagarajah, A. Suresh. 2012. "Autoethnography in the Study of Multilingual Writers." In *Writing Studies Research in Practice: Methods and Methodologies*, edited by Lee Nickoson and Mary P. Sheridan, 113–24. Carbondale: Southern Illinois University Press.

Craig, Collin Lamont, and Staci Maree Perryman-Clark. 2011. "Troubling the Boundaries: (De)constructing WPA Identities at the Intersections of Race and Gender." *WPA: Writing Program Administration* 34 (2): 37–58.

Damron, Rebecca, and Ronald Clark Brooks. 2017. "Using Autoethnography to Bring Together Writing Center and Composition Practicums." *Writing Program and Writing Center Collaborations: Transcending Boundaries*, edited by Alice Johnston Myatt and Lynée Lewis Gaillet, 47–66. New York: Palgrave Macmillan.

Flaherty, Colleen. 2018. "Mental Health Crisis for Grad Students." *Inside Higher Ed*, March 6. https://www.insidehighered.com/news/2018/03/06/new-study-says-graduate-students-mental-health-crisis.

Fleckenstein, Kristie S. 1999. "Writing Bodies: Somatic Mind in Composition Studies." *College English* 61 (3): 281–306.

Freedman, Diane P., and Martha S. Holmes, eds. 2003. *The Teacher's Body: Embodiment, Authority, and Identity in the Academy*. Albany: SUNY Press.

Greenfield, Laura, and Karen Rowan, eds. 2011. *Writing Centers and the New Racism: A Call for Sustainable Dialogue and Change*. Logan: Utah State University Press.

Grimm, Nancy. 1999. *Good Intentions: Writing Center Work for Postmodern Times*. Portsmouth, NH: Heinemann.

Inoue, Asao. 2015. *Antiracist Writing Assessment Ecologies: Teaching and Assessing Writing for a Socially Just Future*. Fort Collins, CO: WAC Clearinghouse.

IWCA (International Writing Centers Association). 2001. "IWCA Position Statement on Graduate Students Writing Center Administration." *International Writing Centers Association*. http://writingcenters.org/wp-content/uploads/2008/06/graduate-student-position-statement2.pdf.

Kopelson, Karen. 2003. "Rhetoric on the Edge of Cunning; Or, the Performance of Neutrality (Re)Considered as a Composition Pedagogy for Student Resistance." *College Composition and Communication* 55 (1): 115–46. https://doi.org/10.2307/3594203.

Long, Mark C., Jennifer H. Holberg, and Marcy M. Taylor. 1996. "Beyond Apprenticeship: Graduate Students, Professional Development Programs and the Future(s) of English Studies." *Writing Program Administration* 20 (1–2): 66–78.

Macrorie, Kenneth. "The Graduate Experience in English: An Introduction to Ten Case-Histories." *College Composition and Communication* 15 (4): 209–12. https://doi.org/10.2307/355489.ACce.

Madden, Shannon. 2016. "Introduction: Access as Praxis for Graduate Writing." In "Access and Equity in Graduate Writing Support." Special issue, *Praxis: A Writing Center Journal* 14 (1): 1–8.

Matudela. 2018. "INTRODUCING: nextGEN Listserv for Writing & Rhetoric Grad Students." *Communication, Rhetoric and Digital Media News*, North Carolina State University, April 19. https://crdm.news.chass.ncsu.edu/2018/04/09/introducing-nextgen-listserv-for-writing-rhetoric-grad-students/.

Mountford, Roxanne. 2002. "From Labor to Middle Management: Graduate Students in Writing Program Administration." *Rhetoric Review* 21 (1): 41–53.

Parke, Erin. 2018. "Writing to Heal: Viewing Teacher Identity through the Lens of Autoethnography." *Qualitative Report* 23 (12): 2953.

Ratcliffe, Krista, and Rebecca Rickly, eds. 2010. *Performing Feminism and Administration in Rhetoric and Composition Studies*. New York: Hampton.

Restaino, Jessica. 2012. *First Semester: Graduate Students, Teaching Writing, and the Challenge of Middle Ground*. Carbondale: Southern Illinois University Press.

Royster, Jacqueline Jones. 1996. "When the First Voice You Hear Is Not Your Own." *College Composition and Communication* 47 (1): 29–40.

Skinnell, Ryan, Judy Holiday, and Christine Vassett. 2015. *What We Wish We'd Known: Negotiating Graduate School*. Southlake, TX: Fountainhead.

Taylor, Marcy, and Jennifer L. Holberg. 1999. " 'Tales of Neglect and Sadism': Disciplinarity and the Figuring of the Graduate Student in Composition." *College Composition and Communication* 50 (4): 607–25. https://doi.org/:10.2307/358483.

Villanueva, Victor. 2006. "Blind: Talking about the New Racism." *Writing Center Journal* 26 (1): 3–19. http://www.jstor.org/stable/43442234.

Willard-Traub, Margaret K. 2002. "Professionalization and the Politics of Subjectivity." *Rhetoric Review* 21 (1): 61–69.

Young, Vershawn Ashanti. 2007. *Your Average Nigga: Performing Race, Literacy, and Masculinity*. Detroit: Wayne State.

5.1

DOWN THE RABBIT HOLE

Elitza Kotzeva

Never imagine yourself not to be otherwise than what it might appear to others that what you were or might have been was not otherwise than what you had been would have appeared to them to be otherwise.
—Lewis Carroll

The alarm clock resounds in my ears. It penetrates my dream and resonates with my body—I feel deep inside me the urgency of the alarm. It's 6:00, and I need to wake up the kids, make breakfast, and send them to school. The well-known course of the day begins. The clock's hands rush furiously around its face, announcing the beginning of a race—the race between me and the time imparted on my body. As I am preparing breakfast, I think of how time has become part of my body, setting clear limits on what I can and can't do, both taking away and giving me a chance to do things outside the family agenda, and this includes an opportunity to work on my scholarship.

When I get back to my desk later that morning, I slide my finger down the page to the paragraph where I stopped reading the day before. The book is by French philosopher Henri Bergson (1911): "I place myself at once in the material world in general, and then gradually cut out within it the centre of action, which I shall come to call my body" (45). I start thinking about the way we situate our bodies within the material world and how our actions define our bodies within the material, with the material, for the material. The exigencies of the material world prioritize our responsibilities and the actions they require—finishing the housework, doing homework with the children, spending quality time with the family, going to extracurricular kid activities, reading to the children before bed, finishing my chapter, walking the dog. No, wait, walking the dog should come before my chapter work. What is more important? Before I get a chance to work on my scholarship, I need to finish my "other" work. The prioritization of actions has prescribed the way I place my body in the world—the "right," that is the more ethical, sequence of actions.

https://doi.org/10.7330/9781646422340.c005.1

But our bodies are different. Our ethics differ too. The priority of actions within the material then is different because of the diverse ways various bodies choose to be in the world. There are plenty of examples around me. Most of my single colleagues, for instance, or those without children keep complaining about their busy schedules as graduate students or young scholars. I listen to them trying to imagine how they struggle with their priorities and how in prioritizing the actions of their bodies they must, too, leave the work on their scholarship last. I keep listening but fail to understand how they place themselves in the world and "cut out within it the centre of action" (Bergson 1911, 45), which they call their bodies. Their bodies are different from mine, and their material existence has other exigencies.

I, on the other hand, don't have the time to complain about the lack of time. I remind myself that time is in my body, and I shall be in control of it. I am in control of my body and the actions that constitute it. I am in control of time. So I tell myself.

I get to writing. I forget the clock on the wall. The only clock that matters is the one inside me. The actions of my body—my writing—now define the way I experience time, the way I reconstruct time in my mind.

I jump bravely down the rabbit hole.

A few pages further, Bergson (1911) explains how we need to educate our senses in such a way that they can reconstruct a complete image of the material (an object or even our body) with our perceptions, with our impressions of the surrounding images. "The sensations here spoken of," Bergson elaborates, "are not images perceived by us outside our body, but rather affections localized within the body" (51). With the educated use of our senses then, in the view of the French philosopher, we can create a "real action" within us—a reflection of the virtual action on the external objects. We can learn how to train our senses to recreate a different materiality of time within us—distinct and only ours. I begin writing furiously.

Down, down, down. I fall even deeper down the rabbit hole.

I read, I write, I work. I sink deep into my thoughts. I forget the materiality of my body as it exists to others and to the outside world. I feel only the body I choose to construct as a result of my senses, as a result of my real action—that of my mind. Time does not fly anymore because flying time belongs to the world outside me. It does not underpin anymore my temporal experience. I work within my own moment, unmeasurable by the ticks of the clock.

Then, suddenly the alarm on the stove goes off.

"Down she came upon a heap of sticks and dry leaves, and the fall was over" (Carroll 2012, 9).

I look at the clock on the wall. Its linear time has kept moving the hands along in perfectly measured units, time different from the way I experienced it while writing. In five minutes, according to the clock, my children will be home from school. Let me turn off the stove. Let me see if the laundry is finished. The alternative clock inside me has allowed me to experience the action of writing in time not measured by minutes but by the action of my thoughts, by the life of my mind, somewhere else, in a parallel universe, down Alice's rabbit hole. As I slowly crawl back up to the linear time of the day, my body feels relieved it has allowed me to experience this other temporality, different from the conventional notion of time. That is the time of my work life.

REFERENCES

Bergson, Henri. 1911. *Matter and Memory*. London: S. Sonnenschein.

Carroll, Lewis. 2012. *Alice's Adventures in Wonderland and, Through the Looking-Glass and What Alice Found There*. New York: Barnes & Noble.

5.2

WRITING IN THE BODY

Janel Atlas

When I talk about my research, I gain important insights into other people. I can tell a lot about a person by how they react when I say, "I study women's stories of pregnancy loss; my project began thirteen years ago when my second baby died right before she was born at thirty-six weeks' gestation."

I've gleaned these insights in conversations that take place by the buffet table at a cocktail party, on the sideline of a kids' soccer field, and in the corridor at an academic conference. Sometimes the person gets flustered and crestfallen. They may clam up, muttering something like "Sorry for your loss." On occasion they can't even manage that and instead change the subject or excuse themselves. Sometimes the interlocutor asks follow-up questions, like about what that was like or what her name was. The most common response, though, is a glimmer of recognition; I can see in the person's eyes that they or someone they know has endured a pregnancy loss. When I mention my own, their mind and mouth are flooded with a similar story. They want to share some of the details of their own babyloss or the loss endured by a sister, mother, grandmother, daughter, or friend. I often hear something like, "I know someone I should connect you with," or "I have a story you should hear—it relates to your work."

It has been fascinating to conduct scholarly research about something simultaneously so common—at least one in four pregnancies ends in miscarriage or stillbirth, with the real percentage likely much higher—and yet still somewhat taboo to bring up in conversation both within and outside the academy. People often seem to believe they would be breaking a social code by referring to a dead baby unless someone else raises the subject first.

In these conversations, when I talk about my research into pregnancy-loss stories, I splay myself open. I reveal something from my past that is deeply personal and sad but that I decide to disclose: to look at it, turn it over in my hands, describe the experience publicly, and, more important, argue that babyloss is indeed a topic deserving of scholarly attention.

Exposing my own lived experience of stillbirth has been necessary along each step of the journey from bereaved parent to PhD researcher, yet embodied knowledge doesn't neatly fit into academic discourse. Nor is the evolution of my thinking about this subject easily mapped onto a tidy flowchart or a linear timeline. When I write about babyloss—devastating miscarriages, secondary infertility, babies born too soon and too late, my own or others'—I pay an emotional and physical toll. Each time I plan out the next steps for research, writing, and submitting for publication, I'm forced to concede that my work isn't circumscribed within a semester plan or neatly slotted into an editorial calendar.

For example, sometimes when I'm reading or annotating a babyloss story, I drop down from an analytical headspace and stumble across affective traces of grief in my body. Without my notice (or permission), my shoulders have hunched up around my ears as I've read the opening lines, knowing full well where the story of a much-wanted pregnancy will end. Sometimes I find my heart is clenched, ripples of compassion flowing when I encounter a particularly eloquent expression of grief. And there have been many instances when I've read a passage I'm studying through a scrim of hot tears.

Writing about babyloss and asking critically engaged questions about babyloss stories necessitates, for me, a recursive flow: from self to other; from past to now; from the head to the heart. It's not enough to inhabit only one of those spaces because it is actually through the movement across and between, by respecting the imbrication of those two seeming poles of difference, that knowledge from either space can be understood and then communicated. Feminists have been pointing out this paradigm since the 1980s, including Donna Haraway (1988), who famously wrote that all knowledge is "situated and embodied" (583). Yet even three decades after Haraway's powerful argument, producing academic prose still seems to demand a disembodied or at least superhuman ability to think apart from the fleshy affective weight of a physical form.

As within social interactions in which I disclose my baby's death, I must carefully consider the different audiences I must persuade of the validity of both my personal grief and professional aptitude to study and understand babyloss narratives. For instance, when I apply for a grant or submit a report about my progress to an institutional committee, I shift from an affective and embodied realm to an intellectual one. Yet I can't completely eradicate the emotional and embodied aspects of my work from formal discourse settings because to do so would deny both the genesis of and the continued motivation for my research.

Writing in the academy more generally, and specifically in administrative applications for travel funding, grants, and other business-side committees, demands a privileging of certain kinds of knowledge, or at the very least requires adopting discourse practices that neglect embodiment. In a fellowship proposal with deadlines and operationalized intentions, where can I account for the existence of my body? How can I predict the depleted days, the disrupted sleep, the stretches of time when my living children's needs require so much of my time and energy that the thought of reading even a single tragic narrative about someone else's baby dying makes my head ache?

In performing the roles of researcher, critical thinker, and feminist writer, I don't feel there's much room for my body. This is especially ironic because the subject I study places bodies and what happens *to* them and *inside* them right at the center. This proscribed duality requires a continual negotiation, a rhetorical savviness I sometimes find tiresome even as I know it's necessary. I must ask: *Who is my audience? What do they value? What kinds of "data" count as data? Is it safe to reveal emotional or psychological vulnerability to this person, or should I present a confident and objective self in this space?*

The answers to these questions and the pathway I'm continually forging as a scholar and seeker come from both inside and outside the academy. From inside academia, I've been lucky enough to have genuine conversations with advisors, mentors, and colleagues about how they settle into their own research and writing practices with boundaries that acknowledge their physical strengths and energetic boundaries. From the outside world, I devour books, articles, and podcasts about emotional intelligence, vulnerability, and humanness. This wisdom reminds me that the motivation for my academic work and the means of conducting it require acceptance of both my body and my mind, and that the risk of doing this work is also its promise.

The compulsion I feel to engage with these stories inspires me to continually invite others to join the conversation, sharing stories that may at first seem isolated or much too private to tell. Instead of subsuming one under the other, I move along the intersections of knowledges, inviting others to open themselves to grief, knowing, and connection, even as I navigate the blurry lines of my own knowing.

Emotional Pain

6
"NEVER MAKE YOURSELF SMALL TO MAKE THEM FEEL BIG"
A Black Graduate Student's Struggle to Take Up Spaces and Navigate the Rhetoric of Microaggressions in a Writing Program

Triauna Carey

"I have never once gone in search of racism, but racism sure knows how to go in search of me." My mother's words echoed through my head as I sat in the office of an administrator. As academics, we tell ourselves we often treat classrooms, meetings, and conferences as sterile places, clean of discrimination and bigoted language, but the experiences of scholars of color reveal a different truth. The sterilization is a cover, a mask of coded language, systems of power, and hierarchies, but sometimes the cover slips. It was the second time during my doctoral program an ambiguous issue had been reported and I was called into an office with an administrator. This time was in regards to the way I went about addressing a racially charged encounter I had with a student and reporting it to my supervisors and faculty.

The first had been an anonymous report detailing my "issues with the program" and asking me to explain how I could feel isolated, like a burden, and unheard as a graduate student of color. I spent an hour detailing passive-aggressive behavior and discriminatory acts and trying to explain how my lack of belonging was tied to my embodied experiences as a Black student in predominantly white spaces in my research, studies, and as a teaching assistant. I left the room feeling more confused than when I entered because I still was not sure about the original issue reported, the purpose for the meeting, or why I was being questioned. I answered as honestly as I could, even when my answers were challenged and critiqued. I left the room realizing it was not a simple meeting about my progress in the program. It was an interrogation into my experiences for reasons I still do not know to this day. I never heard about the anonymous report again.

https://doi.org/10.7330/9781646422340.c006

As I sat in an office for the second time, feeling like a child being scolded in a principal's office, my mother's voice echoed about racism being in search of me. It didn't matter what I tried to do. I could enter a doctoral program eager to belong and contribute different ideas based on my experiences as a Black woman. I could try to assimilate into the community, which consisted of an all-white faculty. It didn't matter if I spoke up, backed down, or mimicked the culture around me. Racism would find me. This time it was in the form of a student calling me "colored" during a one-on-one session for an assignment and assuring me they were impressed by me because "the coloreds" supposedly did not amount to much where they were from. When the comment was made, I was flustered and did my best to explain why the term was derogatory and unacceptable, but that wasn't what concerned me while sitting in the office with the administrator. The student was deeply apologetic and open to educating themself. The moment was long past, but I was left to rationalize my handling of the situation in a private meeting with an administrator who wanted me to report the student for racism. I was chastised for not reporting it to the proper authorities, even though I assured the administrator I brought it up to the faculty in charge, the program director, and a room full of peers during a meeting. When I originally brought it up, I was met with awkward silence and told the situation seemed quite "tough." When all was said and done, I was the one apologizing for bringing it up and bringing down the mood of the room. I left the second office visit in a matter of months feeling the same, ashamed and like a burden for being addressed in a racist, derogatory way. I was in a doctoral program for rhetoric and writing, and yet the administrators and faculty could not see the irony in placing the burden of racially charged rhetoric on my shoulders as a Black woman.

The other irony was that I preferred the bigoted words of the student over the microaggressions used against me by my faculty and peers. After all, that student was open to educating themself and growing beyond the narrow-minded ideologies they were taught. The academics in question assured themselves they were open-minded and exempt from such things. Racial microaggressions are defined as "brief and commonplace daily verbal, behavioral, or environmental indignities, whether intentional or unintentional, that communicate hostile, derogatory, or negative racial slights and insults toward people of color. Perpetrators of microaggressions are often unaware that they engage in such communications when they interact with racial/ethnic minorities" (Sue 2010, 271). This lack of awareness compounds the power of microaggressions by placing the person on the receiving end in the daunting position of assessing when to endure, when to move on from the environment, and when to bring it to the attention of the perpetrator, which all result in taxing emotional labor. As a Black woman conducting academic research and teaching first-year composition courses, I have experienced many instances of racial discrimination and biases, but I find most of the emotional labor happens in academic spaces outside the writing classroom and does not include dealing with overtly racist slurs. These occurrences take place at conferences, during meetings with colleagues, and in the loaded rhetoric used in evaluations and feedback. For graduate students of color, microaggressions tend to be in the form of complimenting articulation, demeanor, or how comfortable someone feels in the spaces we take up. We are often told in a surprised tone how "articulate" we are or complimented for being "nicer than one would expect." Rhetorically, the power of these types of microaggressions is impactful because of the guise of civility, professionalism, and sincerity, but often microaggressions are accompanied with slights, backhanded compliments, or biased language. While the overt racist language of that student is widely condemned at universities and colleges today, the use of covert racist language, such as microaggressions, continues to target marginalized groups of people and reinforce stigmas, assumptions, and discriminatory, colonial practices well after graduate students and educators of color arrive on college campuses and enter the writing classroom.

This chapter explores how graduate students of color endure the emotional labor it takes to confront microaggressions and discriminatory practices in writing programs, how we can use our bodies to take up space, the challenges of doing so, and how microaggressions continue to work for deeply rooted systems of discrimination and colonial practices in writing programs, departments, and the spaces of academics beyond the writing classroom. By exploring these issues, the goal is not simply to criticize our institutions and writing programs but instead to continue to contribute to making space for institutional embodiment. I take up space through this work by making these situations visible and analyzing how the experiences impact my embodied rhetoric.

TAKING UP SPACE

Experiences like the ones detailed above continue to remind us of the importance of taking up spaces in both physical and metaphysical ways. People of color must constantly, painstakingly at times, work to speak up, hold positions of power, and take up spaces not often available. We must also remember to share our experiences and narratives in our research and writing because, no matter how inconvenient or uncomfortable such sharing may be, our bodies will be used against or for us depending on our assertion over the spaces we reside in. This is particularly significant in sharing our experiences, narratives, and works in writing programs because as Jasmine Tang and Noro Andriamanalina (2016) state, "Race and writing are inextricable: Racial formation cannot be removed from writing program administration in the US nation-state" (10).

In addition, these scholars outline four ways writing programs can assist graduate students of color and provide resources as they navigate through a program: "(1) equal emphasis on research and practice on the part of the WPA, especially with respect to local contexts and histories of communities of color; (2) acknowledgement of how nonmainstream epistemologies connect to writing practice; (3) relatedly, recognition that for many students of color, connection to community is inseparable from one's academic identity; and (4) the integration of writing support in a robust, institutional effort that focuses on the academic and personal well-being of graduate students of color" (Tang and Andriamanalina 2016, 10–11). These points of emphasis are imperative in assisting graduate students of color as they find ways to take up space and contribute to ongoing conversations often uncomfortable and risky for students already deemed lower in the hierarchy of graduate school.

To approach writing programs, classrooms, and departments as spaces to think critically and creatively, and to express new ways to address issues, means thinking of the writing classroom as a physical space to engage in and thinking of scholarly research as metaphorical spaces to share, voice, and listen through. This sharing of work connects marginalized groups of people from different cultures and embraces the concepts of *inclusion* and *diversity* institutions continue to work toward, but does not focus merely on statistics or numbers to account for a certain race, gender, or category institutions can mark as *Other*. This effort to take up space then becomes a method of challenging and critiquing practices in writing programs, but the method, even when encouraged, is often vague on the details and opportunities to do so. For example, even when encouraged to speak up and take up space, the people I could look to for guidance were mainly white faculty members keen on ignoring the systems of power at play, dynamics of and the factor of race. In fact, the only examples of people of color in faculty positions I can recall were faculty members who left or were ostracized. In this way, it is a case of theory versus practice, and practice is often overlooked.

In terms of theory, as a writing instructor, researcher, and scholar, I lean on theorists that push back against false narratives of what it means to be a female scholar and person of color. Scholars such as bell hooks (1981), Audre Lorde (2007), and Gloria Anzaldúa (1999) are often taught and acknowledged, but the theories of their works are not often put into practice in writing programs, which is counterproductive to the theories and experiences of these scholars. In *Ain't I a Woman: Black Women and Feminism,* hooks (1981) states, "The inability of American women to understand racism in the context of American politics is not due to any inherent deficiency in woman's psyche. It merely reflects the extent of our victimization. No history books used in public schools informed us about racial imperialism" (119). To this point, mainstream books in the education system not only do not prepare us for microaggressions, addressing cultural differences, or systemic oppression but also fail to outline ways for students of color to approach these issues. The mere existence of us in these spaces is treated as good enough, and we are often stifled, spoken over, and ignored, which is why it is important for graduate students of color to share our narratives, explore our histories, and make our experiences known.

In "The Master's Tools Will Never Dismantle the Master's House," Lorde (2007) reminds us that we need more scholarship and narratives "dealing with the role of difference within the lives of American women: difference of race, sexuality, class, and age. The absence of these considerations weakens any feminist discussion of the personal and the political" (110). Meanwhile in *Borderlands/La Frontera: The New Mestiza,* Gloria Anzaldúa (1999) writes about her experiences with education as a child and asserts, "Wild tongues can't be tamed, they can only be cut out" (54). These scholars use their writing and narratives to empower future generations of scholars and marginalized groups of people to not simply take up the spaces allotted to them but to exist in environments and spaces not automatically given as well. However, in writing and doctoral programs, these theories are treated as just that, theories, rarely accompanied by practical guidelines, resources, or assistance in overcoming the issues addressed.

In practice, many experiences and narratives point to the difficulties of taking up space, addressing racism, and explaining how it is necessary to outline ways to do so with productive, rhetorically effective approaches. In "Want to Retain Faculty of Color? Support Them as Faculty of Color," Larissa Mercado-Lopez (2018) argues, "While we wish for students to see the possibilities that exist for them as educators, researchers, and policymakers in higher education, we are not successful at showing students those possibilities in our faculty" (para. 2). I can personally speak to this as a Black woman who was taught by only a handful of women of color in my entire academic career, including K–12, a bachelor's degree, two master's degrees, and while working as a doctoral student. However, that does not mean I did not take courses that focused on scholarship and theories by people of color.

My experiences remind me of Shawn Wilson's (2008) in *Research Is Ceremony* in that regard. Wilson tells a story about his experiences in college, where he was taught solely by white professors. He found it odd since there were plenty of Indigenous people in town he believed knew more about the subject matter. For Wilson, the issues of who teaches students of color and for what purpose are about more than the race of people teaching the courses. Wilson speaks to the bigger issue scholars like hooks, Lorde, and Anzaldúa point out as well: these are educators who have little experience with the marginalized voices they are teaching about and who assign books written about the people, not by or for them. He concludes by joking, "I figured it out. If white guys teach all the courses about Indians and they teach in the way white people think, then to find Indians teaching the way Indians think, all I had to do was give up Native Studies and join the White Studies program" (19).

Wilson's story reveals what happens when people of color are not given opportunities to take up space, share their narratives, and be validated in the way white intellectuals and theorists are valued. A challenge to this critique is that this should not be an issue because the race of the educator should not matter. However, as Mercado-Lopez (2018) explains, the claim that race and demographics should not matter in terms of the diversity of educators at institutions is one of the common missteps in the pushback against scholars of color taking up space:

> Yet, there is a timidness to initiate programming and resources for faculty who name and appeal to their specific racial and ethnic identities. Universities, instead, tend to take on a catch-all All Faculty Matter approach to supporting faculty: we support ALL faculty, therefore we support faculty of color. The loose use of "diverse faculty" in institutional language thereby becomes an expansive umbrella under which any faculty can claim membership. While I recognize white faculty can experience oppression on the basis of sexuality, gender, disability, and so forth, disparities on the basis of race and ethnicity are more historically embedded in and reproduced by institutions and their hiring and promotion processes. (para. 5)

This pushback tends to omit the voices of marginalized groups of people, neutralizes and diminishes perspectives, and, far too often, speaks of us, about us, or even for us but rarely views us as integral in our roles in these conversations. The best way to take up space in practical ways is to make our narratives known in spaces that usually conform to the status quo. This means exploring the work of scholars often omitted, pushed aside, or minimized. It means challenging narratives that speak about and not with people of color. It also means allowing graduate students of color to share their experiences through their work.

CAN WE TAKE UP SPACES WE DO NOT FEEL SAFE IN OR TRUST?

When thinking of the concept of taking up space in meaningful ways, it is important to consider the risk involved in doing so as a graduate student of color. This reminds me of a conversation I had with an advisor about power relationships and hierarchies in doctoral programs. The advisor assured me such things were not an issue in the writing program, and I had to point out how convenient it was for a faculty member in a position of power to say that to a doctoral student. I still had to rely on the faculty for feedback, grades, and approval of procedures and progress, which meant my behavior, rhetoric, and types of engagement were constantly being evaluated. This would all determine not only whether I successfully defended my dissertation but also future funding opportunities while still in the program. Downplaying the risks of being a graduate student in general, let alone a graduate student of color, did not change the issues of power. So, can we take up spaces we do not feel safe in or trust? In my experiences, the issues of safety and trust hinder the ability to take up space in meaningful ways, especially when the way one takes up space by speaking up or being vocal begins to risk the chance for success and availability of opportunities moving forward.

The policing of the voices of graduate students of color is one of the most challenging and intellectually dangerous consequences of downplaying tactics used to hinder graduate students of color from taking up space, and the most rhetorically effective tactic I have encountered while trying to take up space involves the use of microaggressions. According to Staci Perryman-Clark (2016), "Microaggressions often reveal themselves when negotiating issues of power, authority, and ethos" (20). The rhetoric behind a microaggression relies on its ability to be subtle enough to pass as sincere but obvious enough to create tension, anxiety, and/or feelings of discrimination. They exclude individuals and at times create a gaslighting effect. When experienced incessantly, what could be disregarded by some as an innocent misunderstanding or dismissed as unintentional becomes a weight placed on the target to bear and carry around in their classrooms, around peers and colleagues, and even in their research. This becomes emotional labor that must be processed by the subject of the microaggression, who must also be mindful of the burden it could place on others if it is brought up.

In addition, microaggressions place doubt on the validity of the accounts and experiences of the target and make their perspective appear irrational. Often, microaggressions play into racial stereotypes and are used to restrict and omit voices that do not embrace the status quo or assimilate into a dominant culture in a writing program, department, or classroom. When microaggressions and similar rhetorical strategies are deployed, they do not simply prevent graduate students of color from speaking up and voicing concerns. They make these students second-guess their abilities to perform academically. They create a deteriorated sense of self-worth, and these doubts often enter into graduate students' classrooms as they teach. This weight is carried with us into the writing classrooms we take up space in and beyond in ways rarely voiced due to fear of retaliation, distrust of the spaces we find ourselves in, and the risk of taking up space appearing to outweigh the reward.

BEYOND ONE SPACE

Unfortunately, issues regarding taking up space as scholars and graduate students of color are not prevalent merely in one writing program, at one university, or in one region. As a scholar in the field of rhetoric and composition, I saw it in the conversations before, during, and after the National Council of Teachers of English's announcement that it was moving forward with the 2018 Conference on College Composition and Communication in Kansas City, Missouri, despite the NAACP's initial travel advisory against the state of Missouri. I see it in the response to Vershawn Ashanti Young's (2018) 2019 CCCC's Call for Proposals, in which scholars were challenged to view language in a way other than the status quo: "We gon show up, show out, practice, and theorize performance-rhetoric and performance-composition. Ahm talkin bout buttressing the public good and engaging communication pedagogies that open possibilities, many of them yet unknown—in reading, writing, speaking, listening, visuality, and digital communication. I prod you to raise new questions about performance-rhetoric, performance-composition, or you can ruminate on one of mine."

Instead of rising to the challenge and thinking about the productive conversations to be had, there were many responses that focused on the vernacular, its role in the conference, and whether it was proper or formal enough in an intellectual space. Some of these discussions included the larger issue of racism: lack of resolutions about discriminatory practices at institutions, the mere existence of racism, cultural appropriation, and frustration about the call not representing all academics through its use of language. Instead of focusing on what the call encouraged scholars to think about, the questions involved, and the perception of language, many responses became spaces to argue over who felt excluded, who felt uncomfortable with the vernacular, and how rhetorically effective such language would be moving forward. The issues with the call, like with most conversations about race, were brought up by scholars of different races and went beyond only one concern to extend the conversation to larger issues scholars had with the way race is addressed by NCTE and other groups in academic circles. This became a microcosm for the issues facing graduate students of color in doctoral and writing programs.

Due to the amount of tension, recent developments in political and academic circles, and cultural shifts that continue to occur in society, one call became a debate about race, language, and tensions in the way we assess, address, and use writing in general. The concerns brought forth for NCTE demonstrate how even writing programs and departments continue to struggle with conversations about discrimination and language use through writing. Examples of this struggle are evident in pieces of feedback that demand minorities prove and validate their struggles with representation in programs and scholarship, while also demanding they only share their narratives in certain ways and in certain spaces that make their peers and faculty feel comfortable with the conversation. So the question becomes, How do we address these issues?

Asao Inoue (2015) focuses on the concept of *local diversity* to not only acknowledge the systems historically situated in writing programs but also recognize how perceptions of language and experiences differ for individuals. This approach confronts many of the issues arising in microaggressions as well, which rely on ignoring discriminatory language and refusing to acknowledge how different groups of people interpret cultures and rhetoric.

The concept of local diversity ultimately means classroom writing assessments must engage meaningfully with the diverse students in classrooms. It means teachers really cannot develop assessment procedures or expectations without taking into account their students' literacies. And this means local diversities should change the academic discourse, change what is hegemonic in the academy, but this is a difficult task, one requiring a more holistic sense of classroom writing assessments, a theory of classroom writing assessment as an ecology (Inoue 2015, 75). This ecology can and should extend beyond the writing classroom to include doctoral programs, writing programs, and departments.

Viewing Inoue's (2015) concepts of *habitus* and *ecologies* for writing-classroom assessment steers us down the right path, but at some point we must be willing to take the next step as well, which is an even more daunting task, that brings us back to the importance of taking up space. As scholars, educators, and researchers of color, we must use our writing, classrooms and research to share our experiences. We must educate the academy about the language and rhetoric weaponized to speak for or against marginalized groups of people. We must not shy away from the conversations when they become difficult or make us feel uneasy, as they often do. More important, as graduate students embodying these experiences, we must take up space, especially in spaces not originally intended for us.

In addition, writing programs must rise to the occasion in the acknowledgment of microaggressions and other rhetorical strategies used to perpetuate discriminatory, colonial practices. It is not enough to merely acknowledge the existence of difference. We must go beyond this to confront the uncomfortable tensions within our programs because what many of us have learned is that microaggressions and discriminatory behavior in the academic world do not only come from the stereotyped white male portrayed in popular culture and media. They come from white women. They come from people of color. They come from graduate students of color through the way we interrogate, restrict, and confine our own voices and the voices of other people, which is why it is important that we hold ourselves and others accountable. However, the onus should not be placed solely on graduate students of color to educate others about these issues. As Lorde (2007) reminds us, "This is a diversion of energies and a tragic repetition of racist patriarchal thought" (113). Instead, we should acknowledge, discredit, and educate to combat the discriminatory language of these rhetorical strategies through active listening but not taxing emotional labor, through better representation, not statistics praised for diversity that place the burden of representation on a few minorities in programs and classrooms.

As Inoue (2015) argues, "Understanding explicitly interconnection is important in antiracist writing assessment ecologies, because seeing the ways all aspects of the ecology are interconnected (including students, teachers, and their discourses) helps everyone pose problems about language and judgment through their differences, through the local diversity revealed in writing, assessing, and the material bodies in the classroom" (93). This explicit understanding of interconnection is evident beyond the writing classroom in doctoral programs, writing programs, departments, and research on writing assessment. I challenge us all as academics to think about how we are complicit in these practices and rhetorical strategies rooted in discrimination and to continue the difficult conversations. We must all take up spaces in ways that allow us to challenge the systems we are in and learn about the ways these systems still affect our teachings, practices, and embodied rhetoric.

As I think about my experiences as a graduate student of color and the number of times I was called into an office to validate my experiences with racism or defend my choices in response, I think about Inoue's (2015) insistence on making racism visible. "Don't tell me we can ignore it and that doing so will make it go away. Don't tell me we shouldn't see race and that's the answer to racism. Doing so tells me that my experiences of racism in school and out are just figments of my imagination, that they must have been something else, that we just cannot know if there is racism anymore, that we just have to ignore it and all will be well, that we just wait a little while longer" (24). Each time I was called into an office to speak about racism, I found myself staring across the desk at a white administrator in a much higher position of power than mine as a graduate student and thinking, How am I supposed to explain this? How are my experiences supposed to mean something to them if the very nature of the disbelief relies on their inability to experience it? When writing program administrators and faculty question the validity of racial tension, this doubt tends to be rooted in their inability to relate to the issue. "Well that hasn't been my experience here" is a sentence I have heard far too often in these situations, and it is problematic for two reasons. One, it assumes that because someone has not personally experienced a discriminatory act, the act does not exist. Two, it gives the power and authority to someone else to bestow validity on issues they may not want to acknowledge or may not comprehend.

And yet, with all the reasons to not speak up or voice concerns, taking up space is still the most liberating form of resistance to this type of thinking, and I was encouraged to do it by one of the only faculty members of color I ever encountered. After a particularly confidence-crushing comment from another faculty member, which resulted in my conceding a point and moving on, I was pulled aside and told, "Never make yourself small to make them feel big." This advice came from one of the only faculty of color I encountered in my entire academic career, but their guidance and mentorship continues to impact me to this day. That is the power of people of color taking up space in academic circles and writing programs. This presence does not only help the individual. It spreads to all those who watch, go forth, and continue on in their careers, and that is far more powerful than any office meeting or microaggression.

REFERENCES

Anzaldúa, Gloria. 1999. *Borderlands/La Frontera: The New Mestiza.* 2nd ed. San Francisco: Aunt Lute Books.

hooks, bell. 1981. *Ain't I a Woman: Black Women and Feminism.* Boston: South End.

Inoue, Asao. 2015. *Antiracist Writing Assessment Ecologies: Teaching and Assessing Writing for a Socially Just Future.* Anderson, SC: Parlor.

Lorde, Audre. (1984) 2007. *Sister Outsider: Essays and Speeches by Audre Lorde.* Berkeley: Crossing.

Mercado-Lopez, Larissa. 2018. "Want to Retain Faculty of Color? Support Them as Faculty of Color." Spark: Elevating Scholarship on Social Issues. https://medium.com/national-center-for-institutional-diversity/want-to-retain-faculty-of-color-support-them-as-faculty-of-color-9e7154ed618f.

Perryman-Clark, Staci. 2016. "Same Song, Different Verse: A Sista's Experience with Microaggression and the Need for Allies." *WPA: Writing Program Administration* 39 (2): 20–22.

Sue, Derald Wing. 2010. *Microaggressions in Everyday Life: Race, Gender, and Sexual Orientation.* Hoboken, NJ: Wiley.

Tang, Jasmine Kar, and Noro Andriamanalina. 2016. "'Rhonda Left Early to Go to Black Lives Matter': Programmatic Support for Graduate Writers of Color." *WPA: Writing Program Administration* 39 (2): 10–15.

Wilson, Shawn. 2008. *Research Is Ceremony: Indigenous Research Methods.* Manitoba: Fernwood.

Young, Vershawn Ashanti. 2018. "Call for Program Proposals: Performance-Rhetoric, Performance-Composition." *Conference on College Composition and Communication.* http://cccc.ncte.org/cccc/conv/call-2019.

6.1
BODIES IN CONFLICT
Embodied Challenges and Complex Experiences

Nabila Hijazi

In their 2015 article on embodiment, Maureen Johnson, Daisy Levy, Katie Manthey, and Maria Novotny (2015) posit that "to think about rhetoric, we must think about bodies. To do this means also to articulate how scholars' own bodies have intimately informed our disciplinary understanding of rhetoric. . . . One approach is to cultivate an even more expansive view of embodied rhetorics" (39). I take up this notion of embodiment to include the experiences of not just me, an immigrant and a successful college-educated Syrian Muslim woman—who embodies many roles of a daughter, mother, housewife, academic, and tutor to Muslim women, especially refugees—but also other Syrian refugee women, nontraditional students with whom I share languages, culture, religion, and many material circumstances. I evoke the notions of "fleshy presences" (Price 2011) and "sweaty concepts" (Ahmed 2017) through embodied experiences that make the body, the physical body, a source of knowledge—by recalling, reliving, and reexperiencing pain to make meaning out of displacement and loss.

As a Syrian immigrant Muslim woman who came to the United States in the late 1980s, I've seen the struggles many Syrian women face in this country because of religion, culture, and gender-role clash. I personally have maintained a Syrian cultural lifestyle and some of the assumed gender roles—as a housewife and a mother. I've also spoken and taught Arabic and its Syrian dialect to my children and have taken care of a household according to Muslim values. I have had to extend myself to succeed in both personal and academic spaces; of course, my journey has not been easy or smooth, and I am not a young graduate student in her late 20s, ready to defend her dissertation, look for a job, and seek a tenure-track position. Rather, I am the mother whose education was disrupted when I started a family and who finds happiness in her bilingual children's success, the daughter who finds solace in her

https://doi.org/10.7330/9781646422340.c006.1

aging mother's approval and endless *duaas* (Islamic invocations), the community member who loves giving back to her Muslim community, the graduate student who wants to finish her doctoral degree and meet deadlines, the college instructor who values her students' progress, and the researcher who hopes to continue her academic projects with potential publication. My academic journey has been demanding—but it is one that confirms the different roles female academics embody.

I have worked with nonprofit organizations that help refugees settle in the United States. My dissertation builds on this work as it explores the experiences and challenges of adult literacy learners, especially women refugees from Syria, a war-affected country. My embodied journey through this project has been challenging. Before I decided to base my dissertation on the work of refugees, I had the chance to work closely with them in several volunteer projects at the mosque these refugees attend. I was on the mosque's board of education and was invited by the mosque's religious leader, the Imam, to create literacy programs for refugees, men and women, especially Syrians since the community helped many Syrians relocate and settle. Through close interactions and materially being there, I was able to create a rapport with many of them. I have spent hours and days contacting local mosques to enroll their children in free Quran and Arabic classes, collecting donations from friends and family, sponsoring fundraising events, and giving rides to doctors' visits. These efforts were taxing not just to my physical body but also to my academic self.

Through my interactions with these refugees, I felt their urgent need to enroll in literacy classes in order to become independent and manage their own affairs. Some were already enrolled in literacy classes through government-sponsored agencies, but many expressed lack of interest, either because of the location or because of not seeing the value of these classes.

Ultimately, through my conversation with the Imam of the mosque and the members of the mosque's board of education, we decided to host a literacy class at the mosque since we saw the women's gratitude and emotional attachment to the mosque and its community. Due to my academic qualifications, I was invited to start this literacy program. To solicit interest, I visited one of the Syrian refugees in her home. Embodying the spirit of this community, she invited all the Syrian refugee women who lived in the same neighborhood to her house. I asked them if they would be interested in attending literacy programs and if they would be interested in enrolling their children in Arabic and Quran after-school programs. Based on interest and commitment,

I drafted a budget plan and was able to start a literacy class, which met weekly for three hours for a whole semester. The Syrian refugee women students attending the class were provided with free transportation and childcare by the mosque to ensure attendance and full commitment.

When the class started, I felt a sense of accomplishment—my labor would soon yield positive results—but unfortunately, that was not the case. Even with all the incentives provided, retention became a serious issue. I began to wonder why enrollment was so low, and this question became the focus of my dissertation. I decided to interview the women to understand how language programs can attract and retain students. I know cultural perspectives have something to do with it—education may not be a woman's first priority—children come first. And many Syrian refugee women, especially from rural areas, possess a limited Arabic education. But to succeed in this country, I've always believed that women need education and that literacy and higher education are the decisive factors for achieving agency in society and a sense of autonomy.

Once I had IRB approval, I started collecting data through interviews. Even though I had a list of questions to use during the interviews, I did not use all of them, especially since open-ended, in-depth interviews have a flexible and unstructured format, allowing for more informal settings and spontaneous answers from interviewees. Knowing that one aspect of these interviews involved asking these women, who reeled from horror and fear and survived traumatic violence, to recount their ordeal, intruding on their private pain, I agonized about how to conduct these interviews without retraumatizing them, how much detail to push for about the brutality they witnessed, when to stop, and whether to offer comfort. I knew it was important to invoke the trust we'd built and to put myself on the spot by sharing similar experiences and not acting as a cold academic who was there to get the job done. I could not maintain a "professional" distance.

I conducted the interviews in Arabic, Syrian dialect, and in the students' houses since all my interviewees have children and travel would be difficult. The interviews were done over Turkish coffee and Syrian sweets, the norm for Syrians during a visit. Holding the interviews in their homes gave the interviews a more personal, intimate feeling, as these women, including me, felt comfortable taking our Islamic veils off, adopting an informal setting and feeling relaxed.

While reading the questions to my participants in Modern Standard Arabic, I decided to tone down some of the language and use Syrian dialect to make the questions more understandable and accessible. During the interviews, we had moments of tears and laughter. My participants were comfortable sharing bitter memories of embodied hardships the transcripts do not and cannot capture. Some described how their towns were destroyed, how their fathers and brothers were gunned down, and how they spent days and even months with a scarce supply of food or with no food. Some even shared memories of being held hostage before fleeing their towns and escaping death. One further described how her family was held hostage for over a month and how miraculously they were let out to flee barefoot in the cold winter. Some of their children are still in a state of fear and insecurity and panic if their siblings go outside to play with other children in the neighborhood, agonizing over the fact they may not come back or might be harmed. I cried with them and shared their anxieties.

All of them opened up and related cruel moments of their lives in Syria even before the breakout of the civil war. Many recounted more horrific experiences than mine, but I was able to relate to them by sharing my family's stories of displacement: the imprisonment of relatives who were captured and tortured before being able to flee Syria, the destruction of my family's and relatives' houses, the loss of many sweet memories, or even the deteriorating health and emotional status of some of my family members due to the violence they witnessed and the loss of relatives, friends, and property. To embody their pain, I had to relive my experience and theirs and their stories of displacement. We wept together and consoled each other, appreciating the opportunity to claim our lives—something many Syrians have not been able to do owing to all sorts of displacements.

These interviews became healing sessions in which we shared pain over what happened, especially the loss of bodies, humans, and even properties—the foundation of our roots that many of us cannot go back to reclaim. During the interviews, I had to stop several times, feeling choked and unable to speak or get the words out as I relived the picture of my father on his deathbed, fretting over his inability to go back to his birthplace and his house, where all family members, even extended ones, used to co-live; I had to imagine my mother, who is still depressed because she cannot go back to her house, the neighbors who were family to her, or even the plants she cared for as her children. When our dialogue became hard to continue or tears came down and our throats clogged up, I felt the need to change the subject, discussing our current lives and experiences raising our children, who have had a hard time identifying as Muslims and speakers of languages other than English. Because I shared with them my experience and how I navigated these issues to successfully raise my bilingual children to be confident, proud Muslims, these women became more interested in continuing the conversation.

During these interviews, I naturally and simultaneously adopted different roles: the immigrant Syrian woman whose personal life has been affected by the Syrian civil war regardless of the physical distance, the community member who needs to show support, and the researcher who needed data to complete her project and propose a solution to an existing problem: low levels of literacy among Syrian refugee women. Because many of the experiences my interviewees shared were painful, I deliberately found places I could invite them to tap into positive experiences in which they felt successful navigating their new environment and the conflicting gender roles and finding refuge in enhanced language learning.

Even though success was not realized for each student, and I am still having a hard time convincing these women to seek education, I realized their narratives contest my positionality and resist the dominant discourse and image of women refugees, especially Syrian refugees, of being subjugated or submissive. These women validate their own definition of literacy and occupy spaces that allow them to disrupt the existing systems and norms around literacy studies and academic discourses. The "sweaty concepts" and the challenges, physical and mental, these women embodied during the war, in their displacement, and on their road to settlement, have paved the way for their legitimate place. Regardless of the warfare and the horrific violence they witnessed, these women demonstrate resilience—challenging discourses of power by holding to their Syrian values and cultural practices. Their own definition of literacy does not follow a Western definition, which equates literate to being well educated and learned. Syrian refugee women are exercising rhetorical agency in the dominant culture as they invest in literacy, *functional literacy*, which empowers them to pursue new but different educational and employment opportunities. Their stories disrupt a mainstream definition of the "business of intelligence": "the way we decide who's smart and who isn't, the way the work someone does feeds into that judgment, and the effect such judgment has on our sense of who we are and what we can do" (Rose 2004, xi). These narratives follow what Mike Rose suggests in *The Mind at Work*: they offer "an analysis of physical work and intelligence and a reflection on how we might think more clearly and fairly about" (xvii) women refugees who do service jobs and physical work. Their stories argue against any reductive view of women refugees and their work and put emphasis on the importance of *functional literacy* and the mental work these women perform.

REFERENCES

Ahmed, Sara. 2017. *Living a Feminist Life*. Durham, NC: Duke University Press.

Johnson, Maureen, Daisy Levy, Katie Manthey, and Maria Novotny. 2015. "Embodiment: Embodying Feminist Rhetorics." *Peitho* 18 (1): 39–44.

Price, Margaret. 2011. *Mad at School: Rhetorics of Mental Disability and Academic Life*. Ann Arbor: University of Michigan Press.

Rose, Mike. 2004. *The Mind at Work: Valuing the Intelligence of the American Worker*. New York: Viking.

6.2

OUT OF HAND

Jennie Young

It was 2003, and I was thirty-two years old. I was married with a five-year-old son who had just started kindergarten, and I was pursuing a master's degree in English education. There were days it was stressful balancing full-time motherhood and full-time graduate studies, but for the most part I was handling it.

What I'm saying is that there was nothing particularly wrong when my right hand began to twitch. It was the muscle between my thumb and my forefinger, and it twitched periodically until it twitched constantly. Initially, I watched it pulsing in and out, in and out, with a sort of detached fascination. After a few days, I began to sit on it—as much to hide it as to flatten it out. I don't know why, but I didn't want anyone to know about this new feature of myself, this thing that felt like a strange and shameful secret pet.

After a few weeks I began to struggle with activities that required fine motor skills—tweezing a splinter, threading a needle. During this time I also started to feel untethered, as though I might lose my grip on reality along with my ability to grip anything with my right hand. The metaphorical implications of losing one's right hand did not escape me.

It's hypocritical the way people like me—academics who embrace holism, who champion the mind-body connection—present our bodies to the world, always trying to highlight the strengths, to cloak the weaknesses. But I guess I've always been a closet Cartesian, unable to shake my midwestern, mind-over-matter ethos.

There were so many papers to write, and yet my right hand had grown useless and claw-like by three months into the twitching period. Typing took twice as long as it should have, but I somehow submitted everything on time; it never occurred to me to ask for an extension, to tell anyone at school what was happening.

I went to the doctor once and told him I was feeling nervous and struggling to eat and sleep. For reasons that remain inexplicable even

https://doi.org/10.7330/9781646422340.c006.2

to me, I did not tell him about my hand. He suggested I was anorexic and needed to "work on my issues with myself," so I left and never went back. It wasn't that I was *trying* not to eat; I just couldn't.

This went on for nine months, until even my smallest jeans were slipping from my hips. My face started twitching, and then there was no more hiding it; people were staring—people were asking questions.

I went to a new doctor, and, finally, revealed the origin story (which, of course, was not the origin story—it was just the way my body was manifesting it): I presented my hand. The doctor watched it twitch, too. He ordered tests for hyperthyroidism, hypoglycemia, multiple sclerosis. They all came back normal. He said that when all the physical suspects are exonerated, we must assume an emotional/psychological origin.

He prescribed an antianxiety drug, which I resisted—*this is in my hand not my head!!*—but I took it just to prove him wrong. Within three weeks I felt like a different person—humbled, but healthier. I took the medicine for six months, during which time my hand began to relax, I began to eat, I began to sleep. Life went on.

Fifteen years later: it is the fall semester of 2018. In the interim I've gotten divorced, gotten a PhD, and gotten a tenure-track position directing the first-year writing program at a state university. The kindergartner is finishing his last year of college. Professionally, this is a high point of my academic career. I love my new job. My colleagues are kind and welcoming and generous, and my students are hard-working and engaged. My dissertation—a critique of high school culture in the United States that argues we've mapped fear and paranoia onto student bodies—has been published as a book, and I am invited to give a TEDx talk based upon that book.

My long-term partner, though, is coming undone. He's drinking heavily, and he's not working. The financial pressure of supporting both of us on my own is crushing. We talk, we fight, we go to counseling; we're committed to save this thing. But internally, I am getting scared. He's drunk much of the time now, and he is a mean, mean drunk. He follows me around, he yells for hours, he accuses me of all kinds of things, he threatens to come to campus and do "something," though the threats are vague; he monitors my phone, my laptop, my friendships. He begins referring to himself as "we." I'm trying to teach, to administrate, to write and memorize a TED talk. I tell no one at work what's going on at home because I'm new and because I don't want to be associated with drama. And because I am ashamed; I'm embarrassed that feeling physically and emotionally vulnerable at home renders me less capable of being professionally effective at work. I'm supposed to be directing this program, giving this presentation, guiding these students. Why would anyone trust me to do these things when I can't run my own life, when I've somehow become the woman who must answer the "Do you feel safe in your home?" question in the negative. I manage to keep my secret, but my nerves are shot.

During a particularly rough night with him, I feel myself shift silently into some other gear. What I feel more than know is that I cannot, cannot stay here. I wait until he's spent himself and passed out, and then I take my dog and what I'm able to toss into a laundry basket and I leave without making a sound. I never go back. I rent a one-room apartment because it is available and it is all I can afford. My dog and I sleep curled up on blankets on the wood floor of the new apartment for several days until I'm able to hire movers to go back and get my things. My neck and shoulders throb when I wake early in the morning on teaching days, but I don't miss any classes. I don't want my students to know anything is wrong with me.

During those initial days after I leave, I pace the wood floor and recite the TED-talk script. There's nothing else to do anyway—no internet, no cable, no furniture, no food, no pots and pans in which to cook food even if there were food to cook. I find the pacing and the recitation comforting; it's like repeating an incantation or a prayer. It requires no actual thought.

The talk goes well. My colleagues remark that I seemed calm, unruffled. They don't know this talk is the easiest thing I've done in weeks. I don't want to minimize how frightening it can be to stand up in front of people, but it's not the same as being afraid of the person sleeping next to you. It's just not.

When I wake the morning after the TED event, my entire right arm is on fire. I can't do anything with my hand—can't apply makeup, can't grip a pencil, can't pick up a cup of coffee. It's so bad that I, someone who never visits the doctor, walk to the Urgent Care Center across from my new apartment building. The doctor palpates my arm all the way down to my hand and pauses at the muscle between my thumb and forefinger. "What's going on here?" she asks. "There's a hard muscle knot right here—I think that's what's wrong. How long has this been happening?"

I don't know what to say: "Three weeks"? "Fifteen years"? It's my body's old signal. I hadn't even realized it had started again, and now it's worse than it ever was. The canary had been screaming its head off, but I was too focused on other things to even realize it had flown back into my life.

Academics, I believe, tend to get mired in a paradox of our own design when it comes to issues of embodiment: as a group, we probably have a higher-than-average awareness of what it means to live an embodied life, yet we are perpetually at war with the reality of our embodiment. We resist being defined by our appearances, our dis/abilities, our aesthetic Otherness even while we frequently engage these concepts as the salient features of our scholarship. We fight for causes like body positivity or the right to breastfeed in public while denying the facts of our own, personal, embodied lives. Hell, I wrote a book grounded in embodiment theories while behaving as though I'd never even encountered the very ideas that frame my work—always insisting "I'm fine, I'm fine!" when it came to physical manifestations of emotional pain. My own emotional pain had transmogrified into a literal fleshy presence, and even that I tried to deny.

At the time of this writing it's been several months since that last clenching, and things are easier now, relatively speaking. It's taken a lot of physical therapy and several painful massage sessions to return my right hand to an almost-normal condition.

And it will come again, this little caution bell clearly meant to signal something to me, to slow me down or switch me onto another track. I want to believe I will heed it sooner next time. I hope I will.

Culture of Whiteness

7
BODIES, VISIBLE

Joshua L. Daniel and Lynn C. Lewis

This chapter examines the neoliberal ethic permeating writing program administration. While scholars such as bell hooks, Michael Bérubé, and John Trimbur have described the perils of the neoliberal university, Nancy Welch and Tony Scott's 2016 collection, *Composition in the Age of Austerity*, notes that professionals in writing studies are often unsure of how to respond to neoliberal trends such as the state defunding of public education. This is because, as Scott (2016) argues in a recent *College Composition and Communication* article, these trends operate covertly by transforming daily conditions teachers encounter. He writes,

> The neoliberalization of composition does not happen through explicit arguments that are more persuasive than their counter arguments; it happens operationally through the transformation of learning environments and the terms of labor of the people who work within them. Effective activism therefore involves being in positions that enable us to understand with the help of robust disciplinary frames that provide models for intervention at the level of practice. (33)

We situate writing program administration in a liminal space where authority and power are often structured through neoliberal logics contrary to programmatic goals. Embodiment is denied when students are rendered faceless consumers, learning processes are explained purely as means to the ends of certification and job preparation, and teachers are assessed through efficiency metrics. One way WPAs might counter neoliberal logics is by deliberately cultivating programmatic practices that foreground the experiential, teaching, and scholarly practices of different bodies and embodiments within their writing programs. In this chapter, we describe the practices we have developed while directing an FYC program at our home institution of Oklahoma State University, a large, land-grant university. With no shortage of sites where neoliberalism could be interrogated, we discuss our approaches to making individual bodies visible and countering the neoliberal ethic as WPAs

https://doi.org/10.7330/9781646422340.c007

committed to developing programmatic outcomes, graduate student mentorship, and FYC orientation. These sites involve intensive work with graduate students whose encounters with neoliberal logics will only intensify as they go forward as professionals. We concur with Melissa Nicolas and Anna Sicari, who point out in their introduction to this book, "The body is required for meaning making" (5). Therefore, any successful and ethical FYC program must be attentive to various forms of embodiment in writing and the teaching of writing.

Writing is quantified through standards by neoliberal discourses that discipline and regulate the body. Standards suggest all student bodies should meet one-size-fits-all curricular benchmarks. While Kathleen Blake Yancey (2004) and others have noted standards are "informed by a desire to level the playing field for all students" (19), a one-size-fits-all approach presumes all bodies can/should teach and be taught in the same way. Contrary to NCTE's 2019 "Resolution on English Education for Critical Literacy in Politics and Education," in which political dialogue is identified as an "educational mandate," this logic of standards implies that the apolitical classroom is desirable. Standardized curricula and apolitical classrooms threaten to render the body invisible by denying education should engage body politics.

Neoliberalism further espouses a radical individualism wherein, as Margaret Thatcher famously claimed, "There is no such thing as society, only individuals" (quoted in Harvey 2007, 82). Social collectivities and collaborative spaces are elided in this logic. Individualism inheres to consumerist values: our first-year composition instructors are cogs in the machine of production and their students subject to gatekeeping mechanisms. Structures such as ACT-test cutoffs, long lists of fixed goalposts students must reach, and the elision of difference through nonreflexive teaching and assessment practices drenched in whiteness structure a culture of consent to neoliberalism.

To counter consent to neoliberalism, David Harvey (2007) draws on Antonio Gramsci and argues that communities might establish political consent through appeals to common sense grounded in cultural values and traditions. For FYC programs—particularly large ones such as ours that involve instructors and administrators from different disciplines—this means working to establish collective goals and identities to counter the pervasiveness of neoliberalism's radical individualism. Across the three sites we describe, we discuss strategic interventions for writing program administrators. We argue that revealing and challenging neoliberalism's logics in FYC programs is not only possible but is critical for writing program administrators in a moment when politicians are actively working to erode, replace, and decimate educational institutions and undermine social justice.

OUTCOMES

In this section, we consider how outcomes might be used in writing program administration to promote productive diversity. This means diverse bodies are not only acknowledged and seen but are also valued as sources of knowledge.

Traditionally, the Council of Writing Program Administrators has approached outcomes as a means to articulate both what teachers of writing *know* and *value* about writing instruction and the different curricular pathways individual programs/instructors might take to achieve those outcomes. The outcomes initially emerged in response to a question asked by Ed White on the WPA-L (WPA listserv) in 1997: "Is it an impossible dream to imagine this group coming out with at least a draft set of objectives that might really work and be usable, for instance, distinguishing comp 1 from comp 2 or from 'advanced' comp? We may not have professional consensus on this, though, or even consensus that we should have consensus. How could we go about trying?" (Behm et al. 2013, ix). The WPA Outcomes Statement (WPA OS) as originally adopted in 2000 articulated such values as audience sensitivity, the synthesis of ideas, and an awareness of one's own composing processes. The WPA OS is "simple yet complex" (Harrington et al. 2005, xvi), and a common refrain is that it remains a "living" document (Behm et al. 2013, xvi), one that adapts to local contexts. Or, as Kathleen Blake Yancey (2004) has put it, outcomes tend to focus on student performance with an "implicit recognition within outcomes assessment that there are many legitimate ways to get to Rome" (22–23).

The WPA OS was revised in 2008—with a relatively minor revision adding a category of outcomes titled "Composing in Electronic Environments"—and then again with a major revision in 2014. The 2014 task force remarked that one important revision to the OS was a change from using terms like *writing* or *writing ability* to an embrace of the word *composing* that includes a wide range of processes, products, and technologies. The Council of Writing Program Administrators described the revision when it was approved in July 2014: "In this Statement 'composing' refers broadly to complex writing processes that are increasingly reliant on the use of digital technologies. Writers also attend to elements of design, incorporating images and graphical elements into texts intended for screens as well as printed pages. Writers' composing activities have always been shaped by the technologies available to them, and digital technologies are changing writers' relationships to their texts and audiences in evolving ways." The writing and revisions to the WPA OS move from valuing a diversity of *pedagogical and instructional practices* to a valuing of diversity of *compositional modalities and technologies*. But what about the diversity of student bodies within writing programs, including administrators, instructors, and students?

These are the questions writing program administration scholars are tackling today. Genevieve García de Müeller and Iriz Ruiz (2017), for example, recently used survey data to call attention to how race functions in writing program administration. They illustrate that many writing programs lack the resources to implement antiracist agendas, which places an undue burden on scholars of color. They note a "perception gap" between white scholars and scholars of color pertaining to the existence and effectiveness of theory, teaching models, and pedagogical practices to dismantle racism, with white scholars tending be unaware of their own complicity in ignoring diversity (36). A growing body of scholarship currently works toward antiracism goals in writing program administration, including how better serving people of color might address the racial gap in graduation rates (Sanchez and Branson 2016), how assessment practices might reinforce the structures of racism (Inoue 2016; Inoue and Poe 2012; Perryman-Clark 2016), and how the field should best serve teachers of color (Kynard 2015).

Additionally, in a plenary address to the CWPA, Melanie Yergeau (2016) points out how the field has tended to not see disabled bodies. She argues, "I am making the case ableism is the structuring logic of Rhetoric and Composition, of higher education writ large, and we can keenly feel that ableism even in a well-meaning, mentorly space like the CWPA" (158). This, along with work in feminist studies and gender studies, represents another vein of research through which scholars work to make bodies visible (Brewer, Selfe, and Yergeau 2014; Dolmage 2014; Hamraie 2013).

This scholarship makes two things clear: (1) writing program administration has historically failed to ensure the visibility of diverse bodies in the writing classroom, and (2) now is the time to address and correct this failure. While scholarly conversations around issues such as gender, race, and disability are not new to rhetoric and writing studies, these conversations are only now emerging as a major priority in writing program administration. In a recent article that calls on writing program administration to more purposefully articulate antiracism and social justice as goals, Carrie Leverenz (2016) discusses these issues in terms of their absence from the WPA OS. She writes, "Although the revised WPA

Outcomes Statement does not prevent individual teachers from treating a broader range of differences as assets, given that literacy education has historically sought to erase such differences and the very real difficulty of attending to difference in our age of standardization, we must do more in our classes to support difference, more than simply practice different modes." (42).

From valuing a diversity of pedagogical and instructional practices to valuing a diversity of compositional modalities and technologies, outcomes now must value a diversity of *bodies and embodied knowledge*. As administrators, it must be our goal to not only promote diversity and difference in our programs but to also tap the knowledge stored across such difference.

Neglecting this goal is not only a moral failure because our students are not treated with due respect but also an intellectual failure because we lose knowledge embodied by different people.

So what does this mean for us, the authors of this chapter? We are cisgender, able-bodied, writing program administrators who are white, one female and one male. We believe the body of knowledge referenced in this section charges our administrative duties with four vital tasks: (1) we must assume our privilege prevents us from perceiving the full scope of problems different bodies encounter; (2) we must actively work to value and promote those bodies; (3) we must not place undue burden on persons who embody those subject positions to solve all the problems; (4) we must continually focus on developing political consent to the value of collectivity and to a culture of collaboration among instructors.

Our own program has mirrored the brief history of the WPA OS offered earlier in this chapter. When Lynn became FYC director in 2015—with Josh serving as associate director—both courses in the two-course sequence included long lists of objectives students were expected to meet, such as "correctly use MLA citation" or "use topic sentences to construct paragraphs." We moved to outcomes in order to emphasize the potential diversity of *pedagogical and instructional practices* we saw in our instructors. We are housed in an English department with five programs: creative writing, linguistics, literature, rhetoric and writing studies, and screen studies. Because we run over 250 sections of composition each academic year, we draw instructors from across these areas. Though we provide them training at orientations and workshops, we know these instructors have different pedagogical backgrounds. Because a creative writer might bring different skills to the table than a linguist for teaching a literacy narrative, we believed outcomes would usefully articulate that our instructors might use different pathways to arrive at similar goals. Over time, we revised the common curriculum to include more opportunities to utilize different *compositional modalities and technologies*, such as visual images, infographics, and digital archives.

Outcomes are one way to articulate that not only do we see the diversity of bodies across our students and teachers but also that treating them justly and learning from one another are core goals. We have recently revised our programmatic outcomes to do just this. As Leverenz (2016) has written, nothing prevented us from doing such work, but naming it as an outcome has benefits. First, it creates the expectation that curricular or pedagogical innovations designed to dismantle systems of oppression are not only interesting ideas—they are foundational for our program. Hopefully, this brings our instructor focus to this vital work. But, more than that, it creates a mandate for Lynn and Josh. When we assess ourselves and the program, we cannot say we are doing our jobs well unless we find evidence of success on this front. Second, it acknowledges that we, as white writing program administrators, have benefitted from our whiteness and that our complicity with the neoliberal university has likely harmed diverse student bodies. As Inoue (2016) says, "If you're white, you're likely harming your students of color because of something you can't control, your whiteness and your white language privilege. This isn't a hopeless situation, but it takes acknowledging it, then concerted action" (136–37). By making the valuing of a diversity of bodies and embodied knowledge a stated outcome, we signal to our instructors that the necessary response to acknowledging white privilege is not to throw our hands up in hopelessness but to dig in and resolve to improve. Third, we hope naming diversity as an outcome helps student and instructor bodies feel seen. While difficult to verify, perhaps simply acknowledging their difference and the structural disadvantages they face might put us and them in a better position for a more just relationship.

When administrators emphasize the potential for outcomes to open curricular possibilities, we contend these outcomes can become a powerful means of challenging neoliberal logics while having to work within them. For us, outcomes have provided a way to work toward the consent mentioned earlier so we can emphasize what we as a program believe and are working toward while also acknowledging that instructors can and must shape classroom spaces and practices through their own embodiment.

Outcomes are just a first step. What we name as goals for the program matters little without action. We now turn to two areas in which writing program administrators can take action: mentorship and orientation.

MENTORSHIP

Mentorship happens at multiple levels within our FYC program across many years. Incoming graduate students without previous teaching experience serve as writing center tutors in the fall and are also paired with an experienced instructor in a composition classroom. These instructors include advanced graduate students, visiting assistant professors, and lecturers. The graduate student prepares for and attends all classes, takes notes on the outcomes for the class and which activities helped the instructor meet their outcomes, and teaches two class sessions of their own in order to receive feedback. They also regularly meet with program directors to reflect on what they observe in the classroom, and they compose reflections on practices they want to cultivate for their classrooms. In later semesters, they work with an experienced graduate student, an assistant director in our program, and receive one-on-one mentorship.

Early scholarship on mentorship tended to describe it in magical, almost spiritual terms. As an example, see the following passage from an often cited piece by Kaoru Yamamoto (1988) on mentorship. He writes, "Teaching is a familiar yet elusive, common yet extraordinary, prevalent yet esoteric human phenomenon. It is an everyday experience, but its secrets have never been exhausted even in voluminous studies over the years from varied perspectives. . . . The mystery lies in the inventive mind that weaves a fabric of complex pattern in the name of teaching. One of the many yarns that goes into this effort has been called mentoring" (183). Early scholarship often explicitly references magical or spiritual metaphors (Carter 1988; Hardcastle 1988). However, writing studies has an established body of scholarship on mentorship practices (Baake et al. 2008; Eble and Gaillet 2008; Micciche and Carr 2011; Lu Lui and Matsuda 2008; Simpson and Matsuda 2008), and this work demystifies the supposedly mysterious aspects of mentorship, such as how mentor/mentee relationships are created and maintained. E. Shelley Reid (2008), for example, argues mentorship should be seen as a "formal, institutional, learnable, activity" because "the real magic in mentoring comes in attention to details, in attentiveness and planning, in learning and practicing and reflecting" (70–71).

However, has the field appropriately considered mentorship as one space in the university where white privilege is maintained? Inoue (2016) has pointed out how standard practices often sustain oppression. In his recent plenary address to the Council of Writing Program Administrators, he argues, "If the dominant discourse of the academy is taught exclusively by white, middle-class teachers, then isn't it possible that such conditions will affect the discourse valued in writing assessments, in writing programs, in writing journals? Is it possible that those who achieve such positions, such credentials, might have achieved them because they can use and favor dominant, white middle class discourse, that they embody the discourse the field comes to expect?" (138). Extending this logic to mentorship, if the academy tends to value the discourse of white, middle-class teachers, then isn't it possible such conditions will affect mentorship practices in graduate programs? Is it possible that those who tend to become mentors will also tend to favor white, middle-class discourse, which will be more effective for mentees who practice and expect that same discourse? Is it not possible that this is one way oppression could be maintained for disabled bodies? For bodies of color? Thinking back to notions of mentorship as magic, we can see that effective mentorship might just be white magic practiced only by a chosen few. Although our field understands mentorship as teachable, our contention is that there is opportunity still to tap its potential to dismantle racist structures and make more diverse bodies visible.

We are early in our process with this work, but we think of mentorship in two ways that might open possibilities. Specifically, we contend effective mentorship should build and maintain space for reflection and should involve goal setting. Both practices make it possible for program directors to strategically intervene when issues related to embodiment emerge.

In our program, we first create spaces for reflection in order to troubleshoot emergent issues in mentor/mentee relationships. One of the most challenging issues is how to pair new mentees with mentors. We do not know the new mentees well enough to know their needs. Moreover, because mentors volunteer to participate, it is difficult to know year to year who will be available. Structure has been our main solution. Once graduate students are paired with their mentors, they meet with program directors early and often to discuss the mentor's class. Moreover, they compose regular logs of each class, along with their own reflections, which are shared on a Google Doc with program directors. This process allows us to troubleshoot any emergent problems, track a graduate student's developments, ideas, and concerns in the program, and it also helps us plan additional support for students who might need it. We see this approach as a way to make the body visible in our mentorship program. Students of different ages, races, genders, or ethnic backgrounds often have different concerns as beginning instructors. In the early stages of their teacher training, planning and reflection help make those concerns visible. Again, requiring reflection is a small gesture but one that can be helpful. Say, for instance, a transgender mentee has a mentor who—for whatever reason—is not using the mentee's preferred pronouns. These reflection logs are a place for that mentee to make that information available, at which time Lynn and Josh can intervene.

Selective intervention acknowledges individuality but also the potential for variability in the mentor/mentee relationship: one mentee may find a mentor's laid-back, folksy style alarming while another may find it inspiring. Dialogue about these differences helps new instructors articulate their desired future positionality as a teacher without insisting they fit a cookie-cutter definition.

Second, students who report getting the most out of their mentorship are those who set and define goals with their mentor. Mentors, who sometimes think they are unqualified to mentor graduate students, tend to express more anxiety about participating in the program than do their mentees. One way we address this is by holding a goal-setting workshop for mentors at the beginning of each fall semester. Mentors read some of the current scholarship in writing studies on effective practices, and they leave the workshop with a plan to meet their mentees to talk through goal setting. In addition to helping mentors see there are many resources available, the workshop also gives them a plan to understand what help their mentees need. Last year, for instance, a talented new instructor from Italy wanted to work with her mentor to develop more confidence in presenting to students because English was not her first language. Other students might develop goals such as learning to project authority in the classroom or developing a larger tool kit of activities. Goal setting can make the body visible on both ends of the mentorship relationship. The mentee is able to work toward goals resulting from their background and experience, and the mentor is able to see they have much to offer based on their own.

Both moves described are simple and easy to implement. At the same time, much can be done when teachers and program directors simply make concerted efforts to promote and value diversity. Reflection and goal setting are probably things many, if not most, mentorship programs do. Our point is that when reflection and goal setting are done in the context of the program that sees valuing a diversity of bodies and embodied knowledge as a primary outcome, these traditional tools not only refuse the neoliberal ethic but might also be applied toward social justice ends.

FYC ORIENTATION

While the specifics of FYC orientation vary across institutions, ours is a week-long process in which graduate students teaching for the first time participate in workshops about teaching composition within our programmatic and institutional contexts. In recent years, we have added two types of sessions particularly suited to making bodies visible through writing program administration: antiracism and corequisite teaching. Because the state of Oklahoma is nearly 75 percent white and our university is nearly 70 percent white, students of color are often underserved. We see antiracism and corequisite initiatives as powerful ways to make Black and Brown bodies more visible at our institution. Putting this work in FYC orientation—an early and intense time of graduate student training—signals to students that serving and supporting students of color is high-priority work for our program and provides opportunities for our beginning instructors to consider and develop pedagogical strategies explicitly attentive to those students.

Antiracism is new to our writing program, as Lynn gave the first presentation on it during our spring 2018 orientation. In this presentation, she described work by whiteness scholars Tammie M. Kennedy and Krista Ratcliffe, as well as antiracist scholar Asao Inoue, and asked instructors to work in groups to consider how assessment practices may reify whiteness and/or work against antiracist goals. Discussion was lively, with many instructors offering ideas. Although a number were more comfortable discussing how their practices aligned with antiracist goals, a significant and vocal minority asked questions, critiqued their own practices, and noted the need for further program work. Lynn's purpose was to begin the conversation, and she indicated she hoped others would be interested in tangible efforts to reflect on and re-vision pedagogical strategies.

Following the day's orientation, surveys were handed out to the instructors to gauge how well the sessions met their stated outcomes. Lynn read the survey comments on her session with interest: many instructors wrote of a desire for more concrete suggestions and strategies; they were already seeing the need for and valuing a call for attention to antiracist practices. One survey comment was an outlier: an instructor wrote Lynn's session was "shallow and self-serving." Reading this, Lynn became wryly aware of her own body—female, white, privileged—and the identity ascribed to her by those words. That is, this white, male instructor (these markers were evident from evidence the survey provided) was calling out Lynn for lacking scholarly weight as well as pushing her own "political agenda." This response was an important reminder for us that graduate students can arrive to our program already vested in neoliberal logics. The response assumes first that Lynn had a particular political agenda in her presentation and, second, that having any sort of political agenda is bad. It rehearses the familiar neoliberal myth that classrooms are supposed to be apolitical. The comment pays homage to neoliberal values insisting on the apolitical classroom where transactions between instructor and students can only be color blind.

During the following weeks, Lynn and Josh sought opportunities to speak with first-year instructors about what antiracist pedagogical strategies might look like. We made use of casual conversations, as well as more formal post-teaching observation dialogue, to seek ideas, praise instructors' ongoing work, and generally forefront our commitment to antiracism as praxis.

Months later as we planned our next orientation, four graduate student instructors approached us and offered to plan a session on antiracist strategies. These graduate students developed scenarios based on their own experiences with racism. Discussions were energetic, engaged, and oftentimes passionate. Lynn and Josh joined as quiet participants while these four risked their personal experiences—and bodies—for the eyes of their fellow instructors. Postsession surveys praised the dialogue that ensued as enormously useful, as well as revealing.

What happened was evidence of consent to the culture of collaboration we had been working towards: a rebuttal to neoliberal logics. We believe this moment might not have been possible without our earlier revisions to outcomes-based assessment and to the mentorship program. Nor would it have been possible without our holding the door open for these conversations and freely offering our own reflections as we interrogated our own practices and thinking.

Now in the fourth year of our collaborative partnership as director and associate director of first-year composition, we are marking additional evidence of consent in increasing willingness to participate in—and lead—curricular-review discussions, workshops on such topics as power and gender, and new program initiatives.

Corequisite teaching was another session we added to orientation in 2018 and, like antiracism, it is essentially an introduction to program initiatives moving forward. The corequisite, or accelerated learning program (ALP), initiated first at the Community College of Baltimore County in 2007, replaces the usual model for developmental writers. In the traditional model, students deemed to be developmental writers are typically required to take and pay for a no-credit course that will allow them to master the skills needed to pass first-year composition. Success rates, measured in numbers of students persisting and passing this sequence, have been abysmal. In the ALP model, students take both the developmental writing course and the traditional first-year composition course side by side with the same instructor. The traditional FYC class is a mix of students: some whose test scores suggest they would normally be involved in developmental writing courses and some whose scores do not. The smaller ALP course consists of only those students who would not normally place into FYC.

Our university did not previously offer developmental writing courses. Students whose test scores did not meet the cutoff were directed to take classes at a local community college, which lacks the resources of OSU. These were the students underrepresented on our campus. They lacked access to resources available to others. And they tended to be people of color.

Relegated to an underfunded community college, they were utterly invisible at OSU. In our version of the corequisite model, we have been able to provide six hours per week of writing instruction for these students. They are on campus, participating in activities and in classes, but they are also supplied with guided support and the extra time they need to master the writing tasks of a first-year writing classroom. In effect, we replaced a neoliberal model of efficiency, where invisible bodies push through needed tasks in the minimum amount of time, to a slowed pace with attention to relationship building and providing the amount of time needed to accomplish our program outcomes.

When Lynn announced this initiative, she wasn't sure how easy it would be to find graduate student instructors interested in taking on such a project. However, at the first organizational meeting, twelve graduate students attended and registered strong enthusiasm for an initiative that would, as one student put it, "allow us to walk the walk, not just talk the talk." Two writing studies PhD students spent the summer writing our side-by-side curriculum under Lynn's supervision and then led an orientation session introducing their work to our volunteers. Lynn was struck by the easy collaboration, laughter, and sharing spirit in the room. The students involved are in diverse fields: creative writing, literature, and rhetoric and writing studies, but this was common ground. As a group, they decided to call the initiative the CoRe. By inviting graduate students to participate in and develop antiracism and corequisite strategies in orientation, our intent is to make such work sustainable and normalize it as a central component of the job duties for teaching in our program.

CONCLUSION

We open this essay suggesting a neoliberal ethic permeates the day-to-day work of writing program administration, and we claim this ethic often manifests through a one-size-fits-all approach to pedagogical practices that can put considerations of the body out of sight. We see this as built around a larger ethic of radical individualism that works against the values of not only our own program but also the values espoused by the field of writing studies, which supports collaborative writing, casts the composition classroom as a political site, and urges both instructors and administrators to support genuine diversity and to work purposefully to dismantle structures that propagate oppression. We argue that revealing and challenging neoliberal logics in FYC is both possible and critical in this political moment, as politicians actively work to erode, replace, and decimate educational institutions and undermine social justice. Our goal is to identify places where we have attempted this work in our own program with the hope that other administrators might see how the traditional work involved in administration—programmatic outcomes, mentorship, and graduate student training in workshops and orientation—can be productive sites to challenge neoliberal logics and make the body visible.

This work is not easy. The chapters bookending this chapter, "Out of Hand" by Jennie Young (chapter 6.2) and "Dancing with Our Fears" by Mary Lourdes Silva (chapter 7.1), point to the cultural impetus demanding academics ignore their embodiment, as well as to how and why the body makes meaning. Young struggles to listen to her body despite scholarly engagement with embodiment theories. Lourdes Silva struggles with her embodiment as female, first-generation writing teacher whose English is accented. Each scholar finds a way forward when they permit their bodies to be visible: Young learns to think of her body's pain as alarm bell; Silva learns to let her body lead in the *machista*-permeated dance of the tango. Their stories exemplify how the neoliberal ethic of rendering diverse bodies invisible can damage and how paying attention to embodiment can heal. We need to listen to their stories and imagine the new practices they make possible and essential.

In John Trimbur's (2008) foreword to *The Promise and Perils of Writing Program Administration*, he argues that administrators should "see how they fit into the corporate structures that have come to dominate academic work more generally in the era of neoliberalism" (x). Moreover, he claims administrators are, in fact, well situated to challenge this neoliberal ethic through our ability to create programs that critique neoliberalism, to find ways to work productively within the limitations of our own institutional contexts, and to align ourselves in "solidarity with broader struggles for social justice" (xii–ixiv). While the current political moment makes it easy to feel there is little we can do, we believe the positions we occupy as administrators carry a special responsibility to do what we can to make things even just a little better for our students and our instructors, especially those from traditionally underserved or unseen student bodies.

REFERENCES

Baake, Ken, Stephen A. Bernhardt, Eva R. Brumberger, Katherine Durack, Bruce Farmer, Julie Dyke Ford, Thomas Hager, Robert Kramer, Lorelei Ortiz, and Carolyn Vickrey. 2008. "Mentorship, Collegiality, and Friendship: Making Our Mark as Professionals." In *Stories of Mentoring: Theory and Praxis*, edited by Michelle F. Eble and Lynee Lewis Gallet, 52–66. West Lafayette: Parlor.

Behm, Nicholas N., Gregory R. Glau, Deborah H. Holdstein, Duane Roen, and Edward M. White. 2013. *The WPA Outcomes Statement: A Decade Later*. Anderson, SC: Parlor.

Brewer, Elizabeth, Cynthia L. Selfe, and Melanie Yergeau. 2014. "Creating a Culture of Access in Composition Studies." *Composition Studies* 42 (2): 151–54.

Carter, Kathy. 1988. "Using Cases to Frame Mentor-Novice Conversations about Teaching." *Theory into Practice* 27 (3): 214–22.

Council of Writing Program Administrators. "WPA Outcomes Statement for First-Year Composition (3.0), Approved July 17, 2014." http://wpacouncil.org/aws/CWPA/pt/sd/news_article/243055/_PARENT/layout_details/false.

Davila, Bethany. 2017. "Standard English and Colorblindness in Composition Studies: Rhetorical Constructions of Racial and Linguistic Neutrality." *WPA: Writing Program Administration* 40 (2): 154–73.

de Müeller, Genevieve García, and Iris Ruiz. 2017. "Race, Silence, and Writing Program Administration: A Qualitative Study of US College Writing Programs." *WPA: Writing Program Administration* 40 (2): 19–39.

Eble, Michelle F., and Lyneé Lewis Gaillet, eds. 2008. *Stories of Mentoring: Theory and Praxis*. Anderson, SC: Parlor.

Hamraie, Aimi. 2013. "Designing Collective Access: A Feminist Disability Theory of Universal Design." *Disability Studies Quarterly* 35 (4): http://dsq-sds.org/article/view/3871.

Hardcastle, Beverly. 1988. "Spiritual Connections: Protégés' Reflections on Significant Mentorships." *Theory into Practice* 27 (3): 201–8.

Harrington, Susanmarie, Keith Rhodes, Ruth Overman Fisher, and Rita Malenczyk. 2005. *The Outcomes Book: Debate and Consensus after the WPA Outcomes Statement*. Logan: Utah State University Press.

Harvey, David. 2007. *A Brief History of Neoliberalism*. Oxford: Oxford University Press.

Inoue, Asao B. 2016. "Friday Plenary Address: Racism in Writing Programs and the CWPA." *WPA: Writing Program Administration* 40 (1): 134–54.

Inoue, Asao B., and Mya Poe. 2012. *Race and Writing Assessment*. New York: Peter Lang.

Kynard, Carmen. 2015. "Teaching While Black: Witnessing and Countering Disciplinary Whiteness, Racial Violence, and University Race-Management." *Literacy in Composition Studies* 3 (1): 1–20.

Leverenz, Carrie S. 2016. "Redesigning Writing Outcomes" *WPA: Writing Program Administration* 40 (1): 33–49.

Lu Lui, Steve, and Paul Kei Matsuda. 2008. "It Takes a Community of Scholars to Raise One: Multiple Mentors as Key to My Growth." In *Learning the Literacy Practices of Graduate School: Insiders' Reflections on Academic Enculturation*, edited by Christine Pearson Casanave and Xiaoming Li, 166–85. Ann Arbor: University of Michigan Press.

Micciche, Laura R., and Allison D. Carr. 2011. "Toward Graduate-Level Writing Instruction." *College Composition and Communication* 62 (3): 477–501.

National Council of Teachers of English. 2019. "Resolution on English Education for Critical Literacy in Politics and Media." https://ncte.org/statement/resolution-english-education-critical-literacy-politics-media/.

Perryman-Clark, Stacy. 2016. "Who We Are(n)'t Assessing: Racializing Language and Writing Assessment in Writing Program Administration." "*Toward Writing Assessment as Social Justice*," special issue, *College English* 79 (2): 206–11.

Reid, E. Shelley. 2008. "Mentoring Peer Mentors: Mentor Education and Support in the Composition Program." *Composition Studies* 36 (2): 52–79.

Sanchez, James Chase, and Tyler S. Branson. 2016. "The Role of Composition Programs in De-Normalizing Whiteness in the University: Programmatic Approaches to Anti-Racist Pedagogies." *WPA: Writing Program Administration* 39 (2): 47–52.

Scott, Tony. 2016. "Subverting Crisis in the Political Economy of Composition." *College Composition and Communication* 68 (1): 10–37.

Simpson, Steve, and Paul Kei Matsuda. 2008. "Mentoring as a Long-Term Relationship: Situated Learning in a Doctoral Program." In *Learning the Literacy Practices of Graduate School: Insiders' Reflections on Academic Enculturation*, edited by Christine Pearson and Xiaoming Li, 90–104. Ann Arbor: University of Michigan Press.

Trimbur, John. 2008. Foreword to *The Promise and Perils of Writing Program Administration*, edited by Theresa Enos and Shane Borrowman, 5–20. West Lafayette: Parlor.

Welch, Nancy, and Tony Scott. 2016. *Composition in the Age of Austerity*. Logan: Utah State University Press.

Yamamoto, Kaoru. 1988. "To See Life Grow: The Meaning of Mentorship." *Theory into Practice* 27 (3): 183–89.

Yancey, Kathleen Blake. 2004. "Standards, Outcomes, and All That Jazz." In *Debate and Consensus after the WPA Outcomes Statement*, edited by Susanmarie Harrington, Keith Rhodes, Ruth Fischer, and Rita Malenczyk, 18–23. Logan: Utah State University Press.

Yergeau, Melanie. 2016. "Saturday Plenary Address: Creating a Culture of Access in Writing Program Administration." *WPA: Writing Program Administration* 40 (1): 155–65.

7.1

DANCING WITH OUR FEARS
A Writing Professor's Tango

Mary Lourdes Silva

My feet plant deeper into the wooden floor; seventy-year-old sounds of the *bandoneón* fill my legs like mercury. I grow more tense when the singer cries out in pain about the loss of his first love and mother country. Within my tango embrace, that safe space a leader creates for the follower, she grows in my arms, light as ivy but also deeply rooted into the ground where I feel her free leg move because of the subtle gestures of my torso and arms. In the improvisational dance of Argentine tango, at a *milonga*, the leader connects with the follower through the embrace and has several simultaneous responsibilities: navigate the *pista*, always inching forward in complex circular patterns on the crowded dance floor; listen to tango *orquestas* from the golden era of the 30s and 40s, locating the dominant beat, the *compás*, while also interpreting the playful *síncopas* and silence in between; provide half a frame for the follower to slip into place like that final puzzle piece to complete the full picture; listen to each other's bodies in a whisper to share out loud stories of past and present; and *la entrega*, total surrender to the follower and music and a private protest of what tango should look like.

Within the *machista* culture of Buenos Aires, in the first one hundred years of tango's history, female leaders were nearly nonexistent. During Argentina's economic crisis in the late 90s, women began to learn how to lead in order to teach classes. In the mid-2000s, young male and female dancers began to challenge the gender norms of tango at queer *milongas* throughout the city (McMains 2018, 176). In 2019, although most *milongas* in the city are still quite heteronormative, where men invite the women to dance and most dances are between men and women, it is not uncommon for two women to dance together. I first learned to follow, like most women in tango. However, it wasn't until I learned to lead, empowered by my own creative agency on the dance floor and empowered by countering gender norms that still define the

https://doi.org/10.7330/9781646422340.c007.1

sociopolitical fate of women around the world, that I gained the confidence to stand as an authority figure in front of my writing classroom.

I did not truly understand the extent of my impostor-syndrome symptoms until after the tenure process was over. That story ended on a positive note, with my obtaining tenure and living in Buenos Aires for one year during my sabbatical, where I write this chapter. The part of the story that remains silenced is the part in which I had to undergo years of student evaluations at an all-white private liberal arts college. Without fail, in every class, 27.5 percent of students found the required writing course a waste of time, and at least one or two students criticized my pronunciation of certain words—a painful reminder of childhood years in school when peers made fun of my English. And for years, I tried to overcompensate for my limitations in education, knowing my immigrant parents, with only a primary school education, couldn't provide me the same opportunities as the parents of my wealthier American friends. Like any first-generation female student, I worked harder than everyone else, read more, wrote more, studied more, took more classes, participated in more extracurriculars, earned more degrees, more, more, more. But no amount of more could fill this void I had; and year after year of having to read cruel anonymous reviews by students, with whom I developed a strong rapport in the classroom, sucked the light out of me. Study after study continues to illustrate the unfair gender bias of anonymous student evaluations, and administration after administration continues to impose these student evaluations onto women faculty because, as one male administrator at my college told me, "It's not a perfect tool, but it's the best we have."

Tango is a truth drug that fills our void. It's a form of escapism that allows our bodies to experience strength, love, laughter, altruism, sadness, pain, failure, and fear. In tango, we learn to embrace our failures and fears, dancing into the late hours until the sun rises, because we are chasing that next high, an embodied sensation of pure joy and unconditional love. As a writing professor at an all-white college, I realized I was afraid to expose my genuine self, afraid to be called out as a fraud, afraid to teach, afraid of my own students. The editors of this collection describe how too often we silence our fears and anxieties "because of the shame associated with having certain bodies and/or the knowledge that no one will listen" (Nicolas and Sicari, chapter 1). Unlike tango, where a "fleshy epistemology" (Nicolas and Sicari, 5) is the norm, where the nature of the dance is to engage in "dialogue with differing bodies, embracing the contradictions and complications that come from bodies," in the writing classroom, our individual bodies stand open and bare, unprepared for the cruelty of student criticism.

A common critique on my evaluations when I first began to teach at this all-white college was my lack of clarity in and organization of curricular assignments and classroom activities. Although I valued deliberate chaos in the learning process (the unexpected couple entering the dance floor and the leader needing to shift the follower's axis in a split second) and intentionally made space for ambiguity in order for students to co-construct with me a pathway toward their own learning goals, I valued job security more at this point in my career, so I did the most reasonable, logical thing—I designed a flawless prescriptive curriculum with copious models, clear directions, and various forms of feedback. And it worked. I learned to teach to the test and my evaluations improved, enough to help me earn tenure. But I also learned I had to compromise some of my values, beliefs, and integrity as a writing professor to meet the expectations of my administration. Writing is a recursive, nonlinear, situational, rhetorical process of knowing and ambiguity (Purdy 2014, 613). For a white male professor, it is a privilege to embed ambiguity, cognitive dissonance, and nonlinearity in the classroom (all necessary elements to learn tango). For many female professors, however, to espouse these same writing principles, we are expected to nurture, console, apologize, and be flexible with deadlines and classroom policies.

The student criticism did not stop with tenure. There was always at least one student who would protest publicly, "But YOU said . . . I am not sure what you want from us."

Without hesitation, panic would set in, breaths shortening, as if a straw was shoved into my mouth and I was ordered to breathe normally. I couldn't. I worried that any form of student confusion or anxiety would spiral beyond my control, and once again, regardless of the hours of student conferences, pages of reviews of student drafts, and regular participation at professional-development events on campus, I would have to read caustic comments about my personality or identity. Of course, one could write this off as collateral damage that comes with the job. At the University of California, Santa Barbara (UCSB), my alma mater, one writing program administrator commented that it was a sign of good teaching when a small percentage of students hate you. At my college, it is a call for administrative intervention.

My fear of teaching drove me thousands of miles away to the dimly lit dance floors of Buenos Aires. Most tenured faculty would celebrate their recent promotion, but I knew I needed this year to rediscover my joy for teaching and writing. It wasn't until I experienced in my body the *absence* of fear when experimenting with failure on the dance floor that I realized I needed to dance with my fears in the writing classroom.

I realized each class, each student was an individual dance in which my job as the leader was to create that safe space for my students to express their own agency and take risks by experimenting with different ideas, writing technologies, and genres. And as the cliché goes, it takes two to tango; I also needed to feel safe to experiment with my curriculum and express my own creative agency as a writing professor.

Halfway into my stay in Buenos Aires, I was assigned to teach an online summer course on academic writing, as well as coordinate a writing technology institute at UCSB for K–16 writing instructors. Here was my chance to reconnect with students; I had the opportunity to take the lead and redesign my course, and more important, I had a chance to follow their lead and listen to their actual interests. After hours of conversation, one student, who had begun with an erudite topic like *Social Media Influencers and Their Impact on Female Users*, asked a more meaningful question, "Why did my best friend resort to cutting after spending months on Snapchat?" Another student researched *Body Modifications in the Workplace* and later confided, "Will my tattoos limit my job prospects as a classical guitarist?" These authentic questions emerged from hours of writing, reading, discussion, research, and yes, some resistance. Students tried repeatedly to regurgitate the prose of their secondary sources to suit the expectations of academia. Convincing students to experiment with genres and make mistakes required a different process for each one. But once I started to hear their voices, I could also hear mine, and this time, it wasn't the critic repeatedly second-guessing herself. Later, when I stood in front of a classroom of fellow colleagues and peers at UCSB, I heard it again. In the middle of my opening talk, I trusted my intuition and modified the ice-breaker activity, which then set the tone for the entire institute. They talked and I listened.

In tango, the best leaders are those who learn to listen and listen to learn—listen to the music, listen to the crowded dance floor, listen to your follower, listen to your body. Both in the writing classroom and packed *milongas* of Buenos Aires, we long to share our stories, whether it be through words or the body. Regardless of the modality we choose, we fear exposing our vulnerabilities and insecurities. The beauty of tango and writing is that we don't have to experience them alone. I would like to believe my dance with fear will result in better student evaluations or remission from the impostor syndrome. Nothing I do in the writing classroom or dance floor can promise that outcome. In fact, I promise you there will be more cruel evaluations to come. More self-doubt. However, I know now that I do belong in the classroom, mispronunciations and all—ready to listen.

REFERENCES

McMains, Juliet. 2018. "Rebellious Wallflowers and Queer *Tangueras*: The Rise of Female Leaders in Buenos Aires' Tango Scene." *Dance Research* 36 (2): 173–97.

Purdy, James P. 2014. "What Can Design Thinking Offer Writing Studies?" *College Composition and Communication* 65 (4): 612–41.

7.2

"DO NOT DISTURB—BREASTFEEDING IN PROGRESS"
Reflections from a Lactating WPA

Jasmine Kar Tang

Complete with an unassuming black bag, the Medela Pump in Style breast pump has many parts, including the adapter, tubing, flanges, connectors, valves, membranes, bottles, caps, and bottle stands—in total almost twenty parts to assemble at each lactation session. The protocol for pumping and storing breastmilk, which varies from parent to parent, is just as convoluted as the assembly process and easily takes a couple hours each day:

- Assemble, disassemble, two times a day.
- Refrigerate pump parts in Ziplock between pumping sessions. Always have extra parts at work just in case.
- An absolute must for pumping at work is a hands-free pumping bra. (Bonus: have a breastfeeding cover around just in case someone ignores the sign you put on the door.)
- For the commute home, use a cooler with an ice pack.
- When traveling with milk, don't run: shaking the milk can destroy the proteins.
- At home, carefully transfer milk from the pumping bottles to the feeding bottles: milk will separate in storage, but, again, don't shake it! Just swirl it around gently.
- Transfer milk to five different bottles for daycare. Write a number and date on each bottle and record on the fridge to keep track of freshness. If there's extra milk, freeze in Lansinoh storage bags, with dates written on each bag.
- Store flat and in increments of two to four ounces to prevent leaks when thawing.
- Wash all pump parts, pumping bottles, and daycare bottles in hot, soapy water.
- Sanitize above items in the steam bag. (Frequency depends on the age of the baby.)
- Pack up all parts when everything is dry the next morning.

https://doi.org/10.7330/9781646422340.c007.2

I have been breastfeeding for over five years over the course of having two kids. When my firstborn, Danny, arrived, I was working half time with no benefits at a "start-up" writing program serving Indigenous graduate students and graduate students of color (Tang and Andriamanalina 2016). Two days before my water broke, my then boss mentioned I qualified for parental leave in some way. I had no idea what a big deal that was, and up until that point, I had not even thought to ask HR about my rights. I dismissed the thought of looking into it further, thinking my four weeks off (which I had banked) would be enough. I was only part time, so how hard could it be to come in only a few days a week, especially when I had family coming to town to help, too?

When my son was three weeks old, and as I recovered from a botched epidural (complete with a spinal headache and two blood-patch procedures), I found myself cowriting a grant application to help fund the continuation of my already-puny position for the following year. The crisis of new parenthood was compounded by my preparations to return to work a matter of weeks after giving birth. This is not unusual. And, like many parents who breastfeed exclusively, I was terrified of cultivating nipple confusion, of Danny refusing a bottle, and of me not producing enough breastmilk for him to have while I was at work. When I returned to campus, I resumed providing individual writing consultations and organizing writing workshops for Indigenous graduate students and graduate students of color. Here I was—writing, researching, and teaching about how the body is inextricable from writing/research, especially for writers of color like myself. And here I was, a woman of color and a struggling new mom, going to work with at most three hours of sleep the night before. I could not make sense of this dissonance: as I encouraged writers to *listen to the body*, I denied my own. This disembodiment, I have come to believe, is a function of the academy: it is how the academy runs, and I complied, ignoring my own intuition and commitments.

Since I didn't have my own office, I pumped in the conference room of the Graduate School, in a space where higher-ups made important administrative decisions, where the fate of fellowship applicants was decided, where formal meetings were held. Lined with giant windows and fancy videoconferencing equipment (close the blinds, and make sure the camera is turned off!), it was also a room everyone walked past in order to use the women's restroom, make copies, check their mailbox, make tea, or grab their lunch from the fridge. In other words, anyone who did any of these things would see my "Do Not Disturb—Breastfeeding in Progress" sign (a typical, prefabricated sign that's actually inaccurate—if only I could be breastfeeding my baby!).

Unexpectedly, over time I felt quietly radical, as if my little wrinkled-up sign and my Google Calendar room reservations were disrupting the third floor of Johnston Hall. I was pumping and *taking up space*. For me, lactating on the job was connected to my being a mother of color in academia, an identity that by itself felt radical, complicated by being a WPA in an underdog unit that served Indigenous communities and communities of color.

Fast forward a couple years. One month into a new full-time job as codirector of the writing center on the same campus, I became pregnant with my daughter Mingyi. Though I barely qualified for FMLA, I knew better this time. I asked for and received nearly five months of (mostly unpaid) leave, with my colleagues generously taking on more work the whole time. Returning to work meant dutifully pumping every day again, which I did until my daughter was almost a year and a half old (bringing my grand total to twenty-four months of pumping at work). With my new workplace, I was able to pump in a private lactation room or in my own office.

Equipped with my angled Pumpin' Pal flanges and my new and improved hospital-grade Lactina Electric Plus pump, I became a lactating machine. This time around, I mastered the art of pumping and storing breastmilk with maximum efficiency.

Even with the support of my colleagues (and the privilege of an extended parental leave), I still faced an internal struggle about what it meant to not be with the very child the milk was intended for. It's a set of emotions that literally can affect milk production. The tricky thing about pumping is that milk volume is related to your ability to relax. In other words, the more milk you pump, the shorter the session—and the faster you can get back to work. To get the milk going, you are literally supposed to smell a onesie and look at photos or videos of the kid (Bonyata n.d.). But how do you simulate a mother-baby connection if you're pumping on the clock? With so much on my to-do list, I constantly found myself trying to get work done while pumping. However, if feeling connected to your baby is necessary for pumping, is it possible to actually work and pump at the same time? (That's what the hands-free pumping bra is for, right?) And, *how much* work can I get done during a pumping session? Can reading and writing emails reduce my milk production? (Yes.)

My boss requested I put lactation breaks on my Google Calendar so my immediate circle of colleagues would know to *not* schedule meetings with me during those times. This made perfect, practical sense for me, and I was glad to comply. I realize now that this ongoing calendar event was an act of feminist praxis: my pumping breaks became protected *and* visible, a strange simultaneity that valued and normalized breastfeeding but also forced it onto everyone's computer screens.

I also started feeling more strongly that breastfeeding is connected to my commitment to racial justice and equity (Faison et al. 2019) and to my experience as the first full-time person of color in the history of my writing center. I am already highly visible at my workplace. I feel my body and my tongue and how they are different from those of my colleagues. What do I decide to voice, and what do I let go? These are everyday questions that can feel mundane or explosive or somewhere in between for people of color.

Taking and supporting lactation breaks in the workplace allows us to render visible the embodied dimensions of parenthood, opening up spaces and opportunities for our workplace cultures to more fully recognize and prioritize the humanity, the embodied histories, and the wellness of our staff. I have the privilege of co-supervising an outstanding team of almost fifty consultants (including a couple lactating parents), and my thought is that we cannot deny the representational value of an administrator of color who makes and takes time to pump. This is the fullness of supporting the breastfeeding colleague: it enables the parent to bring their whole, embodied self to the work and to literally feed their family. And still, the daily, sustained act of pumping is a constant reminder the parent isn't home with their child. My emotions are further complicated by my experiences navigating the spaces of a PWI, where I am cautious of overstepping—of the possibility of asking for "too much" or taking up "too much" space. This is the emotional cost of fully bringing our bodies to work.

REFERENCES

Bonyata, Kelly. n.d. "Let-down Reflex: Too Slow?" KellyMom.com. Last modified April 8, 2020. https://kellymom.com/bf/got-milk/supply-worries/letdown.

Faison, Wonderful, Talisha Haltiwanger Morrison, Katie Levin, Elijah Simmons, Jasmine Kar Tang, Keli Tucker. 2019. "Potential for and Barriers to Actionable Antiracism in the Writing Center: Views from the IWCA Special Interest Group on Antiracism Activism." *Praxis: A Writing Center Journal* 16 (2): 4–11.

Tang, Jasmine Kar, and Noro Andriamanalina. 2016. " 'Rhonda Left Early to Go to Black Lives Matter': Programmatic Support for Graduate Writers of Color." *Writing Program Administration* 39 (2): 10–15.

Relationships

8
THE CIRCULATION OF EMBODIED AFFECTS IN A REVISION OF A FIRST-YEAR WRITING PROGRAM

Michael J. Faris

In January 2018, I was appointed co-writing program administrator (WPA) of our first-year writing (FYW) program and placed officially in charge of leading a massive, one-year revision of and recommitment to FYW at Texas Tech University (TTU). In spring 2017, our then-incoming department chair had assessed the program and determined it wasn't working: students were dropping, withdrawing from, and failing the course at alarming rates; students were telling their peers to take English 1301 and 1302 elsewhere; even academic advisors were telling students to take the courses at a community college over the summer; graduate students working in the program were largely dissatisfied; and despite increasing university enrollment, enrollment in FYW was declining. Our chair mandated a radical and rapid change, and I became the leader of that change. Now, three years later, I am tired. Leading a rapid revision of a writing program that now serves about three thousand students per semester, is, of course, exhausting work. In 2017, we planned new delivery models, new curriculum, and new professional-development and mentoring programs for graduate students teaching in the program. We piloted some of these changes in spring 2018 and implemented a whole new program in fall 2018.

In this chapter, I explore some of the affective dynamics of writing programs, suggesting writing programs might be best understood as sites of embodiment and the circulation of embodied affects. I started the first administration-team meeting of our FYW program in January 2019 by announcing, "Welcome to the first of sixteen meetings where I announce that I am already tired." Fatigue and exhaustion circulate through writing programs, becoming contagious. (This is not necessarily a bad thing.) So, too, do excitements, elations, revelations, joys, incitements, cares, compassions, and successes. And let us not forget

https://doi.org/10.7330/9781646422340.c008

frustrations, fears, terrors, anxieties, angers, rages, resentments, bitternesses, shynesses, obnoxiousnesses, failures, depressions, disappointments, inabilities, and failures. Patricia Bizzell (2009) argues, polemically responding to Stanley Fish, that composition can save the world. But I would add we can only do so if we attend to—if we are attuned to—our and our students' bodies.

I am, of course, not the first to call attention to bodies and affect in writing programs and writing program administration (see, for example, Micciche 2002; Miller-Cochran 2018; Worsham 1998). Lynn Worsham (1998) argues that pedagogy is primarily affective and emotional, so much so that "our most urgent political and pedagogical task remains the fundamental reeducation of emotion" (216). Like Bizzell (2009) and Worsham (1998), I too understand writing courses (and consequently writing programs) as sites of struggle in which our future is at stake. I too desire "to reclaim education as a terrain of struggle crucial to the reconstitution of public political culture" (Worsham 1998, 217).

I believe WPAs must keep bodies (their own, teachers', and students') central in programmatic design in part because we should understand writing and the teaching of writing as a matter of embodied being in the world—a matter of relationality. Our programmatic designs, then, must afford teachers the support and the space to work in their classes in order to foster this relationality, potentially developing new ways of relating and of being in the world for their students. Perhaps I could be accused of utopianism. Not much can happen in a fifteen-week semester, but also, I believe, a lot can. Lives (of teachers and students) can be changed through our courses, and that change happens through the interactions and new (potentially surprising) relationships in those classes.

However, such "on-the-ground" change becomes difficult, if not impossible, when administrative decisions are driven by perspectives that promote technological innovation and disruption and ignore the ontological, embodied nature of writing and teaching writing. I consequently first turn to a brief critique of our previous model of FYW, arguing it relied on a managerial and technocratic logic that, in rationale and in practice, effaced how writing and the teaching of writing are embodied and material—casting bodies as what Melissa Nicolas and Anna Sicari call "institutional bodies" that "stay in the background" (see chapter 1 of this volume). I then share some of my own administrative and composition philosophy, informed by feminist and queer thinking, about bodies and writing pedagogy. I further argue writing and pedagogy are ultimately ontological endeavors—about being together in the world—thus warranting our attention to bodies. From there, I turn to sharing some of our revisions in the FYW program at TTU, outlining how I've attempted to make bodies central to the work of rhetoric and composition at TTU.

ERASING BODIES AT TEXAS TECH: THE DISTRIBUTED-GRADING MODEL

Since 2002, FYW at TTU had been administered as a distributed-grading program in which instructors of record taught their classes (capped at thirty-five students) as hybrid courses, meeting once a week, and student projects were graded by anonymous document instructors (DIs)—graduate students and instructors—in the program. This program was designed to address exigencies caused by real material constraints: enrollment increased rapidly in 2002, but the university didn't provide more funding to employ more instructors. Further, the department had to employ our first-year master's students, who couldn't be instructors of record under accreditation rules. The solution was a distributed-grading model that could respond to these economic and institutional constraints by having experienced instructors teach relatively large classes, having students submit their work in a database-driven online portal, and having DIs respond to and grade student work anonymously. Further, this model could (ideally) ensure fairness in grading because each student document was assessed by two anonymous DIs who would evaluate student work based on criteria, not influenced by relationships with students (Kemp 2005b; Lang 2005; Rickly 2005; Wasley 2006).

Besides early explanations for the program, most of the scant scholarly attention to distributed grading has been quite critical. Vicki Hester (2007), who taught in the program, argues it was a model that favored economic rationality and pragmatism over questions of what it means to teach writing, ultimately reducing "teachers to technicians" and decontextualizing student writing (137). Joe Moxley (2008) argues that the database infrastructure for the program reproduced a top-down model of administration rather than a collaborative, networked one (189–90). And in her argument that we need to be thoughtful and critical as we develop hybrid writing courses, Catherine Gouge (2009) critiques the program for relying on a myth of objectivity for assessing student writing. Further, she argues the program relied on and reproduced consumerist logics of efficiency and standardization (Gouge 2010), an argument similar to Tony Scott's (2009) critique in *Dangerous Writing*. As Scott argues, the program was "in line with fast-capitalist logics of authority, organization, and production" and "maximized managerial control" of a deprofessionalized labor pool (181).

I won't reproduce these critiques in detail; let me just briefly say I agree with and endorse these perspectives. When I first learned about how the program was running, I was flabbergasted. It ran afoul of all the theory I had learned and experiences I had about learning to write, process and postprocess pedagogies, peer feedback, teacher preparation, feminist administration, theories of and approaches to teaching with technology, and more. I quickly learned from my undergraduate students in upper-division courses how much they hated English 1301 and 1302 and from graduate students how dissatisfied they were working in the program. It seemed to me the program had made an ontological error in understanding writing pedagogy, failing to understand pedagogy is about being in relations with people: that is, writing, teaching, and learning are ontological, embodied practices about being in the world and being in relations with others.

In "The Aesthetic Anvil: The Foundations of Resistance to Technology and Innovation in English Departments," Fred Kemp (2005a) provides an indirect administrative rationale for the distributed-grading model. He contrasts an aesthetic, humanist, and literary mode of administration—which he sees as elitist and Romantic, unable to respond to the fast-paced economic, technological, and social changes of our times—to an administrative model based on entrepreneurialism, disruption, and innovation. Likening an English department to "a kind of state-run small business" (80), Kemp advocates an administrative model that values innovative and disruptive technological solutions rather than the status quo, believing that "the entrepreneurial spirit actually sees nothing as being wrong or in error so much as it sees a continuing opportunity for relating more effectively within one's operating context" (92). That is, for Kemp, the proper response for English-department and writing program administration to rapid economic, technological, and social change is to think like a businessperson.

At face value, Kemp's argument seems almost commonsensical: certainly we cannot continue to justify the work of English departments based on nineteenth-century models of aesthetic humanism, and certainly (at least from today's perspective) we cannot be reactionary and simply reject technological change, nor can we ignore the larger socioeconomic context surrounding shifts in higher education. But what does Kemp's entrepreneurial logic lead to? Ultimately, at least at TTU, it led to the distributed-grading model of administering FYW—a model more technocratic than pedagogical, serving to efface how writing and writing pedagogy are always embodied.

In a great irony, Kemp (2005a) critiques humanist approaches for their "disdain for materiality and carnality" (87), yet the entrepreneurialism he advocates makes embodiment and materiality invisible and inconsequential to writing pedagogies in the program. In a classroom of thirty-five students that met once a week for eighty minutes with no interactivity online, students became imagined docile bodies (or "institutional bodies") receiving knowledge from their instructors, who had become disciplined to lecture, rather than teach, writing so as many students as possible could receive knowledge to put toward their essays they'd turn in online later (an irony, given Kemp's [2005b] concern that inexperienced teachers were likely lecturing more than teaching writing when given more freedom [111]). Document instructors' bodies were reduced to sitting at a computer and responding to anonymous student writing for twenty hours a week, a sort of drudgery of "heavy grading" Maxine Hairston (1986) warns about, becoming "composition slave[s]" (118). (As M. Jimmie Killingsworth [2010] observes, technorhetoricians too often forget about or ignore bodies that sit at computers to do their work [84].) Further, the materiality of writing was ignored in the program: students submitted their work online as plain text, so students had no control over the visual aspects of their writing—in effect disavowing that writing is always material, designed, and multimodal (see Ball and Charlton 2015; Wysocki 2005). (No multimedia here, despite Kemp's defense of technological change!) Ultimately, the administrative framing of distributed grading served to make invisible the day-to-day, embodied, material practices of teaching, writing, and learning, which instead became "instrumentalist management techniques" (Scott 2009, 55).

QUEERING PROGRAM ADMINISTRATION

As I mentioned above, everything I witnessed about the distributed-grading model ran afoul of the theories and practices I had learned as a graduate student and while contributing to the FYW program at previous institutions. As a queer man, much of my thinking about writing studies, administration, and pedagogy has been informed by feminist and queer scholars, activists, and theorists who have emphasized the poetic, affective, material, and embodied nature of pedagogy, relationality, writing, and public work. Following queer theorists like Michael Warner (1993, xiii), Leo Bersani (1995, 7), and José Esteban Muñoz (2009, 189), I believe there is something about queerness that leads to implicit critiques of the social order as it is known (in this case, neoliberal managerial logics deployed in rhetoric and composition administrative theories and practices). Sarah Ahmed (2006) calls this a "disorientation" toward the world, one caused because queer bodies do not quite fit into the social order (157–63).

Queer perspectives on composition afford critiques of standard composition curricula and administration. If, as Jeanne Gunner (2002) argues, writing programs are ideological in that they categorize and hierarchize students as types of writers, then queer approaches ask how traditional composition and administration privileges not only composed texts but also composed bodies. Robert McRuer (2006) argues that the same logics that value and enforce composed writing also value and enforce composed bodies—straight and able-bodied (150–55). From another queer perspective, Eric Darnell Pritchard (2017) argues that "literacy normativity"—or "the use of literacy to create and impose normative standards and beliefs onto people who are labeled alien or other"—serves to harm those most marginalized in society, particularly Black queer and trans people (28). In effect, the norms of writing programs, even in process-based approaches, still tend to privilege final products that conform to normative standards. As Geoffrey Sirc (1997) writes of professionalized composition, "Writing could no longer just *be*, it had to be a certain way" (11).

William P. Banks and Jonathan Alexander (2009) observe that very little literature has explored the relationship between queerness and WPA work (88–89). They suggest a queer writing program might be impossible because "abstract antinormative theories" might be too inimical to program administration (97). Thus, "the real value of a queer WPA lies in how the WPA validates or welcomes the sort of queer guerrilla tactics that would act at the local levels, in individual classrooms and assignments" (97). I agree a queer writing program is likely an impossibility, but I want to suggest queer (and other nonnormative or marginalized) administrative bodies benefit a writing program: they bring an attunement to the sensitivity of bodies and how relationality is always made and refigured anew, a (dis)orientation toward themselves, their students, and the program. (See also Stacey Waite's chapter 3 in this volume on queering administration and pedagogy.) Of course, I want to avoid any sort of essentialized view of identity and bodies here. I am merely pointing toward the potentiality of queerly or otherwise marginalized bodies to challenge composition administration as it has too often become: neoliberal, abstract, bottom line, formalist, even when it attempts not to be.

WRITING AND WRITING PEDAGOGY AS BEING TOGETHER IN THE WORLD

How, then, to be a WPA in ways that might encourage guerrilla tactics or other antinormative practices in composition courses? I believe one way forward is for WPAs to understand that bodies are central to pedagogy and administration and that writing and the teaching of writing are ontological practices. Here, I have in mind Robert P. Yagelski's (2011) argument in *Writing as a Way of Being*. While Yagelski's book barely addresses program administration, he makes a powerful case that we should understand writing and the teaching of writing as ontological practices. As he argues, the power of writing is in "the experience of writing itself," not in the product of writing (xiv). Writing pedagogy has been reduced to a set of procedures or processes (whether in process pedagogy or postprocess pedagogy) that ignores the ontological power of writing: "We teach students that writing is a procedure rather than a way of experiencing themselves as beings in an inherently interconnected world" (xv). Yagelski contrasts his nondualistic view of writing to Cartesian views, which see writing as separate from the writer, reproducing "the classic Cartesian subject: an autonomous, thinking being" (3). (At this point, readers should see Yagelski's argument as an implicit critique of distributed grading, which was founded on the premise that writing should be judged as a product, fully separate from the writer, and that any personal relationship with a student can only interfere with that assessment.)

Yagelski's (2011) perspective means refocusing our pedagogical attention away from "the writer's writing" (the products or texts) and towards "the *writer writing*" or "the experience of writing" (7). Focusing our writing pedagogy on texts or products "neglects the effects of the *act* of writing on the writer's sense of being" (7). To attend to the ontological nature of writing—which is about being in the world—means "writing instruction, like schooling in general, is an ontological process; it is part of how we learn to *be* in the world" (30). Yagelski's view of education—and of writing education in particular—is that its goal should be "about creating a better world" (139), and in order to reach this goal, writing pedagogy should be about being in the world together. Yagelski provides a useful example: peer-review sessions are not solely about students helping each other to improve each other's texts. Instead, through peer response and other pedagogical practices, "Writing thus becomes a collective process of inquiry, and the experience of writing becomes a collective act of being together in the world" (161).

Yagelski's (2011) view of writing and writing pedagogy has much in common with emancipatory and feminist pedagogy, especially views espoused by Paulo Freire (2003) and bell hooks (1994). One of hooks's primary contributions to feminist pedagogy, as I understand her, is that teaching is about embodied practices with students, not about instilling disciplinary knowledge. As she argues, teachers and students must engage with each other as whole beings (15), and "education as the practice of freedom is not just about liberatory knowledge, it's about a liberatory practice in the classroom" (147). Likewise, Freire's (2003) critique of the banking model of education and his advocacy for liberatory pedagogy is grounded in changing our classroom practices. As Yagelski (2011) writes of Freire, "At the heart of Freire's analysis is a critique of what is really the ontology of conventional schooling: 'Implicit in the banking concept is the assumption of a dichotomy between human beings and the world: a person is merely *in* the world, not *with* the world or with others'" (29, quoting Freire 2003, 75).

Consequently, I believe part of a WPA's role is to facilitate or make it possible for teachers to design their writing classes as spaces where embodied relationships can be developed and fostered. A class of thirty-five students that only meets once a week, with feedback on writing not from the instructor but from some anonymous grader, makes this endeavor more difficult (and for novice teachers, close to impossible). Of course, this argument likely carries no weight with upper administrators who might pressure WPAs for larger class sizes, but it should carry weight with rhetoric and composition scholars. Nor, I should add, does this argument foreclose the possibilities for hybrid or online classes designed with the sort of interactivity among students and between teachers and students online writing instruction scholars advocate. But it does challenge the assumption that writing can be taught to thirty-five students in eighty minutes a week when students aren't interacting with each other outside class meetings. And it challenges the practice instituted under distributed grading wherein teachers were assigned up to six sections a semester (for a total of 210 students!).

How, then, can we as WPAs foster programs in which teachers are encouraged to consider how to design their classes as spaces of embodied relationality? I'll admit I don't have the perfect answers—or even near-perfect answers—but I'd like to share some of my practices as a WPA and some of the revisions we've implemented at TTU in order to make bodies a central aspect of composing at TTU.

EMBODIMENT IN PROGRAMMATIC REVISIONS

As I worked in coordination with colleagues to plan a new curriculum, new delivery models (including smaller class sizes), new mentorship and professional-development programs, and other new aspects of the FYW program, I was cognizant of how important bodies are to teaching, learning, writing, and rhetoric, and I attempted to keep this awareness in mind as we planned and implemented the new program. First, we've made bodies an explicit point of discussion in our preparation and mentoring of new teachers. Over the course of the first full year of our new program (2018–2019), these discussions took a variety of forms, but they've largely focused on teachers' bodies, students' bodies, and the construction of space. I've found, first of all, that strategically hiring experienced teachers (especially feminist and race-, class-, and ability-conscious teacher-scholars) who can work with and mentor new graduate instructors to be vitally important for a collaborative approach to making bodies visible and a site of practice important. (See also Joshua Daniel and Lynn Lewis's related argument about making bodies visible in writing programs, as well as their discussion of mentoring, in chapter 7 of this volume.) In 2018, our program hired assistant professors of practice who would work with and mentor first-year MA students through their first year of teaching. During orientation in August 2018, a new graduate student asked a fairly complex question about teaching. Without thinking, I sat down in a chair in front of the room to contemplate. I had been standing and moving about the room for the previous hour or so as we had discussed writing pedagogy. Callie Kostelich, our new assistant professor of practice, interjected, observing how I had physically repositioned my body in order to refigure the space for a different type of conversation. And so began a year of attending to our bodies.

How teachers perform their bodies has become central to the practicum I teach for first-year teachers. Consistently, our new teachers and I bring up our own bodies. I stress taking care of their bodies: Are you sleeping? Going to the gym? Cooking? Doing what makes you feel whole and healthy? We discuss how some of their bodies are read differently and interacted with differently by students because of their race, age, gender, and other aspects of their perceived identities. We make spaces in the program for young women to discuss and brainstorm together the challenges of being a young woman and developing an authoritative presence in the classroom. Some of our experienced teachers and professors organized meetings with women graduate students (some at a bar, some at homes) to discuss the challenges of teaching as young women. (Kelsie Walker, Morgan Gross, Paula Weinman, Hayat Bedaiwi, and Alyssa McGrath's chapter 5 and Triauna Carey's chapter 6 in this volume also explore how gender and race power dynamics play out for graduate instructors in their classrooms. See also Jacquelyn Hoermann-Elliott's chapter in this volume, which shows gendered power dynamics are not limited to relationships with students; they are also at play in relationships with colleagues.)

Our students' bodies, too, have been points of discussion during professional-development and mentoring activities. During practicum, we've also discussed and shared our experiences as teachers working with students who are depressed, anxious, angry, disaffected. These become not simply problems to solve but also opportunities to discuss how we interact with other humans and how we help support them. And we've shared ideas for designing lesson plans and activities for universal access. For instance, I encourage new teachers to see accessibility accommodations not as burdens but as opportunities to make their classes as inviting and accessible as possible.

And spaces and practices have been continual points of discussion and exploration with new teachers. Our program has attempted to make writing practices a central aspect for our philosophical approach: our custom textbook stresses practice as a central component to developing as a writer, and we continually discuss writing practices during our practicum. We encourage our teachers to have students write during every class period (a practice I picked up, after some resistance, from Cheryl Glenn when I was a graduate student at Penn State). The notion of writing as an embodied, ontological practice led one new teacher to encourage her students to intentionally design their writing spaces. She told them to gather what made them happy (coffee or other drinks, snacks, certain music, devices) in a space and time they wanted to set aside for writing. And her students reported back (unanimously, evidently, which I can hardly believe) that it worked for them. They wrote, and they didn't write last minute but were in tune with their writing.

Spaces and how spaces encourage ways of relating to each other have been central to our teacher preparation. I consistently call attention to how the architecture of the room shapes our relationships with each other during practicum, and I encourage us to (at times) refigure this space by moving our bodies or the furniture when possible. And our new teachers take notice.

One first-year MA student observed that because she taught in a low-tech classroom in fall semester, students engaged with her and each other (and she engaged with them) differently than in the spring semester, when she was able to show more PowerPoint slides and videos. She scaled back on the digital-technology presentation and found her class interacted differently when certain technologies mediated their experiences.

Further, in our programmatic revisions, we've made materiality a central aspect of students' composing practices and products. Our final assignments in both courses—a podcast episode in English 1301 and an essay or new media project that enters a conversation about an issue of public concern in English 1302—require what Jody Shipka (2011) calls a statement of goals and choices that asks students to explain their material, technological, and rhetorical choices for the project, including how it would circulate in public spaces and reach its audience (113–26). In their chapter on a required podcast episode in FYW, Jeremy Cushman and Shannon Kelly (2018) describe how the materiality of audio demands of students a different attitude and approach toward research and audience engagement and demands of teachers a different affective and embodied response to their students' projects. We've found this to be true in our writing program: one graduate instructor told me about crying in her office in response to her students' podcast episodes, and many have reported other embodied responses to their students' projects (including elation, discomfort, intrigue, and, as is true of all classes, disappointment).

As Laura R. Micciche (2002) suggests, teacher-preparation courses should complement "content knowledge and practical know-how" with "frank discussions about working conditions and the affective landscape of professional life" (454). And as Bizzell (2009) argues, one of the ways composition "saves the world" is "through contact with the professor's personality and values" (186). As a teacher who loves his students, and as a WPA who loves his teachers—I tell our incoming graduate instructors during August orientation that they will be the most important people in my life for the next year (perhaps an obvious commentary on being a single, queer WPA)—I find Kemp's (2005b) argument against teaching personas surprising in some ways. Kemp argues against the "mentorship model" desired by teachers, arguing instead for a systems approach to administration (120). But I remain firm in my understanding that teaching (and administration) happens through relationships, through bodies being thrown together in new (and hopefully exciting) ways that can elicit new opportunities for engagement with writing and with each other, for potentially new ways of being in the world and being with each other.

CONCLUSION: FYW AS THE CIRCULATION OF AFFECTS

I opened this chapter by admitting to being tired. Exhaustion has recently garnered some attention in rhetorical studies. (Both Rita Malenczyk's and Ryan Skinnell's interchapters in this volume address being tired; see also Rebecca Gerdes-McClain's chapter 10 in this volume on Mina Shaughnessy's exhaustion as a WPA.) Jenny Rice (2018) argues for attending to the circulation of negative affects and how they enable potentially new kinds of publics to assemble. In particular, she attends to how "movement exhausts": the circulation of public rhetoric, she shows, *exhausts* in that it both exhausts its own circulation and exhausts public beings (283). However, exhaustion doesn't lead to disengagement but rather to new forms of engagement, like Matt Haughey's Twitter campaign that "replaced the guns held by conservative lawmakers [in images] with comically large sex toys" (286–87).

I often talk with our graduate instructors about their exhaustion. It is—along with frustration, fear, senses of illegitimacy, and sometimes terror—the most frequent affect circulating in a writing program. I discuss the movement from survival to thriving—from struggling through the day to day toward creating public and semipublic knowledge (Restaino 2012). Do I admit I, too, am just surviving so much of the time? Do I discuss being a pretenure, queer, single, raised-working-class WPA? Do I talk about how I put in twelve-hour days so I can support them, deal with administrative minutiae, teach my own classes, keep up with my email, edit a journal, and continue to research and write? Do I tell them most of my writing is now done after sunset over whiskey and cokes and while chain smoking? Sometimes, yes, and sometimes, no.

Just as Rice (2018) suggests exhaustion leads to new types of engagement (rather than disengagement), exhaustion (and other negative and positive affects) is also productive in FYW programs, circulating in unexpected, transformative, or even mundane ways. But if we don't attend to how affects circulate in our program or how bodies interact with each other in classes and through their writing—if we engage in programmatic design without considering these material aspects of our programs—we risk turning to technocratic modes of administration that ignore embodiment and the ontological nature of writing and pedagogy. WPAs need administrative philosophies that take embodiment and affect into account because WPAs, teachers, and students are bodies, and we come together in surprising ways.

Acknowledgments. I would like to acknowledge this chapter was written within the historical territories of the Teya, Jumano, Apache, and Comanche peoples. While such a statement is only a small step toward dismantling colonial logics and practices, I believe it is a necessary step to call attention to the fact that the work of our writing programs is conducted on lands taken from Indigenous peoples.

I would also like to thank our English department chair, Brian Still, for recognizing that the distributed-grading model for FYW was not working for our students, our teachers, our department, or our university and starting us on a course to improving FYW. I also want to thank those bodies who have supported my body and thinking (and challenged my thinking) through our programmatic revision: Kendall Gerdes, Leah Heilig, Callie Kostelich, Kristen Moore, Jennifer Nish, Monica Norris, Roxanne Mountford, Becky Rickly, Brian Still, and, of course, the dedicated graduate students and instructors in our program. I also want to acknowledge those from my previous institutions who have shaped my understandings of bodies and administration, including Lisa Ede, Cheryl Glenn, Debbie Hawhee, Anita Helle, Stuart Selber, Vicki Tolar Burton, and Shevaun Watson. Readers might observe that most of these figures are women. If composition studies has taught me anything, it is that Beyoncé (2011) is right: "Who run the world? Girls."

REFERENCES

Ahmed, Sara. 2006. *Queer Phenomenology: Orientations, Objects, Others.* Durham, NC: Duke University Press.

Ball, Cheryl E., and Colin Charlton. 2015. "All Writing Is Multimodal." In *Naming What We Know: Threshold Concepts of Writing Studies*, edited by Linda Adler-Kassner and Elizabeth Wardle, 42–43. Logan: Utah State University Press.

Banks, William P., and Jonathan Alexander. 2009. "Queer Eye for the Comp Program: Toward a Queer Critique of WPA Work." In *The Writing Program Interrupted: Making Space for Critical Discourse*, edited by Donna Strickland and Jeanne Gunner, 86–98. Portsmouth, NH: Heinemann.

Bersani, Leo. 1995. *Homos.* Cambridge, MA: Harvard University Press.

Beyoncé. 2011. "Run the World (Girls)." Track 12 on *4*. Columbia, compact disc.

Bizzell, Patricia. 2009. "Composition Studies Saves the World!" *College English* 72 (2): 174–87.

Cushman, Jeremy, and Shannon Kelly. 2018. "Recasting Writing, Voicing Bodies: Podcasts Across a Writing Program." In *Soundwriting Pedagogies*, edited by Courtney S. Danforth, Kyle D. Stedman, and Michael J. Faris. Logan: Computers and Composition Digital Press. https://ccdigitalpress.org/book/soundwriting/cushman-kelly/index.html.

Freire, Paulo. 2003. *Pedagogy of the Oppressed.* 30th anniversary ed. Translated by Myra Bergman Ramos. New York: Continuum.

Gouge, Catherine. 2009. "Conversation at a Crucial Moment: Hybrid Courses and the Future of Writing Programs." *College English* 71 (4): 338–62.

Gouge, Catherine. 2010. "Location, Location, Location: The Radical Potential of Web-Intensive Writing Programs to Challenge Disciplinary Boundaries." In *Writing Against the Curriculum: Anti-Disciplinarity in the Writing and Cultural Studies Classroom*, edited by Randi Gray Kirstensen and Ryan M. Claycomb, 111–26. Lanham, MD: Lexington Books.

Gunner, Jeanne. 2002. "Ideology, Theory, and the Genre of the Writing Program." In *The Writing Program Administrator as Theorist: Making Knowledge Work*, edited by Shirley K. Rose and Irwin Weiser, 7–18. Portsmouth, NH: Heinemann.

Hairston, Maxine. 1986. "Making Assignments, Judging Writing, and Annotating Papers: Some Suggestions." In *Training the New Teacher of College Composition*, edited by Charles W. Bridges, 109–24. Urbana, IL: NCTE.

Hester, Vicki. 2007. "When Pragmatics Precede Pedagogy: Post-Process Theories of Assessment and Response to Student Writing." *Journal of Writing Assessment* 3 (2): 123–44. http://journalofwritingassessment.org/archives/3-2.4.pdf.

hooks, bell. 1994. *Teaching to Transgress: Education as the Practice of Freedom*. New York: Routledge.

Kemp, Fred. 2005a. "The Aesthetic Anvil: The Foundations of Resistance to Technology and Innovation in English Departments." In *Market Matters: Applied Rhetoric Studies and Free Market Competition*, edited by Joyce Locke Carter, 77–94. Cresskill, NJ: Hampton.

Kemp, Fred. 2005b. "Computers, Innovation, and Resistance in First-Year Composition Programs." In *Discord and Direction: The Postmodern Writing Program Administrator*, edited by Sharon James McGee and Carolyn Handa, 105–22. Logan: Utah State University Press.

Killingsworth, M. Jimmie. 2010. "Appeals to the Body in Eco-Rhetoric and Techno-Rhetoric." In *Rhetorics and Technologies: New Directions in Writing and Communication*, edited by Stuart A. Selber, 77–93. Columbia: University of South Carolina Press.

Lang, Susan. 2005. "New Process, New Product: Redistributing Labor in a First-Year Writing Program." In *Market Matters: Applied Rhetoric Studies and Free Market Competition*, edited by Joyce Locke Carter, 187–204. Cresskill, NJ: Hampton.

McRuer, Robert. 2006. *Crip Theory: Cultural Signs of Queerness and Disability*. New York: New York University Press.

Micciche, Laura R. 2002. "More Than a Feeling: Disappointment and WPA Work." *College English* 64 (4): 432–58.

Miller-Cochran, Susan. 2018. "Innovation through Intentional Administration: Or, How to Lead a Writing Program Without Losing Your Soul." *WPA: Writing Program Administration* 42 (1): 107–22.

Moxley, Joseph. 2008. "Datagogies, Writing Spaces, and the Age of Peer Production." *Computers and Composition* 25 (2): 182–202. https://doi.org/:10.1016/j.compcom.2007.12.003.

Muñoz, José Esteban. 1999. *Disidentifications: Queers of Color and the Performance of Politics*. Minneapolis: University of Minnesota Press.

Pritchard, Eric Darnell. 2017. *Fashioning Lives: Black Queers and the Politics of Literacy*. Carbondale: Southern Illinois University Press.

Restaino, Jessica. 2012. *First Semester: Graduate Students, Teaching Writing, and the Challenge of Middle Ground*. Carbondale: Southern Illinois University Press.

Rice, Jenny. 2018. "Circulation Exhaustion." In *Circulation, Writing and Rhetoric*, edited by Laurie E. Gries and Collin Gifford Brooke, 281–88. Logan: Utah State University Press.

Rickly, Rebecca. 2005. "Distributed Teaching, Distributed Learning: Integrating Technology and Criteria-Driven Assessment into the Delivery of First-Year Composition." In *Delivering College Composition: The Fifth Canon*, edited by Kathleen Blake Yancey, 183–98. Portsmouth, NH: Boynton/Cook.

Scott, Tony. 2009. *Dangerous Writing: Understanding the Political Economy of Composition*. Logan: Utah State University Press.

Shipka, Jody. 2011. *Toward a Composition Made Whole.* Pittsburgh: University of Pittsburgh Press.

Sirc, Geoffrey. 1997. "Never Mind the Tagmemics, Where's the Sex Pistols?" *College Composition and Communication* 48 (1): 9–29.

Warner, Michael. 1993. Introduction to *Fear of a Queer Planet: Queer Politics and Social Theory,* edited by Michael Warner, vii–xxxi. Minneapolis: University of Minnesota Press.

Wasley, Paula. 2006. "A New Way to Grade." *Chronicle of Higher Education,* March 10. https://web.archive.org/web/20060822044028/http://chronicle.com:80/free/v52/i27/27a00601.htm.

Worsham, Lynn. 1998. "Going Postal: Pedagogic Violence and the Schooling of Emotion." *JAC* 18 (2): 213–45.

Wysocki, Anne Frances. 2005. "awaywithwords: On the Possibilities in Unavailable Designs." *Computers and Composition* 22 (1): 55–62. https://doi.org/10.1016/j.compcom.2004.12.011.

Yagelski, Robert P. 2011. *Writing as a Way of Being: Writing Instruction, Nonduality, and the Crisis of Sustainability.* New York: Hampton.

8.1

MORE BODIES THAN HEADS
Handling Male Faculty as an Expectant Administrator

Jacquelyn Hoermann-Elliott

It's 4:02 a.m., and I'm wide awake.

Minutes ago, I ran to the bathroom to drop my head over a porcelain bowl of self-pity—a reminder of my body's frailty and my mind's frustration with what I can't control as someone who labors to be an administrator and a mother.

I have five hours to make myself feel human again before cofacilitating an all-morning-long professional-development session for our graduate teaching assistants and adjunct instructors, starting at 9:00 a.m. It's also the day I plan to tell my instructors I'm twelve weeks pregnant.

Today isn't the first time I put my greenest face forward as an administrator. At every one of the three Focus Friday sessions we've held this semester, I've felt brutally ill from the inside out. At the first session, I talked about the importance of student evaluations between stomach spasms so sharply audible the empty writhing of my internal organs drew interest from every corner of the room. I didn't know I was pregnant then. Even the doctor's blood test suggested otherwise.

At the second Focus Friday of the semester, my dear friend, cherished work wife, and the director of our FYC program was traveling for a conference. I was on my own in terms of leading the session. Despite excusing myself to make frequent trips to the restroom and using humor to downplay the severe cold that commandeered my vocal cords—because pregnancy wrecks your immune system, too, in case you didn't know—I managed to finish the training without vomiting on display. Feigning health felt especially victorious at this second Focus Friday because I knew our most recalcitrant male adjuncts would be in attendance, including one white male instructor who had been especially antagonistic toward me in the past. We'll call him Charles.

In the previous semester, I had made the difficult decision to rate Charles's teaching as *ineffective* after conducting a routine observation of his classroom. His lack of preparation, lesson planning, and connecting to student learning outcomes, and his documented flippancy toward his female students and myself, were not evidence enough, in his mind, that this rating wasn't actually about my personal feelings toward him. Or so he expressed in a tirade of complaints to upper administration and any instructor willing to listen.

Months later at this second Focus Friday, I wasn't surprised to hear him disparage the pedagogical topics we'd been talking about all morning long.[1] After nearly three hours of discussing all the research and strategies for implementing growth mindsets in college classrooms, Charles raised his hand to be heard. Once called upon, he let me know he disagreed with every principle we'd discussed that day because he grows "every day by staying the same."

Charles's final comment to me, as he leaned against a wall with both arms crossed, was, "Well, when is a growth mindset a growth mindset a growth mindset?" In that moment, I felt every pair of eyes in the room bolt back to my body, scanning for a nonverbal cue that might be interpreted as an unraveling of my nerves or a surrendering of my authority, just this once, in response to this person's efforts to discredit my ethos as a teacher-scholar. And yet, having dealt with pricklier male faculty than Charles, I knew not to entertain his question. I chose to respond by smiling, thanking him for sharing his thoughts, and moving on.

When I was a younger—much healthier and fiercer—administrator, I would have reacted differently. I would have enjoyed a moment of argumentative sparring with this person or asking him a follow-up question that countered his own. Having spent the last two months physically debilitated by a physical condition I couldn't speak of, though, left me no more energy to care. (I also like to think my toddler-parenting skills were finally paying off in this moment—placing on full display that my buttons were no longer pushable.)

Now, lying in bed at 4:30 a.m. before our final Focus Friday of the semester, I am contemplating how I will share with my instructors that they will see my body undergo a dramatic change in the coming months. It's like announcing, "Hi, you're about to witness me go through a second puberty. I'll try to make this as unawkward as possible for all of us," but finding a blander, more professional statement than that is in order. I spend too long scrutinizing my own words because I know being with child is synonymous to being seen as having only half a brain (or less) in the academy. Elrena Evans (2008) tackles the issue of floating-head syndrome in academia in the 2008 publication *Mama Ph.D.*, in which she explains that people are expected to live in their minds only, where they do their greatest thinking unencumbered by the fleshier, physical needs of their bodies or their families. Evans's point rings true to my experiences working with colleagues of any gender who have chosen to comment on my perceived lack of health and my changing body and to suggest I'm incapable of doing as much work as other full-time faculty members. Being a pregnant administrator means inviting those touched by your leadership to trust you'll remain healthy enough to show up to work every day and to continue supporting them.

I do as the working-mother bloggers say and make my announcement very brief. I collectively thank the instructors in attendance for their support over the past semester as I navigated the health challenges they were able to witness, and I tell them I'll be delivering in October.

Much to my surprise, most erupt in tiny fits of excitement and clapping. Their encouragement makes me wonder if these moments of physical vulnerability have helped me find favor and goodwill with them. After all, what's more vulnerable than telling a room of coworkers that you've been keeping a secret from them? Or that your body is attempting to create another human being and that process doesn't always go as planned? There's rarely the invitation to discuss the vulnerability of your body, your unborn child's body, and what happens if your health takes a turn for the worse.

When I look around the room to find where Charles is sitting, I am almost unsettled by the smile I see inching across his face. The word "congratulations" might have been uttered.

About a month later, I find I have more graduate teaching assistants coming into my office than ever before. Some are just stopping by to ask the obligatory How are you feeling? question with a squealy, drawn-out emphasis on the last word, which is an unspoken way of asking for details on how my body is changing that week. Others are at my doorway needing help with their own pedagogical or personal issues. Even though the emotional labor of lifting them up wears on this already tired mother-administrator, I am honored they trust me with their own stories of vulnerability. Physical vulnerability and what makes me weak in some colleagues' eyes is now strengthening my relationships with these graduate teaching assistants in viscerally meaningful ways.

As for Charles, I can't say yet how our relationship might change. He still goes out of his way to avoid everyday conversations with me, and I try to give him the space he seems to need, knowing full well his avoidance game will end eventually. A colleague of mine suggested my pregnancy announcement made him find favor with me again because he sees me as a weaker-than-before link in the administrative chain of higher-ups.

I have to mindfully choose not to ponder his perceptions of me, and instead I wonder how higher education's collective understanding of expectant female faculty has or has not changed in the last decade since Evans's conceptualization of floating-head syndrome. I wonder if the visibility of administrators' bodies has been put into greater focus because we, unlike faculty without administrative responsibilities, are the ones performing on stage, delivering professional-development content, holding extra office hours, and making site visits to classrooms. And of course, I wonder more now than I did before—when I was a pregnant, less visible graduate student—about how I can use the vulnerabilities of my body to make room for more bodies than heads in academia.

NOTE

1. See Carol S. Dweck's (2007) *Mindset* for extensive research and citation on the concept of growth mindsets in teaching and relationships.

REFERENCES

Dweck, Carol S. 2007. *Mindset: The New Psychology of Success.* New York: Ballantine Books.
Evans, Elrena. 2008. "Fitting In." In *Mama PhD: Women Write about Motherhood and Academic Life*, edited by Caroline Grant and Elrena Evans, 49–54. New Brunswick, NJ: Rutgers University Press.

8.2

ABOUT A LUCKY MAN WHO MADE THE GRADE

Ryan Skinnell

In August 2014, when I signed and submitted an advance contract for my first single-authored monograph, *Conceding Composition*, I was riding a high of joy, relief, affirmation, and anxiety. In the subsequent several months, while the joy, relief, and affirmation persisted, the anxiety came to dominate my life. I was consumed by it for the better part of a year because I needed a book for tenure, and the prospect of not getting tenure terrified me. Consequently, I prioritized my writing over virtually everything else in my life. It could reasonably be called an obsession, one effect of which was that I allowed my singular focus on writing to damage my physical and emotional health and to undercut important relationships in my life.

When I signed the book contract in August, I was still writing. The manuscript was halfway completed, but I needed to write about forty thousand words before December 1. In chapter 8 of this collection, Michael Faris describes the exhaustion that arises from deep, sustained engagement with a whole program's worth of students and colleagues and the importance of thinking about how bodies exist in the world. In her response to Faris's chapter, Jacquelyn Hoermann-Elliott (chapter 8.1, this collection) contemplates what it means to try to stay engaged with others when your body—and some people's projections onto it—radically reshape established relationships. By contrast, as much as possible, I sought to disengage from the experience of my body and from the world around me while I was writing my book.

I was fortunate that my job was oriented to supporting my writing—I was only teaching two classes, both upper-division rhetoric and writing courses I'd taught before. I did little in the way of service work, no administrative work, and almost no committee work. On the other hand, I had several other writing deadlines, including multiple book chapters I'd promised to editors, a journal article to revise and resubmit, and

https://doi.org/10.7330/9781646422340.c008.2

conference papers. I also had three children under the age of eight. The youngest was two years old and did not sleep through the night (she wouldn't regularly do so for at least two more years). And as I would learn much later, I had an undiagnosed case of sleep apnea, a sleep disorder that causes a person to stop breathing when they start to fall into a deep sleep. When the person stops breathing, they wake up, though usually not completely—just enough so they never quite make it into the most restorative phase of sleep. Basically, a person with sleep apnea may "sleep" all night but never enter deep sleep, which results in fatigue and a host of other physical problems. It also often gets worse over time.

I suspect the picture I am attempting to paint is already coming into focus, but I rarely neglect a chance to be overly didactic. I had a major project that would determine my professional future, a short timeline, several other demands on my time, a family life that was simultaneously wonderful and enervating, and a sleep disorder that prevented me from getting deep, restful sleep. That period in my life was, to put it mildly, difficult. I'd been dealing with many of the individual challenges for years and certainly combinations of them. My first daughter was born when I was writing my master's thesis. When she was eight months old, we moved out of state, away from friends and family, so I could start a PhD program. My second child was born while I was writing my dissertation. We moved to another new state when she was five months old so I could start my first job. My third child was born in my first year on the tenure track. The combination of stress, family demands, and professional commitments was not unfamiliar to me. But the addition of the book project ratcheted up my anxiety to new levels.

The physical and emotional toll was profound. I was constantly worn down, of course. I tried to catch up on sleep on weekends or by going to bed early, but all to little avail since I was apparently suffocating nearly to death dozens of times an hour. I also began to withdraw from personal and professional relationships because I didn't have the time or the energy to maintain them. I figured I could pick up where I left off after the book was done (in some cases I did, but in more than I care to admit, I never recovered relationships important to me). I relied very heavily—more heavily than I even realized at the time—on my spouse to pick up a lot of the parenting slack. And I was constantly preoccupied with whatever I was writing and the impending deadlines, so I missed or floated through lots of life events. I know being a cis male in a traditional heterosexual relationship means I got a lot more goodwill in this regard than my wife would have if the situation was reversed.

Nevertheless, the effects were cumulative, and my anxiety continued to intensify as the book deadline approached.

At the beginning of October, about two months after I signed the contract, my anxiety became so acute I practically stopped sleeping altogether. I went to bed every night, tossed and turned for hours because I couldn't turn off my thinking, finally fell asleep for two or three hours, then woke up in a panic. In retrospect, that panic was almost certainly a consequence of the sleep apnea, but at the time I associated it only with the impending book deadline. So I woke up at 1:00 or 2:00 or 3:00 every morning, panicked, and started writing. I could usually get a couple hours of decent writing done on pure adrenaline and coffee, but by the time everyone else was waking up, I was so underslept I could barely carry on a conversation with my family.

Still, we got ready for the day, I took my daughters to school and daycare, and then I went to work until it was time to pick them up at the end of the day. I just kept going, trying desperately to ignore the lessons my body was trying to teach me. A couple of times a week, I was so exhausted I fell asleep right after dinner and (mostly) slept through the night. Then the routine began again.

I missed my December deadline because I was so exhausted, and I had to ask for an extension to January 1. I think I actually sent it in a few days after that, but I don't really remember. Still, the pattern I established in those months before my book manuscript was due persisted well after I submitted the finished draft. The anxiety and insomnia persisted for another four months. I had applied for other jobs, I had conference papers to write, and so on. There were always plenty of triggers. And since I still didn't know about the sleep apnea, and wouldn't for another two years, I continued to wake up every night, usually after a couple hours of sleep, and stay awake. That habit eventually changed in mid-April—I honestly can't say why or how, but I definitely remember when. Still, for nearly seven months, I was a ghost, hacking away at a book project between minor breakdowns while my life sort of crumbled around me.

Looking back more than four years later, I really feel very fortunate. Most important, I (mostly) resumed having a life, which is nice. And I am proud of the book I wrote, though I suspect it would have been better if I'd written it under different circumstances. But with the benefit of hindsight, I'm also alarmed at how poorly I attended to my physical and emotional needs. To be blunt, I was in physical and emotional crisis for the better part of a year, but I couldn't see anything beyond my writing responsibilities—including the effects of my crises on the people around me. I can't help but wonder in retrospect how different the experience might have been if I'd been less consumed by the project and more responsive to my body and my life. I am certain I would have been a better father, spouse, friend, teacher, and colleague. I can't help but wonder whether I would have been a better scholar, too, if I wasn't trying to drag my exhausted self across a finish line that ended up not being as inflexible as I made it out to be.

REFERENCES

Skinnell, Ryan. 2016. *Conceding Composition: A Crooked History of Composition's Institutional Fortunes.* Logan: Utah State University Press.

Trauma

9

A DAY IN THE LIFE
Administering from a Position of Privileged Precarization in an Age of Mass Shootings

Shannon Walters

I began my term as WPA in what most people would call the opposite of a precarious existence: I had just been tenured, I owned my own home, and our first child had been born nine months earlier. I had enjoyed a substantial family leave, with eight weeks paid and a semester's relief from teaching. For my six prior years on the tenure track, I had been well mentored by veteran WPAs. My university supported me through a course at a center for teaching excellence. I was compensated through teaching releases and separate stipends from college and university programs.

One's threshold for precariousness, however, is relative. And—as I came to understand in my two years of program administrating—the shifting terrain of writing administration, the daily challenges of academic motherhood, and the cultural climate of the neoliberal university in an age of mass shootings made me acutely aware of the urgent need for new ways of reacting to the range of precariousness of academic life. For me—and I hope for any writing teacher or administrator committed to making our educational spaces as livable as possible—these new perspectives mean applying a disability studies perspective to questions of precarity.

Political theorist Isabell Lorey (2015) describes three valences of the precarious—precariousness, precarity, and precarization—each of which can be understood as intensified through a disability studies perspective. Precariousness is the common condition of life lived in the context of complex interdependency and shared vulnerability. A common refrain among disability studies activists and scholars is that we will all become disabled if we live long enough, testifying to this somewhat "naturalized" or accepted form of precariousness.

https://doi.org/10.7330/9781646422340.c009

Precarity, which is more complex, operates as a product of social, legal, and political parameters that order shared precariousness into hierarchies, distinguishing between bodies deemed worthy of protection and security and those that are not (Lorey 2015, 18–22). From a disability studies perspective, precarity captures the illogic that defines some (mostly able) bodies as deserving access to healthcare, employment, education, and housing and others (most disabled) as not. Margaret Price (2018) argues that in a particularly difficult position are people with "obscure, unrecognizable disabilities," calling this issue a "crisis of precarity" (192–93).

Even more complicated is precarization, which, according to Lorey (2015), is a mode of biopolitical governmentality specific to the propagation of the neoliberal state, which governs for and through widespread insecurity. As Lorey details, "Contrary to the old rule of a domination that demands obedience in exchange for protection, neoliberal governing proceeds primarily through social insecurity, through regulating the minimum of assurance while simultaneously increasing instability" (2). In the context of the neoliberal university, this often means squeezing the most labor out of instructors with the most precarious existences—adjuncts, teaching assistants, part timers, and those on contingent contracts. From a disability studies perspective, precarization characterizes the feeling of lack of a social safety net, the exhaustion produced by continually having to argue for the value of one's existence, and the fear of asking for accommodations to perform one's job. Contingent disabled faculty, for example, often forgo asking for accommodations so as not to further jeopardize their employment status.

My position of what I came to call *privileged precarization* as a WPA was also shaped by intersections of gender, work, and motherhood, which were sometimes at odds with my perspective as a disability studies scholar. In their study of motherhood and precarity, Julie A. Wilson and Emily Chivers Yochim (2017) write that "ongoing precarization incites new gender sensibilities that impinge on and intensify women's work and their experiences of motherhood" (20). These new gender sensibilities became clear to me as I attempted to juggle family and work, but my position as a disability studies scholar hoping to bring a focus on access to writing program administration became less clear, particularly following a threat of violence to my campus in October 2015. In what follows, I trace the threads of this experience, placing emphasis on difficult moments showing the disparity between my plans, hopes, and expectations for my position and the reality of administrating in a climate of dangerous precarization.

MAKING THE TRANSITION

Personally and professionally, my first year as a WPA was a time of transition. One body of work reached a natural stopping point, as I had just been tenured and my book had been recently published. One of my most indelible memories of that time is hauling my tenure file, a banker's box full of everything I had written in the past six years, to my chair's office ten days before my daughter's due date. Nine months later, in my new administrative position, another body of work began: one filled with new people to meet, policies to navigate, and courses to design and teach. As I prepared for the academic year in the summer, I carried my breast pump in each day and expressed between various administrative tasks.

On various levels of my life—personal, scholarly, and political—I was attuned to the struggles and successes accompanying ongoing efforts toward disability justice. I felt primed to embark on my administrative career with disability as a chief concern. In May, my participant-driven research with neurodiverse students was published, and I was excited to extend this work into administration. In July, President Obama's (2015) remarks on the twenty-fifth anniversary of the ADA reminded me of the ADA's promise and unrealized potential. In August, my eleven-month-old daughter began daycare at a facility using an inclusion-based model in which disabled and nondisabled children from three months on shared classrooms. It would be easy to continue her early-intervention services, including physical and occupational therapy, that she had begun at five months, which are free for Philadelphia residents.

That summer, I was particularly interested in revising the standard syllabus all new teaching assistants and instructors were required to use their first semester. Focusing on urban space, my major revision included a module on disability and accessibility in the built environment and cultural spaces. The syllabus used Philadelphia as an extended classroom, inviting students to think explicitly about our region's relationship to accessibility. This meant bringing student bodies into public spaces to experience how built and affective environments welcomed certain bodies or not. In one assignment, students conducted a site observation of a public space in Philadelphia or on campus, evaluating it for accessibility. Early in the semester, this assignment led first-year students to think critically about their entrance into a new course, new campus, and, for many, a new city.

I was especially looking forward to teaching the composition practicum, the class that met Friday mornings to support new graduate student teaching assistants teaching their first classes of first-year writing. The doubleness of this position intrigued me. Here I could frame the site-observation assignment with readings at intersections of disability studies and composition theory. Here I could guide beginning graduate students toward crafting a teaching philosophy that made accessibility integral. Here teaching assistants, who received full funding for four years towards their PhD, would share a safe, supportive space for both debriefing about that week's successes and challenges in the classroom and preparing for the next week.

I structured my time, vying for that elusive balance between work and home so many academics, particularly academic mothers with small children, seek. I worked four days a week on campus and spent one day working from home with my daughter, juggling doctor's appointments, specialists, and follow-ups. I read every word of *Women's Ways of Making It in Rhetoric and Composition* (Ballif, Davis, and Mountford 2008). I made mental lists of women and allies in administrative positions I could call on when I needed advice. I toted a thick binder from my WPA workshop at CWPA in Savannah into my office overlooking Philadelphia and the Ben Franklin Bridge. When on campus, I reserved my faculty office for pumping breast milk and did program work in my administrative office. The severe gastro-esophageal reflux disease (GERD) my daughter had been diagnosed with at three weeks old made digesting formula nearly impossible.

She also received physical and occupational therapy, so my early days at the office were often spent concerned about her fluid intake, her weight, and her general mobility since the reflux element of GERD had made drinking, sitting, and learning to walk challenging. That fall, placement of first-year students into composition transferred from the first-year writing program to the university's assessment office, a transition requiring many meetings among various stakeholders. I quickly learned I would be spending the bulk of my time facilitating this transition. Somewhere between pumping and placement meetings, I planned classes, oversaw the budget, visited classes, evaluated faculty, and supported teaching assistants.

OCTOBER 4, 2015

Then, on October 4, 2015, something happened. I, along with thousands of other faculty, students, and administrative staff, heard from the ATF and the FBI Philadelphia Field Office, who "out of an abundance of caution" alerted us to the fact that a social media posting threatened violence toward a Philadelphia-area college or university (Moyer, *Washington Post*, October 4, 2015). On the message board 4chan, the same site used to warn students in the Northwest the day before a recent shooting at Umpqua Community College in Oregon, a message appeared warning of more violence. The message read, "On October 5, at 1pm Central time, a fellow robot will take up arms at a university near Philadelphia" (Snyder, Blum, and Nussbaum, *Philadelphia Inquirer*, October 5, 2015). Nine people were killed in Oregon, and the poster of the new message called that shooter a fellow member of the Beta Rebellion. Also included was a warning: "If you are in that area, you are encouraged to stay home and watch the news as the chaos unfolds."

I received many emails from teaching assistants and writing-faculty instructors asking for advice: whether to hold class, make class optional, penalize students who were absent, or hold class online as an alternative. At first, I engaged in what I thought of as "corporate speak," referring TAs and instructors to the university's official memorandum. When pressed, I told to them to use their discretion. They would have to make their own call. I hated to think more contingent instructors might be afraid to use their discretion because of their contingent status. The differing valences of the precarious showed themselves here. The implicit questions underlying the questions to me asked: What are you going to do? Are you afraid or not? How should I decide? And the larger, implicit questions then surfaced: How much fear are our teaching positions worth? How do we weigh other people's need to feel safe, as well as our own, against a threat of violence? Why do our academic spaces feel so dangerous?

My own academic career had been punctuated by school shootings. In high school, I was in the doctor's office when my physician recounted relief upon hearing his daughter was safe during at shooting at Penn State. I was a sophomore in college when Columbine happened, and I heard about it, by word of mouth, while in the dining hall. In graduate school, I was reading for comprehensive exams when the aftermath of the Virginia Tech shooting unfolded on my television. I was in my first year at a new job on the tenure track when Amy Bishop opened fire in a faculty meeting. I was on sabbatical, finishing my first book, when Sandy Hook happened. While I knew the classroom had never been the safe space we imagined—especially for poor students, students of color, disabled students, queer students, and female students—our government's inaction on gun control certainly seemed to contribute to this precarization, increasing instability by offering what often felt like the "minimum of assurance" of safety in our classrooms (Lorey 2015, 2).

On Sunday evening October 4, after reading *Goodnight Moon* and *Goodnight Gorilla* to my twelve-month-old, I learned everything I could about the recent shooting in Oregon, which had made news in the days before, and the message board 4chan, on which the threats of violence had been posted. I read about how Chris Harper-Mercer opened fire in the writing class in which he was a student, killing eight students and an assistant professor. He purposely spared the life of one student, instructing him to deliver a flash drive to police after Harper-Mercer's suicide. This drive contained writings showing he had studied mass shootings, including one perpetrated by Elliot Rodger, who killed six people near the University of California Santa Barbara in 2014 and tried targeting women at a sorority.

Because I was a writing teacher, it wasn't lost on me that Harper-Mercer opened fire in his writing classroom, an introductory composition class. I was drawn to how both Rodger and Harper-Mercer chose to present themselves in writing and other media, particularly their us-versus-them mentality. They both left writing associating themselves with the loosely organized online group called the Beta Rebellion, who define themselves by their sexual frustration and isolation. Self-identified betas separate men into two categories: the alphas, who are sexually active and enjoy power and prestige because of their sexual prowess, and betas, who feel rejected by women and disempowered by alpha men and who blame women for their "incel" status, or being involuntarily celibate. Before the shooting, Rodger uploaded a video on YouTube and emailed a manifesto, both of which described his desire to punish women for rejecting him and to seek revenge on sexually active men, whom he envied. A journalist who read Rodger's manifesto called his writing "clear and precise . . . Rodger was no crank philosopher. Instead he was a memoirist, able to describe the details of his sad, lonely world with surprising candor" ("Fleischer," *Los Angeles Times*, June 6, 2014).

As a writing teacher and administrator also committed to disability justice, my reaction to what I learned was complicated. Harper-Mercer and Rodger were reported to have shared similar mental illnesses and mental disabilities, which raised uncomfortable questions, particularly from my perspective as a researcher in disability studies. Both shooters were reported to have experienced mental illness, and some reports emphasized an autism spectrum disorder diagnosis, while noting diagnoses of other school shooters, such as Seung Cho and Adam Lanza (Anderson, *Los Angeles Times*, September 23, 2017; Nagourney, *New York Times*, June 1, 2014). Media coverage that speculates on the psychiatric diagnoses of school shooters can dominate and limit a cultural conversation that should be much wider. When having to respond to a flurry of emails from instructors on the evening of October 4 about whether to hold class, there was not time enough in the world for me to engage deeply and ethically with the tangle of associations among mental illness, misogyny, neurodivergence, and mass shooting provoked by this situation.

"NORMAL OPERATIONS" IN UNIVERSITY PRECARIZATION

Looking back, I can better understand why I was uncomfortable relaying the "corporate speak" of the university and the FBI's warning when instructors asked for guidance. What does it mean for the FBI/ATF to act out of an "abundance of caution" in sharing with the public a message about a "threat of violence" made "against a university near Philadelphia"? Certainly the fact that the anonymous poster and Harper-Mercer had made threats in the same online forum was troubling, but it was challenging to assess the risk. The vagueness of the government's and university's official statements contrasted sharply with the vivid, specific language used by the anonymous poster, warning of a "fellow robot" who would "take up arms." On online forums where members of the Beta Rebellion posted, it seemed clear who might be targeted. For example, on 4chan's "random" board, /b/, one user's early self-description of the group's ethos blithely combines ableism and sexism: "/b/ is the guy who tells the cripple ahead of him in line to hurry up. /b/ is the first to get to the window to see the car accident outside. /b/ is the one who wrote your number on the mall's bathroom wall. /b/ is a failing student who makes passes at his young, attractive English teacher . . . /b/ is the guy that calls a suicide hotline to hit on the advisor" (Nagle 2017, 32).

As a writing teacher and WPA, I could recall interactions with students and members of the general public who fit this description. I could also tell this user's description was aimed to trade on, highlight, and maybe even critique stereotypes. Betas engage in self-mockery almost as much as mockery of others, such as women, disabled people, and their allies. This user's description highlights the sense of unearned entitlement betas demand while also seeming to draw attention to its absurdity.

In her detailed examination of internet subcultures, including 4chan, Angela Nagle (2017) suggests the betas draw on a long history of using tropes of madness and insanity for transgressive purposes. Describing a tradition of madness as a "creative source, a rejection of mainstream norms and a political act of rebellion," she notes the "throwing off of the id" that characterizes sites like 4chan is often "described as insane or unhinged to baffled outsiders" (32). A disability studies perspective, however, also calls attention to how betas' trolling capitalizes on the precarity of disability and gender. Betas clearly call attention to their perceived subordinate status by further marginalizing others. As a writing teacher and WPA, I had no trouble imagining the combination of entitlement and sexism that would lead a failing student to make a pass at their English teacher, as described on the /b/ board, but it was certainly more challenging to imagine what combination of that might lead someone to claim "incel" status and open fire on a campus or classroom.

In addition, dominant discourses are generally not helpful in making a decision such as the one I and others in the university community faced on October 5. Madness, as a concept, particularly the violence associated with it, has not served us well regarding discussions of school shootings. Psychiatrist Jonathan Metzl (2017) describes a "deep unease" with associations between mental illness and gun violence, writing that "focusing centrally on the psychology of individual assailants ultimately makes it ever-harder to address the larger issues that guns in America represent: the mass psychology of needing so many guns in the first place, or the anxieties, apprehensions, and psychical traumas created by being surrounded by them all the time" (171). Writing about Rodger, Rebecca Solnit (2015) explores unquestioned assumptions circulating in discussions of mental illness, explaining, "Voices in the mainstream insisted he was mentally ill, as though that settled it, as though the world were divided into two countries called Sane and Crazy that share neither border crossing or a culture" (122). The "crazy" lone gunman mythology individualizing shooters deflects attention away from more complicated questions. As Price (2011) writes, "It is easier to focus on individuals, because when we presume that the problem lies within individuals, we can continue to believe that the problem will go away if the individuals are cured. Or incarcerated, or expelled, or eradicated" (175). In fact, people with mental illness are no more likely than those without to use guns to inflict harm on others and are more likely to be victims of violent crimes than to perpetrate them.

The contrast between the vague language of the warning from the FBI and the vivid language on the beta forums was unsettling. For me and other members of the academic community, that discrepancy made it difficult to assess risk. University officials sent out a message around 9:30 p.m. to "reach out" to let the academic community know they heard us regarding "safety concerns" and to note an increase in "security presence throughout the university" (TU alert). Like many of the instructors emailing me, we were all in the position to make a decision: go to campus or stay home? The question boiled down to a question of security, but it involved everyone making their own call, managing their own anxiety, and weighing their own personal thresholds of precariousness.

In her examination of precarity, Judith Butler (2015) focuses on how governing through precarization produces a form of self-government, an angle that helped me understand my position as a WPA in light of the nonspecific threat of violence to the Philadelphia area in October 2015. She asks, "How do we understand the organization of 'security' under neoliberal conditions as requiring and inducing precarity as a mode of life, as an infinite trajectory, as the organizing principle for the process by which we are governed and by which we come to govern ourselves" (viii)? In the neoliberal university, a "security presence"—increased visibility of police officers and, at my university that Monday, the Department of Homeland Security—functioned to ostensibly reassure the academic community that everything was okay. The end of the public-safety announcement emphasized that the university would be having "normal operations" Monday, the day of the threat. In other words, we were encouraged to "govern ourselves" by pretending everything was "normal." As a WPA, I understood administration as a form of government and self-government. Instructors and teaching assistants who were asking for guidance about holding class were in many respects asking how to manage their own thresholds of anxiety while teaching in a time of dangerous precarization. While I couldn't articulate it at the time, I was deeply disturbed by what I saw as the two main choices we all had to decide between: pretend that everything was normal or stay home.

OCTOBER 5, 2015

Like a lot of other faculty and students, I decided to go campus the next day despite the threat. And it was not a day like May 23, 2014. Or October 1, 2015. Or April 16, 2007. But the possibility of violence wended its way throughout my day. Getting dressed, I wore flats, as I typically did, but today I thought they would be good for running. I typically packed my lunch, but I felt a different kind of relief that I could eat in my office instead of trekking throughout campus to buy lunch. Someone dropped a stainless-steel water bottle on the pavement while I was walking to my office and I couldn't help but startle. In the parking garage I noticed a strange smell, or did I? I couldn't tell if I was imagining it, if it was always like that, or if I was just paranoid. I wasn't scheduled to teach that day, but I had administrative meetings, and they formed the tempo of my day. I picked my daughter up at daycare, came home, ate dinner, and got ready for the next day.

I didn't see my graduate teaching assistants until Friday, although I had office hours and answered emails throughout the week, particularly that Sunday as they thought through what to do. We discussed the difficult decision that had arisen for the instructors who had been scheduled to teach on Monday. A few did not hold class. The ones who did said they didn't quite know what they were doing there. What would they do in an emergency situation? Our university's procedures provided once source of direction: "In the event of a Lockdown, **secure yourself** in a room and do not leave until the situation has been resolved" (Temple, "Lockdown" n.d.). This directive, which instructed a form of self-security, couldn't help but remind me of precarization, which governs for and through widespread insecurity. We seemed to have internalized that mode, so attentive to the pervasive sense of insecurity in our lives and schools that securing ourselves seemed just a series of questions without answers.

A "lockdown" is defined as "a procedure used when there is **an immediate threat**" and "a need to stop access" to all or a portion of campus buildings (Temple, "Lockdown" n.d.). But the culture of mass shootings in the United States has made the sense of threat so dispersive so as to be rendered pervasive. How do we "govern ourselves" in this climate? There may be no immediate threat, but there is always the threat of violence. So, how do you "secure yourself?" The objective, to "stop access" for an assailant with a weapon, certainly made sense, but it resonated uncomfortably in our larger conversations about access and disability. One in five college students reports having anxiety or depression, and almost 20 percent of directors of campus psychiatric services report their services as inadequate (American Psychological Association). Whose access counts most here? Rather than prepare for an assailant by stopping access in a moment statistically unlikely to happen, didn't it make more sense to provide better access for everyone to mental health services?

The university's Active Assailant Preparedness plan offered more details, more directives, and more ways to move, or so it seemed. The three main concepts important to remember were "Run. Hide. Fight." My students and I couldn't help but think about who could run, hide, and fight and the able-bodiedness required in these situations. Who can run to find an "escape route," "stay out of view," and "be physically aggressive" (Temple, "Active Assailant" n.d.)? Another form of precarity was at work here in the form of what kinds of bodies were worthy of protection and security and what kinds were not. In spite of all my plans about studying the city of Philadelphia in terms of its accessibility and focusing on popular public spaces like the Liberty Bell and Independence Mall, it came down to us discussing how to survive a hypothetical mass shooting. In spite of all my hopes about shaping new students' teaching philosophies to take access and multimodality as a given, here I found myself discussing an active-shooter scenario with students. There was a long plexiglass-framed piece of art on the wall of our seminar room. We could pull that down and use it to "barricade all entries," as advised. We could hide behind our seminar tables after we turned them on their sides. Windows weren't an option on the eleventh floor, and they didn't open anyway. Access was not what we thought it was, although it did teach us important lessons not only about who was valued in what classrooms and public spaces but also whose lives were more secure and protected. To run, hide, and fight seemed like a plan of last resort, of course, and couldn't we focus our attention differently before that in a way that might prevent it? What would it mean to sit with mental disability rather than run from it? How might we go about not hiding from mental illness and disability, something so many students experience? And in Metzl's words, what would it mean to fight "the mass psychology of needing so many guns in the first place"?

PRIVILEGED PRECARIZATION

October 5, 2015, was not the day that made me resign as WPA the next year, one year before my contract expired; it was more complicated than that. I became pregnant with my second child, which coincided with a dissolution of one of my stipends after a reorganization of the general education program. Tale as old as WPA time, I'm sure, but when I did the math, things just didn't add up, especially once I learned a male counterpart in a similar program would not be facing a pay cut. My department had also just emerged from nearly a year of informal investigations into a hostile-work-environment charge that affected everybody in the department, an oppressive atmosphere that left me exhausted. With two children in daycare, and a 40 percent stipend reduction, I calculated I would be paying the university if I continued in my position, mainly because of the increased hours of childcare needed to cover my administrative responsibilities.

Beyond the math, I considered the pressures of breastfeeding and pumping and the likelihood my second child would also have GERD, and I knew it wasn't an equation I could make work. I made this argument, my stipend was not reinstated, so I resigned. In the end, it was simple precariousness that caused me to resign. A common condition of life—pregnancy—highlighted the complex interdependency and shared vulnerability my pregnant body posed. To resign, by definition, is to voluntarily leave a position. I had the luxury of returning to my tenured faculty position and the privilege of resisting a pay cut rather than accept it. Yet also palpably present was the feeling of resignation. I felt resigned to the fact that little would change in my position and that certain bodies were more amenable to administration and the university than others. My "real" body did not fit the "institutional body" (Nicolas and Sicari in this collection).

Mundane precariousness such as what I experienced with pregnancy coexists with the more complex precarity and even more complicated precarization not only of my overall positionality but also the events of October 5. Every member of the academic community, every day, receives social, economic, abled, and gendered messages about what kinds of people are welcome and what kinds are not. The shooting that didn't happen is also the shooting that will happen if we don't change our uniquely American perspective on gun culture, address our pervasive cultural misogyny, and learn to coexist with mental disability and illness. We share precariousness, each of us subject to the uncertainties and contingencies of our own bodies and minds, but we don't have to share the insidious methods of sorting out which bodies deserve protection and security and which do not. We don't have to resign ourselves to live with the experience of precarity as "an everyday sense of threat, vulnerability, and uncertainty that must be confronted and managed" in our classrooms and academic lives (Wilson and Yochim 2017, 20). October 5, 2015, can teach us this. It is the shooting that didn't happen and maybe won't happen because we still have the opportunity to learn from it.

REFERENCES

American Psychological Association. 2013. "College Students' Mental Health Is Growing Concern, Survey Finds." June. https://www.apa.org/monitor/2013/06/college-students.

Ballif, Michelle, D. Diane Davis, and Roxanne Mountford, eds. 2008. *Women's Ways of Making It in Rhetoric and Composition*. New York: Routledge.

Butler, Judith. 2015. Foreword to *State of Insecurity*, vii–xi. London: Verso.

Lorey, Isabel. 2015. *State of Insecurity: Government of the Precarious*. London: Verso.

Metzl, Jonathan. 2017. "Let's Talk about Guns, but Stop Stereotyping the Mentally Ill." In *Beginning with Disability: A Primer*, edited by Lennard Davis, 169–72. New York: Routledge.

Nagle, Angela. 2017. *Kill All Normies: Online Culture Wars from 4Chan and Tumblr to Trump and the Alt-Right.* Alresford: Zero Books.

Price, Margaret. 2011. *Mad at School: Rhetorics of Mental Disability and Academic Life.* Ann Arbor: University of Michigan Press.

Price, Margaret. 2018. "The Precarity of Disability/Studies in Academe." In *Precarious Rhetorics*, edited by Wendy S. Hesford, Adela C. Licona, and Christa Teston, 191–211. Columbus: The Ohio State University Press.

Solnit, Rebecca. 2015. *Men Explain Things to Me.* Chicago: Haymarket.

Temple University Campus Safety Services. n.d. "Active Assailant Preparedness." https://safety.temple.edu/emergency-preparedness/get-educated/preparedness/active-assailant-preparedness.

Temple University Campus Safety Services. n.d. "Lockdown." https://safety.temple.edu/emergency-preparedness/get-educated/emergency-procedures/lockdown.

Temple University Public Safety Announcement. https://news.temple.edu/announcements/2015-10-04/temple-university-public-safety-statement.

White House. 2015. "Remarks by the President on the Americans with Disabilities Act." July 20. https://obamawhitehouse.archives.gov/the-press-office/2015/07/20/remarks-president-americans-disabilities-act.

Wilson, Julie A., and Emily Chivers Yochim. 2017. *Mothering Through Precarity: Women's Work and Digital Media.* Durham, NC: Duke University Press.

9.1

WHEN DISCOMFORT BECOMES PANIC
Doing Research in Trauma as a Survivor

Lauren Brentnell

There is a strange kind of invisibility that comes with doing research as a trauma survivor at an institution going through the crisis of sexual violence. When beginning my dissertation project, I felt excited by my chosen topic, which was to explore how writing program administrators could implement trauma-informed, care-based practices, particularly at institutions impacted by trauma, like my home university of Michigan State (MSU). I knew studying institutional responses to sexual violence would be emotionally taxing at times, but I'd written about such topics before. As an abuse survivor, I didn't see the topic as something to avoid because of my past—instead, I saw it as necessary to add my voice to the scholarship, to openly represent others like me.

At first, I found it easy to dive into the topic. MSU was in the middle of a sexual-violence crisis of its own, and I let the pain, the anger, the sadness fuel my writing. But after a point, it became impossible to wake up every day, to read about trauma, to go to campus and feel the pain of hundreds of people around me, to be reminded of my own experiences in every one of those stories. I was constantly talking about abuse, whether it was the abuses at MSU or the harassment being revealed everywhere as people came forward with their #MeToo stories. I was dwelling in violence. It became impossible to see the inaction and ignorance of those in power and not feel it in my body—to not feel it as an attack against myself, my work, my life.

Survivors often learn recovery means learning to listen to the body first, to listen to what is comfortable and what is not. The fact is that academia is not always comfortable. And in some ways, it shouldn't be—learning can happen in spaces of *productive* (i.e., carefully scaffolded and moderated) discomfort. However, there is a difference between a discomfort zone, which offers challenges, and a panic zone, which is overwhelming. While writing my dissertation, MSU became

https://doi.org/10.7330/9781646422340.c009.1

a panic zone, a space overwhelmed with traumatic stories. When the extent of MSU's institutional complicity in covering up Larry Nassar's abuse became clear, those of us working and studying there experienced our own kinds of trauma, the trauma of trying to find a way to respond to an institution that had so completely failed us—and continued, in many ways, to fail in its response.

MSU, like many universities before it, enacted what Carly Smith and Jennifer Freyd (2014) term "institutional betrayal," or the tendency of institutions to respond to traumatic situations by enacting further harm to members of its own community rather than acknowledging its wrongdoings and making amends for its faults. Institutional betrayal, they argue, results in a variety of responses from the community, including "disrupted memory, . . . decreased physical health, . . . delayed service seeking or reporting, . . . [and] disengagement from previously valued institutions as a whole" (576). Institutional betrayal, in other words, results in very real physical, emotional, and mental symptoms for those impacted. For myself, it meant the recurrence of post-traumatic stress disorder that hugely impacted my dissertation work.

I fell into a deep depression, one of the worst I've experienced. My days were spent sleeping for almost twelve hours and then waking up, pulling myself onto my couch, and opening up books on rape and abuse and staring at them, uncomprehendingly, for hours before I gave up. No one knew how bad it got because I had so much practice with saying, "This is fine." I finally reached a breaking point at the end of the summer when I was contemplating more than just self-harm and decided to reach out to a doctor for help. I was put on antidepressants and some other medications to help—and they did, at least for a little while. I got some energy back, just in time to dive into the job market with a partial dissertation and a growing sense that I might not *want* to be in academia, not if what it would require of me was the sacrifice of my mental health.

"*We are all moving, breathing, thinking, rhetorical bodies*" (Johnson et al. 2015, 42). But what about when we aren't? What happens when we are so depressed or disabled we stop moving? When panic attacks set in and we can't catch our breaths? When fogginess clouds our minds or flashbacks and dissociations prevent us from thinking clearly? Margaret Price (2009) asks, "How does one speak (either aloud or on the page) if one's mind spins with anxiety, grapples with depression, freezes with panic, or is occluded with brain fog?" (13). What do we do with the disparity of being a rhetorical body that does not produce rhetorical work—that is, of being a body employed by the university if we fail to publish rhetorical scholarship? I am a nonbinary, disabled queer person—I am also white, and, as Christina Cedillo (2018) reminds us, because "ways of being and knowing employed by disabled and racially minorized students are still largely devalued in the academy," these questions become even more critically important to ask when considering orientations around race and disability.

Melanie Yergeau (2016) argues that "ableism is a structuring logic of Rhetoric and Composition, of higher education writ large" (158) and, drawing on Tanya Titchkosky's concept of "reasonable exclusion," Yergeau shows disabled people are systemically excluded through the normative standards of the institution. It is also worth noting that strict standards of conformity and punishment for deviance are precedents for institutional betrayal, so institutional inflexibility is one catalyst for making already traumatic situations worse (Smith and Freyd 2014, 580). Constantly having to fight for our place within the university—often while balancing precarious positions as graduate students, contingent faculty, or nontenured faculty—while also trying to find ways to perform our jobs, which often were not designed with us in mind, is exhausting (which Shannon Walters discusses in this section). I do not often feel I am moving, breathing, thinking, or rhetorical within institutional spaces.

Not only does our current structure remove and exclude people (reason enough to reform our tenure and labor structures), but it also means even those few of us who remain produce research that may suffer for it. I am reminded of the call for slow research practices by Julie Lindquist (2012), practices that allow time to form relationships with participants; understand and interrogate markets, ecologies, and histories; and productively collaborate and form networks within communities. I add that slow research practices allow the researcher to interrogate and, as necessary, limit the impacts of research on our own bodies, to continue to form productive and healthy relationships with ourselves as research participants in our own projects.

I learned while writing my dissertation that doing trauma research as a survivor couldn't be put on a timer, at least not without endangering my own recovery. I was left with a decision. If I pursued a "traditional" tenure-track position, with all the research requirements that come with it, I knew I would likely have to stop researching trauma for my own well-being. One mentor pushed me in this direction, remarking that I should never feel I must self-flagellate for academia. I appreciated her advice, although I noted that her own work also dealt with these difficult issues and that she continued to do it anyway, often at the cost of her own emotional health. I suspect she continued her work for the same reasons

I knew I would: because she knew she would always be called upon to advocate for her community, even at the sacrifice of herself.

So, I pursued another option. Instead of a research-focused position, my top choices were teaching-centered positions. Not only would such a position allow me to do the work that I really wanted to do, that I was advocating in my dissertation—caring for students and creating more trauma-informed classrooms and spaces at universities—but it would remove me from the tenure-track publishing calendar. I can do this work on my own time, take the breaks I need, pursue other projects when it is too much, put it down until I am ready to take it up again. However, this option has other problems; by forgoing tenure, I open myself up to the precariousness of non-tenure-track life, which is often unstable and has become even more so during COVID-19. As I reflect upon the impacts of this research on my body—and of my body on my research in turn—I think about the need of scholars to acknowledge when our research is (re)traumatizing, when and how our institutions are failing us as full humans, and how we can build spaces for valuing more humane and slow research practices so we can still do the necessary work on these topics without harming ourselves in the process.

REFERENCES

Cedillo, Christina. 2018. "What Does It Mean to Move? Race, Disability, and Critical Embodiment Pedagogy." *Composition Forum* 39 (1). https://compositionforum.com/issue/39/to-move.php.

Johnson, Maureen, Daisy Levy, Katie Manthey, and Maria Novotny. 2015. "Embodiment: Embodying Feminist Rhetorics." *Peitho Journal* 18 (1): 39–44.

Lindquist, Julie. 2012. "Time to Grow Them: Practicing Slow Research in a Fast Field." *JAC* 32 (3–4): 645–66.

Price, Margaret. 2009. "Her Pronouns Wax and Wane: Psychosocial Disability, Autobiography, and Counter-Diagnosis." *Journal of Literary & Cultural Disability Studies* 3 (1): 11–33.

Smith, Carly P., and Jennifer J. Freyd. 2014. "Institutional Betrayal." *American Psychologist* 69 (6): 575–87.

Yergeau, Melanie. 2016. "Saturday Plenary Address: Creating a Culture of Access in Writing Program Administration." *WPA: Writing Program Administration* 40 (1): 155–65.

9.2
EMBODIED CV (ABRIDGED)[1]

Denise Comer

CONFERENCE PRESENTATIONS

2019: "Research Presentation When I Cried for Four Days in a Hotel Room over My Marriage Ending." Conference on College Composition and Communication, Pittsburgh, PA.

2013: "That Time I Almost Vomited before Speaking Because I Was So Nervous about Sharing My Controversial Research." Council of Writing Program Administrators Conference, Savannah, GA.

2008: "Panel Presentation Scheduled Four Weeks after the Birth of My Third Child, for Which I Had Planned to Fly with My Infant across the Country, but Actually Couldn't, and So Asked a Friend to Deliver the Paper for Me, Only to Have the [Male] Panel Chair Write Me a Snarky Email: 'Didn't You Know You Would Be Having a Baby When You Applied for This Panel?'" Modern Language Association, San Francisco, CA.

PEER-REVIEWED ARTICLES

2016–present: "Article-in-Perpetual-Progress, Suspended Indefinitely Because Every Time I Consider Opening the File My Chest Tightens."

2013: "Article Completed While My Mother Was in ICU and I Was Making a Four-Hour Drive Multiple Times a Week for Two Months."

2003–04: No articles because I was a new, first-time mother, had gained fifty extra pounds during pregnancy, and was suffering from postpartum depression.

PROGRAMMATIC ADMINISTRATION

2016–17: Year when I avoided my office as much as possible because programmatic morale had reached an all-time low amidst labor-related pressures and a problematic proposed redesign of first-year writing.

https://doi.org/10.7330/9781646422340.c009.2

GRANTS

2017: Grant report I wrote while standing at my kitchen counter, groaning from backache caused by my awareness that the project had failed.

PUBLIC SCHOLARSHIP

2017: Digital scholarship site I had to delay several months because I had developed finger-joint swelling from writing too much.

My Embodied CV could have so many more entries, tracing across my scholarly accomplishments the deaths of loved ones, stressors and challenges, pains and illnesses—countless moments of embodied writing.

I write from, with, and through my body. Awareness glides across my fingertips as I feel the keyboard's plastic squares, my lower lip pushes up slightly too much in concentration, my toes curl together, ideas surge through my stomach and throat. Occasionally, I craft a sentence or discover an insight that sparks a tingling sensation across the nape of my neck.

I write in airplanes, cars, hotel rooms, and lobbies, in my office, on treadmills and stationary bikes, sitting in my favorite living-room chair, and lying down in bed. I write in libraries, classrooms, coffee shops, and restaurants. I write alone, with colleagues, and among strangers. I write in the company of my children and, until recently, in the presence of my husband.

My twenty-two-year marriage ended abruptly during spring semester 2019. Actually, as with many marital endings, it was not really so abrupt. Our marriage had weathered several almost endings across the years.

One of these almost endings occurred on a Tuesday evening in June 2016. At the time, I was midway through teaching a three-and-a-half-week compressed-format course, hosting an international scholar and writing partner who was visiting from across the world, leading a team of graduate student research assistants for an ongoing research project, and preparing a conference presentation scheduled for the following week. Against these obligations, my marital crisis simply did not have room to unfurl.

With Tuesday evening's watershed marital moment looping in my head like tinnitus, I nevertheless proceeded as planned and taught class on Wednesday morning. Canceling would have only secured twenty-four hours respite since each day of class constituted a week's worth of material. Unable to form coherent thoughts, I arranged small-group activities. As I circulated among students, my heart pounded, my breathing was rapid and shallow, my stomach wrenched from dread and shock. I heard sounds as though I were under water.

Over the following days, I wrote the upcoming conference presentation while moving in silence around my husband, deciding intentionally not to decide about whether to stay in or leave the marriage. The international scholar visited, and we dined at restaurants instead of in my tension-filled home. My larger, ongoing research project, however, stalled. For a few weeks, I oversaw the qualitative-coding work I had already provided to the graduate student assistants, but I did not distribute anything thereafter. Nor did I analyze their coding. While I have since begun and completed other research projects, I have let *that* project lie completely dormant for three years because I associate it with that June 2016 marital crisis. The mere thought of opening the research file spawns nausea and agitation.

As bodies do, my body found its own way of processing the crisis I had buried beneath my work: over the ensuing three years, I developed a chronic nerve issue in my foot, which ultimately required surgery; endured eight months of physical therapy for a frozen shoulder; suffered through oral surgery for a suspicious but fortunately benign cluster of cells my dentist found; and discovered and treated basal-cell skin cancer on my chest. For me, as I have continued to write, revise, research, and ideate, these three years have produced a gradual skimming of parts of my body. A nerve severed here, scar tissue broken up there, gum tissue removed here, thoracic skin carved away there. Small parts of my body deleted like unneeded, problematic words.

Nearly three years of marriage counseling and an eight-week Mindfulness Based Stress Reduction (MBSR) program later, the actual ending of my marriage occurred on a Monday in March 2019. During the weeks leading up to that Monday, I had been in the midst of preparing my dossier for promotion.

Despite sensing the marriage's end was nigh, I forged ahead with the dossier, feeling more security in that text than in my marriage (a statement that signals the shakiness of the marriage more than any confidence in my bid for promotion). Sitting at Starbucks over several writing nights, I dutifully crafted a professional, intellectual narrative, synthesizing my scholarly trajectory, significant research contributions, academic collaborations, and future areas of research.

But the narrative kept crumbling at the edges—seeming to me only a partial account, a disembodied narrative masking the ways my moving, breathing, aging body had produced, ingested, and digested this scholarship.

What I really wanted to write, as tears sometimes streamed down my face, was the memory of being newly married in 1997, when my husband sat in the audience at a regional conference offering moral support while I read aloud, with trembling voice, my first-ever conference paper. Or I wanted to write about the way his warm, familiar body felt next to mine as I sat on our couch, writing on my laptop while he napped on a Sunday afternoon. Or I wanted to write about how my stalled marriage has mirrored my stalled research project for three years, painfully cemented in that liminal category titled "Work in Progress."

I suppose my Embodied CV could be more balanced if I were getting distracted while writing from the butterflies of a new romantic possibility, or if I integrated more joyful writing occasions, of which there have, thankfully, been many—a writing group that consisted of walks around campus, moments of writing near the ocean or surrounded by mountains, a collaboration with four inspiring colleagues, for which we gather periodically around an oval wooden table, laughing, commiserating, thinking together.

These embodied writing joys most certainly exist alongside my embodied writing pains, colliding across my CV, providing lived testimony to the inextricability of my body and my body of scholarship. And so I turn toward these more heartening embodiments of writing, even amidst the tatters of my twenty-two-year marriage, now no longer a work in progress but instead one more erstwhile section of an ongoing CV, beyond which I hope soon to discover a new, unwritten, but ever-so-promising future area of inquiry.

NOTE

1. Inspired by Haushofer, Johannes. 2016. "CV of Failures."

Cancer and Death

10
WPAS AND EMBODIED LABOR
Mina Shaughnessy, (Inter)Personal Labor, and an Ethics of Care

Rebecca Gerdes-McClain

INTRODUCTION

Mina Shaughnessy stands out as an exemplar of our field. Though her career was cut short by her death from cancer at fifty-four, her impressive research output, reputation as a compassionate and masterful teacher, and accomplishments as a writing program administrator (WPA) demonstrate that she excelled at each of her roles as an academic—as a teacher, as a researcher, and in service to her field and university. Today Shaughnessy is most famous as a basic writing pedagogue, but in this chapter I focus on her work as a WPA and what it suggests about the possibilities and limits of such labor. In particular, I consider her concern for the "fleshy presences" of her teachers. As Melissa Nicolas and Sicari argue in the introduction to this collection, "It is easy for institutional bodies to be everywhere and nowhere because their fleshy presence is assumed and beside the point; institutions need bodies but pay little attention to embodiment" (6). (Shaughnessy is an early example of a WPA attempting an "institutional embodiment" acknowledging the literal, individual bodies of her teachers and the needs of those bodies. At the same time, her own body and its needs are conspicuously absent from our field's understanding of Shaughnessy and her work.)

Shaughnessy began her career as a WPA in the late 1960s when she was hired to direct the writing portion of the Search for Education, Elevation, and Knowledge (SEEK) program at City University New York (CUNY), a program designed to support underprepared students admitted under the new open-enrollment policy (Maher 1997). During her career at CUNY, she ran the writing center as it grew from one location to two and served as director of the writing program in addition to other administrative appointments (Maher 1997). Given the scope of her administrative accomplishments, her legacy as a WPA is not adequately understood by writing studies scholars. Tellingly, this lack is not unique

https://doi.org/10.7330/9781646422340.c010

to Shaughnessy. While our field charts well the intellectual labor of scholars—primarily through published research—we often struggle to adequately capture administrative achievements and the labor that sustains them. By analyzing Shaughnessy's labor as a WPA, I both demonstrate the embodied nature of that labor (as well as the importance of analyzing labor through this lens) and argue that Shaughnessy's embodied labor experiences suggest martyrdom in the form of meeting (or striving to meet) unrealistic labor demands as a WPA, which, contrary to the instincts of many dedicated WPAs, is not an effective tool for improving the labor conditions of other writing faculty.[1] As an intervention into the unsustainable practice of normalizing gross overwork and a disembodied view of institutional bodies, I offer Virginia Held's (2004) articulation of an ethics of care as an ethical guide for WPAs looking to make labor decisions that support institutional embodiment.

Part of the difficulty in appreciating administrative labor can be attributed to the fact that it is comprised primarily of immaterial labor. First described by Maurizio Lazzarato (1996) and further developed by Antonio Negri and Michael Hardt (2004), immaterial labor sustains the white-collar economy of ideas (as opposed to the blue-collar economy of things). While the labor associated with blue-collar work (manning a machine; repairing equipment) produces material objects, the labor of white-collar work (developing an advertising strategy; managing the emotions of employees) produces ideas, feelings, concepts, and other immaterial entities. This way of understanding labor focuses on the products of one's labor, not the physical experience of one's labor. As Shaughnessy's work attests, academics are quintessential immaterial laborers, trading in ideas and concepts. Yet, even if the ideas academics disseminate in scholarship or the experiences they cultivate in classrooms are immaterial, the labor required to produce those ideas and experiences is not. It is these embodied aspects of WPA labor, or the physical experience of this labor, that the field most struggles to represent. Indeed, turning to a focus on bodies and embodied realities is one reason Amy Vidali (2015) argues for the "disabling" of WPA narratives, which she critiques for unintentionally conflating disability with pain and suffering. The interchapters included in this section, which deal with laboring bodies as they navigate illness and grief, are excellent examples of embodied experiences that impact labor, examples often missing from discussions of immaterial labor.

Shaughnessy's WPA labor experiences, reveals the complexity of embodiment. Such analyses are further complicated by the fact that the affective, or emotional, labor (controversially seen as a subcategory of immaterial labor by Negri and Hardt) associated with caring for students and teachers is undervalued in academia. Negri and Hardt's (2004) classification of affective labor as immaterial has been challenged, particularly by feminist theorists interested in caring labor, which they emphasize includes affective labor yet produces *both* immaterial and material outcomes. In other words, the focus on the product of care labor[2] is insufficient for understanding it. For example, the caring labor of a nurse may result in the immaterial feeling of psychological comfort and a material body free from bed sores (Lanoix 2013). Therefore, analyses of WPA labor that rely solely on immaterial or affective labor as theoretical lenses are inadequate largely due to these terms' failure to represent the physical, embodied characteristics of such labor. For these reasons, I suggest the term *(inter)personal labor* for analyzing the embodied experiences of laboring as a WPA. Unlike the existing terms for describing labor discussed above, this term simultaneously accounts for affective, immaterial, and embodied labor experiences and supports more complex analysis, description, and valuation of WPA work. While *interpersonal* highlights the labor required to manage humans and the relationships between them (labor both affective and immaterial), *personal* highlights the individual embodied, physical experience of that labor. (Inter)personal labor is thus simultaneously affective, immaterial, and embodied. In this way the term acknowledges both the physicality of labor and its emotional and immaterial elements.

Furthermore, I argue that by applying Virginia Held's (2004, 2006) ethics of care, which makes explicit not only the labor of caring but its vital role in society, to analyses of WPA labor, we can more fully represent that labor. As a moral theorist, Held is most interested in how an ethics of care offers a feminist alternative to dominant philosophical modes of thinking, such as justice or virtue ethics (2004). Unlike most moral theories, which explicitly resist emotion as a distorting principle, "the ethics of care values emotion rather than rejects it" (Held 2006, 10). As a moral system, instead of focusing on the individual as independent, an ethics of care focuses on people and the relationships between them (Held 2004, 59). Understanding WPA labor through the lens of managing human relationships usefully highlights the (inter)personal labor required of WPAs. At the same time, an ethics of care provides a theoretical framework for discussing this labor in moral terms. While adding a moral component to theories of labor complicates the discussion, it also forces scholars to confront questions about how this labor should look and why. Explicitly embracing an ethics of care as a theoretical framework for understanding (inter)personal labor unifies labor discussions with pressing ethical questions (such as the participation of WPAs in the systematic exploitation of contingent laborers). Shaughnessy is an ideal candidate for highlighting the value of using this framework because the centrality of human relationships is fundamental to her legacy as a WPA and because the personal effects of her embodied labor highlight the stakes of this work.

A NOTE ON METHODOLOGY

The analysis of primary material described in this piece is deeply informed by Jacqueline Jones Royster and Gesa Kirsch's (2012) description of feminist rhetorical practices. While their definition of feminist rhetorical practices includes but is not limited to historical work, it provides a theoretical orientation that unites the diverse methodologies I draw on in this project. Royster and Kirsch (2012) describe feminist rhetorical practices as demonstrating "the capacity . . . to propel general knowledge-making processes in the field at large—if not forward—at least to another, better-informed, more inclusive conceptual space" (18). In an effort to articulate and own my positionality and support such an inclusive conceptual space, I provide context about my situatedness as a researcher and personal connections to this research in my analysis. While this move does not erase the weaknesses of any one person's attempt to make meaning from history, I have worked hard to provide the reader with the context necessary to evaluate my findings, and my methods, as they encounter my research and claims. Additionally, I am not drawing on new information (these archives have been available for some time now), but Lynée Lewis Gaillet (2012) explains that "increasingly, scholars interested in primary investigation are . . . revisiting primary and canonical materials with a new set of research questions in mind [as well as . . .] viewing (and adding to existing) archives in ways that *make* knowledge rather than simply finding what's already known" (36). By focusing on Shaughnessy's embodied labor experience, specifically as a WPA, I thus make new claims about her contributions to the field.

It is also worth noting that the reason I have zeroed in on Shaughnessy as a research subject has at least as much to do with my own attraction to her as with her undeniable importance to the field. Of several WPAs I've conducted archival research on, Shaughnessy has "stuck" with me in a special way. Laura Micciche (2007), in *Doing Emotion*, applies Sara Ahmed's concept of "stickiness" as a way to describe the emotional impact of some research on researchers. Micciche argues that rather than ignoring, masking, or even feeling guilty for emotional responses to the topics or people we research, we should use such emotions as research tools precisely *because* of their stickiness, or the tendency of certain pieces of evidence to resonate, or stick like "bits of glue," with a researcher. She explains: "Stickiness is a useful concept for me because it helps explain how emotion rides in neither persons/objects nor the social world exclusively. Rather, emotion is dynamic and relational, taking form through collisions of contact between people as well as between people and the objects, narratives, beliefs, and so forth that we encounter in the world" (28). In other words, Micciche argues that emotional responses are both personal (and therefore to some degree unique) and affected by our larger contexts (and therefore to some degree related to current trends, conversations, and challenges facing the field). A researcher's gender, teaching experiences, administrative struggles, and/or identification with a topic might predispose them to be struck by different elements of their research subject. At the same time, larger contextual issues also influence "stickiness"—such as recent trends in scholarship or reforms/administrative decrees sweeping the country. Connecting stickiness to other calls for feminist researchers to embrace their emotional responses to research, I argue that by naming and identifying our strong emotional reactions to our research—the moments that "stick" with us—and by complicating those moments by looking for the personal and larger contextual reasons that explain many of those emotions, we can start asking important questions. In the case of my research on Shaughnessy, for example, why did a handful of memos detailing department jostling over office space and feelings of "welcomeness" bother me so much? Does my frustration come from a purely personal place or from ongoing obstacles rooted in professional dysfunction? Resting with moments of stickiness—using strategic contemplation, rhetorical listening, and other research methodologies—becomes a productive technique for understanding both why I, as an individual, am drawn to particular bits of the archival record and whether or not those moments can be productively linked to ongoing professional debates.

Stickiness is therefore a useful tool for all research, but in this chapter, I argue it is especially helpful for dealing with a figure like Shaughnessy, whose emotional resonance in the field has been so significant. By trying to appreciate where her ideas have been the stickiest, as well as what other values and emotions have been picked up by residual "bits of glue" and become part of her legacy, we can unpack her contributions, her labor situation, and her incredible work ethic, as well as consider principles related to labor to be gleaned from her experience.

These close readings of the archival record are also connected to theoretical concepts of labor and ethics with the goal of suggesting best practices that could benefit the field. Thus, before detailed readings of specific archival moments, I provide introductions to theories that are then to be applied to the archival documents in order to productively grapple with the complexities of our current labor situation.

(INTER)PERSONAL LABOR: MATERIALIZING EMOTION

(Inter)personal labor usefully refocuses discussions of labor on bodily experiences of labor. While Negri and Hardt's (2004) work on immaterial labor helps us understand the role of affective labor in today's economy, it also encourages a disembodied view of that labor, which can reinscribe dangerous gender norms. Sharon Bolton (2009), for example, worries that linking affective labor to immaterial labor "misses emotional work's materiality" (2). Bolton's concern that Negri and Hardt's focus on the material nature of the commodity, shared by Monique Lanoix, downplays the physicality of affective labor. Lanoix (2013) writes specifically about care labor—often medical or domestic in nature—and the ways the immaterial aspects of this labor—the providing of things like comfort and emotional support—work to disembody how we conceptualize such labor. She is particularly concerned that "contrary to what Hardt and Negri may have hoped, typifying care labor as immaterial only serves to reinscribe care labor as marginal activity" (86–87). Focusing on the product of labor instead of the personal experience of labor obscures its embodied nature. This, in turn, supports interpretations of affective labor as nonphysical, simple, unskilled, or suited to women—all of which are used to undervalue that labor. (Inter)personal labor incorporates immaterial and affective labor in important ways while also emphasizing the physical labor required.

The usefulness of *(inter)personal labor* as a term can be seen in the complicated relationship between immaterial and affective labor. It's useful to chart the tensions between these concepts—particularly as theorists have struggled to honor embodied labor experiences—if only to contextualize how pervasive the tendency to disembody and devalue affective labor has been. Kathi Weeks (2007), in "Life Within and Against Work," charts several feminist interventions into theories of affective and immaterial labor not only to highlight the successes and failures of those interventions but also to suggest new approaches and ways forward (234).

Weeks (2007) recognizes early feminist interventions into immaterial labor as useful in rethinking "dominant conceptions of what counts as labor" (235) even as she notes these interventions failed to address the "specificities of caring labor," such as its emotional components (236). In other words, though concrete and physical forms of housework were finally being included in discussions of labor, elements of care labor, such as its affective dimensions, remained largely invisible. While including household labor as not only taxing but also economically significant was an important step forward, those discussions did not consider the unique elements of care work or import those elements into the public sphere. The second major intervention she charts comes from applications of standpoint theory in the 1970s and 80s to domestic labor, which "explored the difference of domestic laboring practices, embracing the otherness of caring labor as a potential lever and site of agency" (237). While the power and significance of affective labor began to come into view, Weeks critiques this approach for relegating care labor (and its affective elements) to specific, often domestic, sites and unintentionally reproducing gendered labor divisions. While care work and affective labor were final being theorized, this theorizing tended to reinscribe gender norms, particularly by suggesting caring and affective labor were primarily domestic forms of labor.

According to Weeks (2007), the apparent impasse between caring labor (which includes but is not relegated to affective labor) and the economic significance of this labor outside the home can be resolved by C. W. Mills's and Arlie Hochschild's work on affective labor. Their work brings affective labor directly into a post-Fordist economy, with Mills recognizing the way affective labor shapes consumer and labor experiences and Hochschild considering how such labor is developed and valued. Weeks explains that "whereas Mills 'seemed to assume that in order to sell personality, one need only have it,' Hochschild's analysis makes clear that this 'active emotional labor' is first, a skillful activity and second, a practice with constitutive effects" (240). Crucially for Weeks, their work demonstrates the economic importance and value of affective labor and highlights how the value of this labor has grown in an increasingly white-collar and service-based economy. In this way, affective labor is integrated into the public economic realm as opposed to banished to the domestic sphere. Given value outside a domestic context, it becomes possible to argue about both the materiality (difficulty and skill level) and monetary value of such work. Ultimately, Weeks believes the tensions between economic and social impulses (analyses of labor versus analyses of social relationships) can be a productive analytic lens:

> Social feminism's insistent focus on the antagonisms generated at the intersection of capital accumulation and social reproduction can still function as a compelling point of departure. The sometimes competing requirements of creating surplus value and sustaining the relations of sociality on which it depends, give rise to a series of problems the analyses of which can yield important critical levers. This problematic has, for example, served to frame pressing questions about . . . the undervaluation of caring practices both waged and unwaged. . . . But once "social life becomes itself a productive machine" (Negri and Hardt), the terms of that distinction and its conflicts must be made more complex than once imagined. (246)

To accommodate this complexity, Weeks (2007) suggests a move from theories of production and reproduction to theories of life and work, arguing these more expansive terms make it possible to make visible and contest "the gender hierarchies and divisions of labor" (247). For my purposes—coming up with an understanding of the embodied labor of WPAs that takes into account affective labor and the moral considerations of an ethics of care—I'm less interested in how we divide labor than in how we embody and enact it and what this embodiment suggests about the moral goals and value of such work. For this work, *(inter)personal labor* is a more productive term because it acknowledges and values affective, immaterial, and embodied labor even though it does not fully resolve the tensions among these terms. Instead, valuing labor from several perspectives simultaneously allows us to begin to consider actionable paths forward toward more ethical and sustainable embodied labor conditions.

(Inter)personal labor also reorients discussions of labor from focusing on products to focusing on experiences. When administrative work is examined through the lens of immaterial and affective labor, the emphasis on product forces WPAs to focus primarily on making their labor and the labor of their teachers measurable, or material, to others in the university. The most obvious way this measurement is accomplished is through research. While a scholar's ideas are immaterial, research—at least in the form of publications and citations—can be seen as material.[3] For WPAs and other academics, producing scholarship turns immaterial labor into a material commodity that can be listed on a CV and counted toward tenure. The danger of this commodification is that it makes rewarding scholarship easier than rewarding the other, equally labor-intensive, parts of the job. While scholarship will always be an important and valuable product of academic work, discussions of WPA labor must also account for how that labor is experienced by WPAs and others in their programs. A shift to (inter)personal labor, therefore, helps center conversations about labor at least as much on the experience of labor as on its products.

Concerns about the lack of physicality surrounding affective and immaterial labor are not new. Bolton (2009), for example, complains that recent moves to theorize affective labor downplay its physicality, and he uses the example of a flight attendant suppressing an emotional response to handle a difficult customer with a smile. While nothing material has been produced, the affective labor of repressing an emotional response has created a specific customer experience. Bolton worries that by classifying this kind of affective labor as immaterial we downplay the ways such labor is physically demanding. Repressing an emotional reaction might include clenching one's jaw, sweating, high blood pressure, a racing heart, or a myriad of other physical reactions. Thus, the product of this work might not be material, but the labor itself is nonetheless physical. (Inter)personal labor allows for discussions of affective labor that remain rooted in bodily experience. For WPAs, canceling an adjunct's section days before the semester begins or comforting and advising a student taking a medical withdrawal necessarily require affective labor, whether it is directed internally (managing one's own emotions caused by affecting a valued colleague's livelihood or confronting a young student's mortality) or externally (advocating for labor or enrollment policies that respond to difficult situations with appropriate emotional—as well as professional—moral uprightness). From masking reasonable emotional reactions, breaking bad news, or participating in the systematic exploitation of adjuncts, the affective labor of WPAs is physical and, too often, invisible work. (Inter)personal labor asks us to consider a WPA's labor in such moments from multiple directions. How is this work experienced physically? What does it produce? What kind of affective labor is expended? At the same time, we must to remember the moral dimensions of these questions: What do we owe the human beings affected by our administrative practices?

DOING IT ALL: THE COSTS OF DISEMBODIED LABOR

WPA work is often understood and represented as uniquely painful. For Vidali (2015), this view is problematic because many of these narratives—which position the embodied experiences of many WPAs as negative or toxic disruptions of an otherwise "healthy" (read: desirable and nondisabled) work life—have the unintended consequence of treating disability in WPA work as both reducible to mental health and as an unnatural state to be avoided at all costs, effectively erasing other forms of disability while also suggesting freedom from exhaustion, depression, and anxiety are prerequisite for successful WPA labor and barring those who function with those disabilities in their daily lives from participating in this work. The list of narratives linking personal suffering and martyr-like labor with WPAs is, as Colin Charlton, Jonnika Charlton, Tarez Samra, Kathleen J. Ryan, and Amy Ferdinandt Stolley (2011) note, "overwhelming" (55). They argue these depictions can be disempowering and unhelpful, and they work hard to put forth new narratives. While pushing against this trope in the ways Vidali and Charlton et al. suggest has value, looking at the labor of early WPAs like Shaughnessy helps explain how the original narratives of WPA suffering became ubiquitous.

Shaughnessy's administrative labor was both demanding and, to some extent, undercompensated. In the CUNY archives, documents detail the wide scope of her responsibilities. From arguments about placement procedures and their relationship to writing curricula (Lea 1973), to a dispute about a raise promised to Shaughnessy in light of her extra administrative duties but initially not honored (Gross 1973; Keilt 1973), to difficulty matching contingent hiring practices to union guidelines (Gilbert 1969), the archival documents detail her complex administrative experiences. After her promotion to director of the writing program in 1973, Shaughnessy outlined the responsibilities of her new position to Dr. Saul Touster in a letter summarizing her appointment. She lists coordinating ESL, basic writing, SEEK, and the writing center; reporting to the English department chair on "all matters requiring departmental action or coordination"; coordinating with the SEEK coordinator and the SEEK chairman for the English department; overseeing the promotion and evaluation of SEEK and writing program teachers; coordinating with the dean of Open Admissions, the dean of Humanities, and the SEEK director on writing program projects; and remaining "flexible."

Considering her relatively short tenure, the scope and complexity of this work, and disputes over her compensation, it is not difficult to understand how WPA labor became associated with martyrdom and suffering. At the same time, however, Shaughnessy embodies the "hero" narrative as well, overcoming these conditions through grit and hard work. Indeed, despite ample evidence aligning Shaughnessy's tenure as a WPA with the suffering associated with such labor, this suffering can only be constructed secondhand. In her published research and the archives, Shaughnessy herself appears optimistic and capable of every challenge. It is not my wish to superimpose onto Shaughnessy my understanding of WPA work as painful to embody.

Nevertheless, as I discuss below, Shaughnessy herself, as well as her friends, understood the cumulative stress of the combined demands of her labor as contributing to the health problems that eventually killed her. In these ways, Shaughnessy is simultaneously a hero who overcomes daunting professional demands and an uncomplaining martyr ultimately felled by those same demands.

Vital to this argument is the claim that Shaughnessy's work as a WPA was unsustainable and that embodying it was, on a physical and mental level, not good for her. Vidali (2015) is wary of arguments that WPA labor is "intolerable" because the embodied realities this language shuns are, for many disabled individuals, a fact of life no matter their working environment (32). If the embodied realities of all physical states other than health become inherently problematized, then those with disabilities are shut out of particular workspaces. While Vidali's argument is a smart and necessary one (and has made me reconsider my own deployment of terms like *healthy* as unproblematically positive), this point does not mean labor conditions that cause or exacerbate physical and mental suffering are acceptable. Shaughnessy is an important example of an individual whose WPA experiences negatively impacted her mental and physical health. In fact, many speculated Shaughnessy's death from cancer was either hastened or, at least in part, caused by physical exhaustion related to her labor as a WPA. Shaughnessy was lauded for the astounding amount of work she was able to do, and do well: "Everyone who met or worked with her expressed amazement at her ability to work so hard, with such dedication and without the least resentment of the time and energy she devoted" (Maher 1997, 75). This reputation, however, came at a price. For instance, a friend "remembers that [beginning to teach at the college level] was the beginning of 'Mina's blue period,' because 'she would arrive each weekend at our house in Connecticut and spend hours and hours grading the stacks of essays written in those ubiquitous blue books'" (76). Linking her blue moods to blue books, this friend articulates how Shaughnessy's labor affected her emotional equilibrium. In a letter to another friend, Shaughnessy writes, "I am writing from under water—way down deep in a churning, murky, frenzied world full of sentence fragments, and sweet, betrayed students, and memos and suspicious colleagues" (quoted in Maher 1997, 104–5). In her description of her work as "under water" and "churning, murky, frenzied," I see both emotional and physical exhaustion.

And as she invokes "memos and suspicious colleagues," I see the difficult (inter)personal WPA labor included in heading a controversial new program. The (inter)personal WPA labor of managing emotions and relationships like these is lost in traditional analyses of WPA labor. Their immaterial nature and the ease with which affective labor can be dismissed as gendered make highlighting this labor difficult. But when it is unseen, it is uncounted. Invisible labor is not only unrewarded in salary or tenure negotiations but also particularly susceptible to subtle accumulations that end with killing workloads. A close friend of Shaughnessy's, Ed Quinn, even "remembers that Mina speculated over the cause of her cancer. 'She . . . theorized that the summer before Open Admissions was the most stressful period of her life. Preparing for thousands of incoming students had been such a burden that she actually felt that the stress had made her vulnerable to the disease'" (quoted in Maher 1997, 224). While preparing for thousands of incoming students as a WPA for a newly created program required more than just (inter)personal labor, stress responds to more than just physical triggers. Stress encompasses our physical and our mental states. By continuing to ignore the (inter) personal demands (especially in terms of embodied experience) of WPA labor, we allow this labor to remain unstated, uncompensated, and unlimited—supporting labor conditions that spiral out of control until the embodied experience of such labor is painful.

AN ETHICS OF CARE FOR THE WPA

From these examples of Shaughnessy's (inter)personal labor as a WPA, we can see that the "problem" of (inter)personal labor is not only its undervaluation but also its invisibility. As discussed when charting feminist interventions into discussions of affective and immaterial labor, the invisibility of labor often aligns with societal biases about the gendered nature of particular tasks and their relative importance. By emphasizing (inter)personal labor's tangible and visible forms, we make it possible to question existing hierarchies that downplay the difficulty or value of specific kinds of labor. For this work, Held's (2004) writing on an ethics of care is particularly instructive. Because the ethics of care is focused on "tangible" and visible evidence of caring, this concept is particularly useful for thinking about (inter)personal labor's embodied realities. In "Taking Care: Care as Practice and Value," Held attempts a more precise definition of an ethics of care, focusing on the tension between care as an activity and care as an emotional experience (or, in her terms, as "practice" and as "value"). While Held emphasizes the importance of seeing care as embodied labor, she resists shrinking her definition to labor alone, noting most theories of an ethics of care "do not lose sight of how care involves work and the expenditure of energy" but also arguing that definitions of care are "often thought to be more than this" (60). Care is bodily work that often requires significant labor, but it also encompasses affective and moral elements. Caring includes our emotional attachments and concerns for the future. For Held, an ethics of care is vital because of the ways it blends—to use the terms I've been employing thus far—the material and the immaterial. She writes, "An important aspect of care is how it *expresses* our attitudes and relationships" (61). In this way, an ethics of care can be used to describe and evaluate the (inter)personal labor of WPAs, bridging the divide between immaterial commodities and the embodied labor required to produce them while offering a moral framework for transforming caring emotion into action (or labor).

Held also insists care offers a viable moral framework, one I argue we can apply to WPA labor. In my experience, the most emotionally challenging part of WPA labor—on which I expend a great deal of affective energy—is participating in the exploitation of contingent writing teachers. While I see my role as one of advocacy and support, nothing can erase the fact that I am better compensated (dramatically in many cases) than most of the teachers I oversee. I do not have the means or authority to change these conditions, and were I to resign in protest, someone else would surely take my job. But no matter how I rationalize it, my labor still facilitates this system. I keep the system running, and I make it tenable by providing the best student outcomes for the smallest investment. Thus, as I confront daily challenges and make decisions about how to divide and focus my labor, I often wonder about the moral value of particular actions. What ought to be my primary commitments? What framework should I use to make difficult decisions? While some of these answers—or at the very least some of their nuance—are personal, I argue many of these answers can be found through the application of Held's ethics of care.

Held (2006) argues that an ethics of care is necessary because it goes beyond simply naming and appreciating the labor of caring: it provides a mechanism for evaluating care labor. For WPAs, we need not invent a moral framework wholesale. Position statements ratified by various of our professional organizations already articulate fundamental values of our field.

While I do not have the space to provide a comprehensive list of those values, I would like to look at one key moral value, as captured in our position statements, that relates to my analysis of Shaughnessy's tenure as a WPA: our field's commitment to the embodied experiences of the people affected by our work. This commitment includes not only the teachers and students in our classrooms but also WPAs. The Council of Writing Program Administration's "'The Portland Resolution:' Guidelines for WPA Positions" (1992) outlines dozens of responsibilities associated with WPA work. In listing the various duties associated with writing program administration, the goal of this document is two-fold: to make the labor of WPAs more institutionally visible and to protect incoming WPAs by providing accurate descriptions of the different types of work they must be able and willing to do. Tellingly, one subcategory in this list is "Counseling and Advising." This section references some of the affective labor required of an administrator—labor like overseeing grade appeals, managing personnel disputes, and writing letters of recommendation. While much of the document is dedicated to more traditional descriptions of labor, the fact that affective labor is included at all speaks to the necessity of emotion in this work. Beyond clarifying job descriptions and specific job-related duties, another way the field makes concrete its concern for the people inhabiting writing programs is seen in attention to general labor conditions. In this vein, the Conference on College Communication and Composition's "CCCC Statement on Working Conditions for Non-Tenure Track Faculty" (2016) outlines reasonable limits to the labor of such positions. For example, it is recommended that such faculty teach no more than three composition classes a semester and that classes are capped at no more than twenty students. While these recommendations are supported by research on pedagogy, they are written in this statement as vital to an ethical and reasonable working environment. These are only two examples of how the field expresses its concern for the people who take, teach, and administer our classes, but they nevertheless usefully demonstrate a few of the concrete ways concern for other people permeates our field.

Since an ethics of care is interested in how values are expressed in practice, by using acknowledged values of the field, we can analyze how well we are and are not achieving those values through our labor practices. While no profession perfectly aligns the ideal and real, an ethics of care can contribute to understanding the embodied experiences—both positive and negative—of WPA labor and their moral significance. In this way, the flexibility of an ethics of care is invaluable. Held (2006) notes that "the ethics of care builds relations of care and concern and mutual responsiveness to need on both the personal and wider social levels" (69). The goal is not to create a static understanding of WPA labor or even of a particular WPA's legacy: instead, the goal is to use an ethics of care as a heuristic for understanding how our care can and should shape the work we do.

In highlighting labor guidelines, I'm particularly interested in the tension between these values and the labor required of WPAs and the teachers in their programs. It is by analyzing this tension that I think Shaughnessy's legacy as a WPA is best understood. While the kind of labor Shaughnessy did as a WPA was not necessarily unique, part of what contributed to her success was her deployment of (inter)personal labor that focused on relationships and the people involved. In short, though Shaughnessy was not responding to Held's ideas, Held's focus on connectedness and relationships describes well central moral commitments that shaped Shaughnessy's decisions as a WPA. A letter from English-department chair Edmond Volpe to Shaughnessy in 1967, during her first-year as SEEK director, outlines a dispute and illustrates Shaughnessy's focus on her staff as human beings to whom she has moral responsibilities that include care for their affective states and embodied labor experiences. The letter appears to be a response from Volpe to criticism from SEEK (formerly Pre-Baccalaureate) staff feeling isolated from the rest of the English department. Knowing this, Volpe expresses his disappointment that none of the SEEK teachers have come to several recent English-department events to which everyone was invited: "Now, I want to make clear that I have never pressed anyone in the department to participate in any function, and I do not intend to do so. But, I have been conscious of the strong feelings expressed last year by the pre-bac instructors concerning their sense of isolation, and I had hoped to remedy the problem this year by making very clear that I want the staff to participate in all departmental activities." While Shaughnessy's response to this exact letter does not survive, a subsequent letter, dated a few months after Volpe's, does. In it, Shaughnessy (1966) obviously continues an ongoing discussion with Volpe about how to effectively integrate the SEEK writing instructors into the department. After referencing attempts such as encouraging SEEK faculty to attend English-department events, she launches into a careful explanation of what she identifies as a key component of the feelings of isolation and undervaluation of SEEK writing teachers: office space. She writes:

> I must again bring up the subject of office space. Everyone is aware of the space problem; the disgruntlement rises more directly from the fact that every teacher in the regular English program has some kind office space whereas not one teacher in the Pre-bac program has any office space. The counseling time that is worked into the teachers' schedules is not an adequate substitute: no one can reach the teachers by telephone except in the evenings, and the teachers, in turn, run up their telephone bills at home; they have no place to "land" when they get to campus; they cannot meet student requests for appointments; and most important, their

contention that they are invisible is seriously reinforced by the failure of anyone to allot them space. Is there nothing we can do and no one we can bother about this? (n.p.)

Shaughnessy smartly locates the "disgruntlement" of SEEK writing teachers in their labor conditions, paying close attention to the affective responses of feeling displaced and unvalued. In advocating for her teachers, Shaughnessy highlights the burdens placed on her teachers, both financially in their phone bills and emotionally in their lack of place to "land," and notes the effect on students who do not have adequate access to their writing teachers. Shaughnessy's focus on the people, both students and teachers, it is her job to oversee and her clear commitment to addressing labor conditions like access to office space in ways that support teachers and students illustrate a moment when the "centrality of human relationships" at the heart of Held's ethics of care clearly guides Shaughnessy's actions as a WPA.

CONCLUDING THOUGHTS: (SELF-)CARE IN ADMINISTRATION

While the previous section highlights Shaughnessy's success at using care for others as a guide for her actions as a WPA, she also represents the field's tendency to not apply care to ourselves. In fact, the very things I most admire about Shaughnessy—her clear respect for her students, her research into challenging dismissive ideas about basic writers, her effective administrative abilities and focus on people—also play into problematic aspects of the mythology surrounding Shaughnessy. As a field we love her, we mourn her early loss, and we see her as a kind of sacrifice to turning our field toward students. For people like me, with a penchant toward martyrdom on the behalf of students, she thus became a problematic role model. Rather than internalizing the expectation that great teacher-scholars must sacrifice themselves to their profession, the goal ought to be finding ways to support the kind of work she did with labor conditions that *also* support teachers mentally and physically—in other words, toward labor conditions that honor the embodied reality of (inter)personal WPA labor.

Embracing an ethics of care and applying it not only to those we oversee but also to ourselves can help us achieve this. In all these ways, Shaughnessy exemplifies core tensions surrounding embodied WPA labor. As a field we are proud of both our student orientation and our commitment to people (expressed, for example, by the field's close attention to employment policies that over-rely on undercompensated contingent work and calls for reform). At the same time, our deep investment in these aspects of the field have motivated many to accept labor conditions that overtax and overburden WPAs, which has had the unintended consequence of normalizing unrealistic and damaging labor conditions. Shaughnessy is a prime example of this, demonstrating the value in building relationships with the people around her and focusing closely on student needs while also serving as a warning that pushing oneself to do the seemingly impossible, while potentially achieving much in a short amount of time, can also normalize such expectations. I am inspired by Shaughnessy, but it is important to articulate the complexities of her (inter)personal labor and its costs, particularly in her bodily experience of that labor. I want to be inspired by her to not only care for and respect the humans touched by my work but also to refuse to perpetuate labor conditions that demand more than one person can sustainably accomplish. Her experience offers a lesson: martyrdom, in the form of meeting unreasonable demands on our labor, is not an effective, or ethical, strategy for long-term change. Accepting such labor conditions for ourselves allows those conditions to extend to our colleagues. Self-care and putting limits on our work, as well as advocating for creating labor conditions that enable effective teaching and administration, is a morally significant dimension of our work.

NOTES

1. Amy Vidali (2015), in "Disabling Writing Program Administration," makes a similar point in different terms. Her goal is to resist WPA narratives that present "health"—or nondisability—as the default scholar state, which the trauma of WPA labor disrupts. While her argument is more complex than this alone, she warns that the WPA "hero narrative" in which the hyperable WPA overcomes a disabling work environment "tucks disability away and fails to recognize or rectify the power differential between disabled and non-disabled people" (42). Similarly, I argue hero (or, in my terms, *martyr*) narratives like Shaughnessy's elide unsustainable structural elements of WPA work by positioning unsustainable expectations for WPAs as individual problems solvable through personal excellence.
2. Care labor describes labor centered on tending to the well-being of another person and includes both affective and nonaffective labor. This term is used by many who discuss affective labor (Bolton 2009; Lanoix 2013; Weeks 2007).
3. While scholarship is commonly treated as immaterial, within the economy of academia, publications function as a countable commodity that can be measured. I characterize publications as material to highlight the difference between how research and service are often valued in academia.

REFERENCES

Bolton, Sharon C. 2009. "The Lady Vanishes: Women's Work and Affective Labour." *International Journal of Work Organisation and Emotion* 3 (1): 1–9.

Charlton, Colin, Jonnika Charlton, Tarez Samra Graban, Kathleen J. Ryan, and Amy Ferdinandt Stolley, eds. 2011. *GenAdmin: Theorizing WPA Identities in the Twenty-First Century*. Anderson, SC: Parlor.

Conference on College Composition and Communication. 2016. "CCCC Statement on Working Conditions for Non-Tenure Track Writing Faculty." http://cccc.ncte.org/cccc/resources/positions/working-conditions-ntt.

Council of Writing Program Administrators. 1992. "The Portland Resolution: Guidelines for Writing Program Administrator Positions." http://wpacouncil.org/positions/portlandres.html.

Gaillet, Lynée Lewis. 2012. "(Per)Forming Archival Research Methodologies." *College Composition and Communication* 64 (1): 35–58.

Gilbert, Mirian. 1969. Letter to staff member, December 4. Morris Ralph Cohen Library, CUNY.

Gross, Theodore. 1973. Letter from Theodore Gross to John Keilt, December 12. Morris Ralph Cohen Library, CUNY.

Held, Virginia. 2004. "Taking Care: Care as Practice and Value." In *Setting the Moral Compass: Women Philosophers*, edited by Cheshire Calhoun, 59–71. Oxford: Oxford Press.

Held, Virginia. 2006. *The Ethics of Care: Personal, Political, and Global*. Oxford: Oxford University Press.

Keilt, John. 1973. "Letter Robert Bott Oct 25." Morris Ralph Cohen Library, CUNY.

Lanoix, Monique. 2013. "Labor as Embodied Practice: The Lessons of Care Work." *Hypatia* 28 (1): 85–100.

Lazzarato, Maurizio. 1996. "Immaterial Labor." Translated by Paul Colilli and Ed Emory. In *Radical Thought in Italy: A Potential Politics*, edited by Michael Hardt and Paul Virno, 132–47. Minneapolis: University of Minnesota University.

Lea, Mary. 1973. Letter to Mina Shaughnessy. Morris Ralph Cohen Library, CUNY.

Maher, Jane. 1997. *Mina P. Shaughnessy: Her Life and Work*. Urbana, IL: NCTE.

Micciche, Laura R. 2007. *Doing Emotion: Rhetoric, Writing, Teaching*. Portsmouth, NH: Boynton/Cook.

Negri, Antonio, and Michael Hardt. 2004. *Multitude: War and Democracy in the Age of Empire*. New York: Penguin.

Royster, Jacqueline Jones, and Gesa Kirsch. 2012. *Feminist Rhetorical Practices: New Horizons for Rhetoric, Composition, and Literacy Studies*. Carbondale: Southern Illinois University Press.

Shaughnessy, Mina P. 1966. "Letter to Ed Volpe." Morris Ralph Cohen Library, CUNY.

Shaughnessy, Mina P. 1973. "Letter Saul Touster, April 18." Morris Ralph Cohen Library, CUNY.

Vidali, Amy. 2015. "Disabling Writing Program Administration." *WPA: Writing Program Administration* 38 (2): 32–55.

Volpe, Ed. 1967. "Letter to Shaughnessy." Morris Ralph Cohen Library, CUNY.

Weeks, Kathi. 2007. "Life Within and Against Work: Affective Labor, Feminist Critique, and Post-Fordist Politics." *Ephemera: Theory and Politics in Organization* 7 (1): 233–49.

10.1

SOMATOPHOBIA AND SUBJECTIVITY
*Or, What Cancer Taught Me about
Writing and Teaching Writing*

Julie Prebel

I began my second tenure-track year with firm plans: new courses with opportunities to stretch my pedagogy and curricular archive, a research agenda with a schedule to situate me for a successful tenure review, and active participation in committee work to connect me more fully to the spaces and people of my institution. A cancer diagnosis after an annual screening mammogram at the end of fall semester, however, quickly unraveled these plans, making them seem idealistic and distant from my embodied experiences. As I went through treatment and continued teaching in spring semester, I experienced my body as simultaneously a subject and an object—an ambiguous sense of self in which I was acutely aware of my subjectivity as inseparable from my body while at the same time my body seemed an abstract idea, a transactional space handled and gazed upon by others. This tension between experiencing the body as simultaneously subject and object is well documented in philosophy, feminism, and critical theories of embodiment, and Madeleine Grumet (2003) notes that this tension is also "pedagogically important" in the ways our body performances play out in the classroom (250).

Before cancer, my teaching body seemed a thing somewhat outside myself, even while I understood the familiar sense of objectification, "standing in front of the room, receiving the gaze of students," an appraisal I tried to deflect, as Grumet (2003) describes, by "distracting students with verbal stimuli" (250). During cancer treatment, however, the sense of my subjectivity—especially my teacher subjectivity—as bound up in my body became unavoidable. Too often I found myself unable to focus or lost the thread of class discussion easily; I forgot students' names, which was unusual for me; my extreme fatigue and physical discomfort was visibly evident; and I canceled office hours to leave early (something I always considered a major no-no). Given these changes in my pedagogy, I worried about course evaluations, so critical for a tenure review, even more than usual, and I especially wondered about how I would keep up bodily with the expectations (self-imposed and, so I thought, discipline specific) of my job.

Looking back on this time, I am struck by how readily I seemed to focus on the products of my labor versus the experiences that might affect my labor, a distinction Rebecca Gerdes-McClain explains in the opening chapter of this section through her definition of "(inter)personal" labor.

Despite my heightened sense of my body experiences during treatment, I nonetheless alternated between the body as subject and as object throughout the semester—an alternation amplified by the topics and texts we were discussing in my popular science-writing course, particularly Rebecca Skloot's (2010) *The Immortal Life of Henrietta Lacks*. Focusing student attention on the story of Lacks, whose cervical cancer cells were removed, preserved, and distributed for medical research without her knowledge or consent, shifted student attention away from my subjectivity towards a narrative about the lived effects of bodies as exhibiting the tension of being both subject and object. As we explored the intersections of the bioethics, racism, misogyny, and medical paternalistic power (vis-à-vis Foucault) evident in Lacks's story, I hid behind my pedagogy to evade bodily surveillance. As it turned out, however, my embodied life experiences impinged upon our discussions of ethical actions, power, and knowledge. My body became a source for both witnessing the theories we were discussing in class and interrogating the different and inequitable experiences of white women with power and privilege versus the lived effects of oppression and white supremacy for Black women navigating medical treatment. There may have been some learning moments in this class, as by disclosing my "perspectives and understandings . . . drawn from [my] lived experiences" and encouraging them to examine the ways particular bodies can be vulnerable, stigmatized, and oppressed, I challenged "students' own frames for action and judgment" (Grumet 2003, 254). At that time, though, I perceived this class as a failure in terms of my ability to sustain a pedagogy focused on what Michelle LaFrance, in this collection, calls the currencies "ideas, disembodied and objective" (247)—a common assumption and misconception about classrooms as intellectual spaces. In a writing course designed to help students become more confident and proficient writers, my bodily experiences made it impossible to give their writing or them as individuals the attention they needed. In their course evaluations, they expressed sympathy for what I was going through and also their disappointment that they did not gain more from a professor they had heard (as one student said) was "known for helping students become better writers." I spoke with no one about this course or these evaluations, feeling discouraged at how I let my students and even my department down—I was hired to teach writing *well*, after all.

Fast forward a few years as I prepared my file for tenure review. Instead of providing a fuller narrative about this science-writing course, as my institution requires for all courses in the teaching section of our file, I sidestepped the C word and contextualized the criticisms in the evaluations as somewhat expected given the new course prep. In fact, I did not mention anywhere in my initial tenure narrative my cancer diagnosis or the fact that I did not take a medical leave during treatment. I was determined that my otherwise strong record of teaching, service, and growing scholarship speak on their own. My body simply did not matter. In her work on embodiment, Elizabeth Grosz (1994) summarizes the somatophobia evident in philosophy since the inception of the discipline and argues that "we have inherited in our current conceptions of bodies" this history of devaluing the body, of coding body experiences as negative in terms that "marginalize or exclude considerations of the body" (4–5). More than falling prey to the Cartesian dualism that privileges the mind over the body, I sought a way to express and display my teacher-scholar subjectivity as one of achievement by denying the body a presence at all, or at the very least by narratively containing its "unruly" (in Grosz's terms) and notably feminine corporeality (breast cancer can subject women and the lower percentages of men who develop the disease to an all-too-familiar misogynistic characterization as weaker, more hormonal, etc.—a topic for a different and longer essay). Eventually, I could not detach my body experiences from my work, as the review committee asked about a lag in my scholarship and professional activities. During the roughly twelve-month period following my surgery and throughout my initial treatment, I found myself physically exhausted and emotionally drained, and thus unable to bring some of my projects to completion.

As much as I tried initially to define myself in what Grosz calls "non- or extracorporeal terms" (14), I had to acknowledge my embodied experiences and take a delay in my tenure review, only to later feel a mixture of relief after a successful tenure and promotion application and regret that I had to call upon my body in all its "biologism" (14) as justification for an interruption in scholarly production.

Some of my writing projects from this year of delay are now in print; some I never returned to, including work highly relevant to my interests in feminism and embodiment, such as a piece on nineteenth-century women's literary depictions of "female" cancers: cervical, ovarian, and breast. As Grumet (2003) says of the ways our embodied lives and histories have an impact in our classrooms, "our bodies give us away" (257). Without question, my body gave me away in the writing classroom during cancer treatment and later returned even though I tried to repress it during tenure review. Perhaps I still devalue my embodied experiences or code them as negative, as I carefully adjust the space between my work as a scholar and my embodiment. My work focuses often on issues of embodiment, yet writing about my own embodied experiences as a teacher and a scholar have proven to be challenging (including writing this piece). The effect of my body experiences defines my relationship to writing as I continue to explore the tension between object and subject, a liminal space where I can admit I have a body—even one that sometimes slows me down—while challenging assumptions that my body reduces my writerly subjectivity or negatively impacts my ability to teach writing and now administer a writing program.

REFERENCES

Grosz, Elizabeth. 1994. *Volatile Bodies: Toward a Corporeal Feminism.* Bloomington: Indiana University Press.

Grumet, Madeline R. 2003. "Afterword: My Teacher's Body." In *The Teacher's Body: Embodiment, Authority, and Identity in the Academy,* edited by Diane P. Freedman and Martha Stoddard Holmes, 249–58. Albany: SUNY Press.

Skloot, Rebecca. 2010. *The Immortal Life of Henrietta Lacks.* New York: Crown.

10.2

A SCHOLAR ANEW
How Cancer Taught Me to Rekindle My Embodiment Research

Maureen Johnson

The morning of my graduation, I woke up early. Ours was the morning ceremony, and I wanted my sister Arica to flat iron my long, red, curly hair. My sister also put on my makeup, using a new eye-color palette she purchased for the occasion. I wanted to look beautiful. After all, today I would officially become Dr. Johnson. I also wanted to feel beautiful because on the inside I was an anxious mess. A few weeks earlier, I had been diagnosed with triple-negative breast cancer, one of the most rare and aggressive types. In this moment, I was cancer free, the tumor removed a few days before Thanksgiving. Even so, I did have a piece of gauze taped over the top of my left breast from a newly installed port for chemo infusions. The operation to install the port, which I jokingly said made me a cyborg, had been the Monday before Friday's graduation. The gauze could barely be seen under my gray dress and could not be seen at all under my graduation robes. I didn't even worry about the bandage when my dissertation chair put the hood over my head and the graduate school dean and photographers adjusted the hood to make sure it was on correctly.

Cancer came at a time in my life when I was finally feeling good about myself. I felt confident in my body after years of struggle. Part of that confidence came from my research, which focuses on accepting bodies as complicated and meaning-making entities. I planned on turning my dissertation into a book to promote body-positive attitudes to help those, like me, who have struggled for body acceptance. My December graduation allowed me to spend the spring applying for tenure-track jobs and turning my dissertation into a book. I wanted to send off book proposals by February.

The completion of my dissertation went hand in hand with my diagnosis. I defended my dissertation in late September and had a mammogram in early October. A few days after that mammogram, I had an ultrasound, and then, after that, a biopsy. All of this happened while I was making my final edits and submitting my dissertation to the university. I found out after my biopsy that I needed to have a lumpectomy to remove the tumor, which at the time they thought was type 0, which would have meant no further treatment. Once I had that lumpectomy, they realized the tumor had grown a centimeter in about a month, thus the tumor was type IIA—which is an early stage based on the size of the tumor—and the cancer has not spread to my lymph nodes. The diagnosis meant two rounds of chemo, four strong doses given every other week, followed by twelve weekly doses of a different drug. The chemo would be followed by seven weeks of radiation.

As I went through diagnosis and treatment, I remembered how embodied rhetorics appealed to me because of my own fat body, but the cancer made this relationship even more complex. In my dissertation, I had written a section on scars and embracing imperfect bodies. Now, I had to come to terms with my own scars, some visible and some hidden, as well as my own bodily insecurities. My hair and skin were always parts of my body that made me feel beautiful, and now the cancer treatment gave me scars and caused me to lose my hair. How could I continue to do research on the body when I struggled with my own embodied identity?

These identity struggles worsened as treatment continued. Despite the mental and physical toll from chemo, taking time off work was not an option for me. Because I was no longer a student, I had to work two adjunct positions while undergoing treatment. I taught three classes at my alma mater and two courses at another institution about a forty-five-minute drive from my house. I did as much prep work as I could before the semester, before the cumulative effects of chemo started. The FYC director at my alma mater allowed me to teach Monday/Wednesday classes, with the Wednesday class sessions online. Wednesdays became chemo day. I taught Tuesdays and Thursdays at the other institution. Fridays were symptom days, as the oncologist warned me the symptoms generally began two days after treatment.

While I didn't experience a lot of pain from the cancer, which luckily was caught very early, the chemo was physically draining. No amount of rest could make up for the constant tiredness. I often had to sit while I led class discussion because I lacked the strength to stand for eighty minutes straight. I lost my hair, eyebrows, eyelashes, fingernails, and toenails. Because I lost forty pounds, my clothes were hanging off me, and I didn't have the desire or energy to shop for new clothes. I also experienced what they call "chemo brain," which made my thoughts fuzzy. Chemo brain is kind of like nature's way of causing you to forget the pain and exhaustion as you go through the process. Even though

I knew it was a side effect, fuzzy brain was difficult for me as a scholar. I had always relied on my mind to get me through difficult moments.

Chemo meant both my mind and body were betraying me. During my treatment I just had to focus on getting better and come to terms with my body all over again. Every time I struggled, I thought about my research and how many times I had written about body acceptance or encouraged others to accept their bodies as they were. There was a disconnect between my body and mind. I had to struggle to reconnect and become whole.

A saving grace through this whole process was my incredibly supportive network. My parents flew in to take care of me. My mentors took turns taking me to chemo on the days my parents couldn't be there. Friends checked on me and made sure I was okay. Through this process, I learned how important it is to make connections with your colleagues because they were a literal lifeline for me.

Despite all the support, the weariness led me to take a break from filling out job applications and working on my book. I was so focused on the day to day that I ignored my future. Luckily one of my mentors pushed me to resume the job search. She reminded me of my own internal strength. Shortly after, I got three phone interviews for tenure-track positions in the same week. Two of those turned into campus visits. When I returned home from these campus visits, I was more tired than I can possibly put into words. I spent many days after them in bed. Even though those interviews were difficult, they paid off. About two weeks after finishing all my cancer treatment, I started a tenure-track faculty position.

While the job search worked out, my book remains unfinished. It took months to get back into the writing mindset, and now I am refining my proposal. While I am back on track, I know the book revisions will take time, maybe longer than they would have before I was sick. Nowadays, I take things slower, focusing on what needs to be done and writing in little pieces at a time. My new goal is to finish my book in two years.

Through the treatment and its lingering effects (I dealt with chemo side effects for two years and still have difficult days), I am much calmer about my career trajectory. Before cancer, my laser focus was on accomplishing the scholarship. Now I recognize the even bigger impact of that research. I must embrace my scars, my short hair, and my status as a cancer survivor. During the early days of my treatment, I kept seeing the disconnect between my research and myself.

Now I see my body is my research. My research provides the insight needed to promote body positivity, and my body provides the method to complete that research. Recognizing the strength of my own body is the first step toward promoting body acceptance on a larger scale.

10.3

A COMP TEACHER'S ELEGY
To Carol Edleman Warrior

Michelle LaFrance

> *Embodiment is defined as physical motion and the knowledge that might stem from such motion, sensory, or bodily response, and a metaphorical and physical connection between the body and writing.*
> —A. Abby Knoblauch

I dreamed about my friend Carol last night.

We were talking about the vulnerability and general discomfort of pelvic exams and how hard it is to embrace the whole "I love my vagina" thing, full-on *Vagina Monologues* style, as women of the twenty-first century *should*. I do, of course, embrace my vagina—I read *Our Bodies, Ourselves* as a young woman. I call myself feminist, body positive, sex positive.

But.

The work of undoing the patriarchy—it's not exactly easy.

In this dream, Carol and I joked about showing ours to one another. And we laughed all the more awkwardly because we would *never*, even though we knew exactly why this movement to love *all* of our bodies has power.

I write this a little shy of one year after she died, unexpectedly.

*

I offer this elegy as a reflection on the ways our bodies go unnoticed, unremarked in our classroom spaces and relationships. "Our bodies inform our ways of knowing," Maureen Johnson, Daisy Levy, Katie Manthey, and Maria Novotny (2015, 39) argue—though I'd make a more unambiguous assertion: *Our bodies are how we know and how others know us.*

I'm not at all surprised Carol would be in a dream with me, modeling for me how we might make what is difficult to see more visible. How we might own what is ours.

But, I must pause here.

https://doi.org/10.7330/9781646422340.c010.3

I want to write something like: Even when she was my student, she was my teacher. And as my teacher, she was always seemingly steady, patient, understanding, *and unflinching.*

Yet that statement strikes me as glib. Whose story I am telling? Hers? Mine?

Carol was a Native woman, a registered member of the Ninilchik Village Tribe and of Alutiiq (Sugpiaq), Dena'ina Athabascan, and A'aniii (Gros Ventre) descent, according to her obituary (Glaser 2018). Carol was often crafting, making, growing, gathering, and cooking—the work of her hands, family and community belongings, central to her scholarship. Her scholarly work pushed boundaries—in her article "Indigenous Collectives: A Meditation on Fixity and Flexibility" in *Native American Quarterly* (2017), she explored what we might learn from the "lowly" slime mold, for instance:

> Slime molds . . . look and act at turns like fungi, plants, and animals. It should not be surprising, then, that these organisms inspire disgust or fear, since they may represent what Jeffrey Jerome Cohen calls a "category crisis," earning them a place in the imagination alongside monsters or aliens: "Refusal to participate in the classificatory 'order of things' is true of monsters generally; they are disturbing hybrids whose externally incoherent bodies resist attempts to include them in any systematic structuration." (374–75)

I borrow her words here to make real for you just how brilliant she was—a provocative thinker, a careful and accomplished writer, and an insightful theorist.

We've lost a luminary.

This snippet of her work resonates with the message her death offers us, as well. "All bodies shift and change, sometimes naturally, sometimes violently. And the positionality of any body is constantly shifting within varied power structures and social situations," A. Abby Knoblauch writes (2012, 63).

Women like Carol are often posed as our teachers, muses, and models—fixed into position in ways that neither consider what they would like, or how they view themselves, or the intersecting dynamics of emotional labor, racial dysfunction, gendered expectation, and material contexts that attend embodiment, identity, and also teaching, mentorship, and even most friendships for women. Beneath all the layers of this story, our bodies are always unforgivingly structuring our experiences and movements, rooting us in time and space as the women we are, shaping the work we choose and are obliged to do together inside and outside the classroom.

I met Carol in fall of 2007 when she was a student in my section of English 197 at the University of Washington. Then, she stood out as an older student, already forty and with grown children. I liked her immediately. We shared a history of crooked life lines, hanging out in dive bars, and a love of indie rock. She had returned to school to pursue an academic career later in life, like me. She had not been gifted the name Warrior by an elder just yet. And I knew almost immediately she would go on to do incredible things, make contributions to ongoing conversations, inspire others, live an authentic and proud life. From the first day of our composition class, I saw this about her, the way teachers just intuitively sense when some students have possibility knitted into their auras.

She turned in some of the most insightful work I've yet read in an introductory composition course—and no wonder, considering her life experience and deep intelligence. When she told me a year or so after my class that she'd kept my handouts on writing in English studies to guide her writing in other classes, I preened.

She thought my teaching *was helpful.*

I watched her complete her undergraduate degree (we walked the same graduation ceremony) and apply to graduate school. I was honored when she asked for my advice on her personal statement and the essay she submitted as part of her application. I was amazed by the sketch of her life shared in her personal statement: how long she'd wanted to go back to school and the things that had changed to allow her to pursue a PhD. I never doubted she'd get into a top program. She was one of us, an academic, from the start.

I watched her as she worked toward her PhD, met Chad, a member of the White Earth Anishinaabe tribe, and began to live her Indigenous identity with a tremendous freedom and rightness. I watched as she completed her PhD, took on a fellowship and then a faculty position at Cornell. As her former teacher, I was unabashedly proud of her and the life she had built.

As her friend, I was deeply saddened to hear of her early passing.

*

Chad left a message.

"Hi Michelle. I'm calling to tell you Carol passed." The message knocked the wind out of me.

She had been at a gathering in Colorado. She was surrounded by friends and family when she slipped away. Shortly after his message, Chad established a GoFundMe blog. There, I watched him narrate his return to family life in Ithaca, the house they had shared (with Chad's children), and teaching at Cornell. I watched this all with the sort of frustratingly useless compassion that characterizes many of our relationships with our former students and colleagues at other institutions. I helped where I could. I grieved for Carol's family. I still grieve for our collective loss.

*

Knoblauch (2012) writes (drawing on Deborah Hawhee) that embodiment is a persistently unrecognized presence in writing and rhetoric. Our language, as we "flesh out" terms, watch differences "bleed into one another," "wrestle" ideas, and "embrace" positions, "speaks to and from bodies . . . carry[ing] multiple meanings, acting as a catalyst for both identification and disidentification" (52). As writing teachers, it is easy to forget this—our classrooms are intellectual spaces, after all. Our currencies, in the ideal, are ideas, disembodied and objective rhetorical structures, disciplinary generalizations privileging *the life of the mind*, as if "mind" exits somewhere free of material or emotional entanglements. And yet, as this elegy makes clear, our bodies are a persistent subtext in these classroom relations.

I read a first draft of this piece to the students in the creative nonfiction class I teach, and one told me "the vagina" signifies "the unspeakable" in the language of dreams—and I could not really counter that point, though the poet in me thinks perhaps dreams (and bodies) are translingual, transrational, and never so direct as to really "signify" anything stable or fixed.

It is a tenuous venture, then, to learn to speak about our embodiments and how they structure our relations, particularly as writing teachers. Carol and I did not need to speak or write of our bodies for them to hold power over us, ordering who we were and are, compelling the very ways we came to know and learn with one another.

I offer this elegy, my memory and story, in order to speak the truth of those embodied relations now.

Rest in power, my friend.

REFERENCES

Glaser, Linda B. 2018. "Carol Warrior, assistant professor of English, dies at 56." *Cornell Chronicle*, July 10. https://news.cornell.edu/stories/2018/07/carol-warrior-assistant-professor-english-dies-56.

Johnson, Maureen, Daisy Levy, Katie Manthey, and Maria Novotny. 2015. "Embodiment: Embodying Feminist Rhetorics." *Peitho Journal* 18 (1): 39–44.

Knoblauch, A. Abby. 2012. "Bodies of Knowledge: Definitions, Delineations, and Implications of Embodied Writing in the Academy." *Composition Studies* 40 (42): 50–65.

Warrior, Carol Edelman. 2017. "Indigenous Collectives: A Meditation on Fixity and Flexibility." *Native American Quarterly* 41 (4): 368–92.

10.4
BORN FOR THIS

Elizabeth Boquet

I'm sorry
I slammed the door on my way out.

I could still hear you through the walls, warning
"Don't you dare."

I'm sorry
I picked up the phone and steadied my fingers just enough
to dial 9-1-1.

I'm sorry
they flopped you like a flounder this way and
that,
tangled your oxygen tanks and tore open your gown.

I'm sorry
I couldn't make you presentable enough
before they wheeled you down the hall.

A tweeze here,
A swipe of lipstick there "Just a little color,"
you would have said.

I'm sorry
I overheard
your last words to Daddy,
an absolution for him of a sort.
"I know you-know-who is making you do this"

It's true
I'm your daughter I was
born for this.

*

I wrote this poem in the spring of 2013, almost two years after my mom passed away. It came near the end of a six-week poetry-writing workshop, which came near the end of a semester-long leave, which came near the end of more than six years of academic leadership. It came at what I expected to be the end of the healing I needed to do—from the loss, from the work. I understand it now to be the beginning of the beginning.

During the poetry workshop itself, I had spent my time floating from table to table, in teacher-facilitator mode, as participants read and wrote and shared. I was listening, I was encouraging, I was responding. I was doing anything but writing—and hoping no one had noticed. By our third session, I had written exactly . . . nothing. No description (week 1), no list (week 2), and no false-apology (week 3) poem in sight.

My mom died on a sunny late July morning when I was working round the year, round the clock, as a central administrator at my university. There was no poetry then.

*

7:30 a.m., 07/28/11—Thursday. Kitchen table at home. To: VP@fairfield.edu

From: eboquet@fairfield.edu
Subj: Re: Performance Evaluations Dear M—,
Yes, I did consult on the substantive performance issues. We all agreed.
I understand why the budget cannot come in to my area, so that piece is working fine.
Maybe an improvement would be to ask HR to design a process for all dual reporting-type positions that we then all follow. The AVP seemed to be suggesting something similar in his message. If you and he both think this is a good idea, I'd be happy to raise it with HR.
Thanks for the feedback. Best,
Beth

*

The kitchen table where I sat to compose this early-morning email is the same one that has fed at least four generations of my family. My grandmother bought it in the early 1940s. Growing up, we ate breakfast and dinner there. (Lunch we had in the dining room, with our extended family.) I don't recall anyone working at this table until it came to live with me, unless you call shelling peas work (which it is). My grandfather never flipped through bank ledgers there. My mother certainly couldn't carry her IBM Selectric home on the weekends to continue typing forms in triplicate. No, in the family I grew up in, at the time I grew up, the worries came home at the end of the day, but the work stayed at the office.

Now, work goes where we go. The laptop is aptly named, even though I tend not to set it exactly there. The old models used to heat up, and the new, cooler version still feels perched too precariously on my thighs. But, like all of us, I can work anywhere and everywhere, in my house and out of it. Kitchen, living room, den, library, coffee shop on one side of town, coffee shop on the other, standing in line at the grocery store, at the pharmacy, sitting in the waiting rooms of one doctor after another after another. During my time as a full-time administrator, emailing started in bed with a check of my phone as soon as the alarm went off, and it didn't end until I went to sleep at night.

*

8:17 a.m., 07/28/11—Thursday. My parents' apartment across town.

I didn't always stop by my parents' on my way to work. For one thing, their apartment wasn't on my way to work. It was decidedly out of the way. Fifteen minutes out of the way, on the other side of town. But I tried to see them every day, and I hadn't seen them the day before. That day, my mom had had a nice visit with her neighbor, Jenny. She sounded good on the phone. When I left work, I decided not to stop. I tell myself now that I thought a visit from Jenny was enough visiting for my mom for one day, that she was probably tired, that it didn't matter whether she saw me or not. But I know that is not true: it always mattered whether she saw me. She was never not happy to see me. She would have been happy to see me that day. The truth is, I was trying to pace myself for what seemed like an inevitable long, slow decline. Turns out, I didn't need to.

My mom had made a few friends in their new apartment complex, and I was grateful. It hadn't even been a year since we'd moved my parents from Louisiana to Connecticut so they could be closer to my husband and me. I had been worried she would be lonely so far from home, though I had underestimated how lonely she already was, with both her kids living far away, with all but one of her siblings dead, with cousins and friends increasingly infirmed. When people asked her what it was like to leave the place she had always lived and move all the way across the country, she said only that she wished she and my dad had done it sooner. So do I.

And yet. And yet, the move killed her. There's a term for it, I now know: discontinuity of care. She suffered from it. She suffered.

When I popped by their apartment that Thursday morning, the door was unlocked. They were expecting me. But when I went inside, there was no one moving around. No coffee being made, no biscuits in the oven, no TV blaring CNN. The door to their bedroom was shut. From behind it, I heard my dad say, "I'm having a little trouble getting your mom out of bed this morning."

The tactile memories are the most enduring: the feel of the cheap, hollow knobs on their apartment doors; the weight of the receiver in my left hand, the buttons giving way to the pressure of the index finger on my right when I called for the ambulance; later, the cup of water I took from the nurse and handed to my mom, who handed it back to me when she was done. The last time our fingers would touch.

*

9:02 a.m., 07/28/11—Thursday. Operations Assistant's Desk, Office of Academic Engagement, Kelley Center, Fairfield University.

To: eboquet@fairfield.edu From: hkropitis@fairfield.edu
Subj: Grant meeting being cancelled!! Hang in there EOM [End of Message]

*

The nurse ushered me out of ER Room #6 and pulled the curtain. I didn't ask why and she didn't say. I leaned against a wall in the hallway and let the bricks cool my back. I must have called my assistant Helen on my way to the hospital because the email trail to her begins here, as she updates me on my calendar for the day. Bent over my phone, I was pulling down this message when I heard my mom's plaintive cry: "Why are you doing this to me?!"

*

9:29 a.m., 07/28/11—Thursday. Hallway in Emergency Department, Milford Hospital. To: hkropitis@fairfield.edu

From: eboquet@fairfield.edu
Subj: Re: Grant meeting being cancelled!! Hang in there EOM
Thanks.
Please cancel jim and keep the rest of my afternoon appts. I plan to be in by 1.
—beth
Sent from my iPhone

*

None of this work I was so insistently keeping my eye on, arranging and rearranging like the Shell Game on *The Price Is Right*, was important. It all could have gone on without me—and some of it has. More of it has been ignored or undone by people who came after me. That is a universal truth of administration. Working this way was a coping mechanism. Denial. A way to remove myself from what was happening to my mom, what was happening to me, what was happening to our family. Administrative work made time scarce and money plentiful. I told myself my family needed the money more than the time.

Of course I was popping between work-work and care-giving work all day long. Setting up a self-study while also trying to get my mom on a list for extended care, reviewing grant guidelines while researching how someone qualifies for hospice, drafting annual reports while setting up an appointment with yet one more specialist. Even when my body was with her, my attention could always be someplace else.

As my mom got sicker, I got healthier, if appearances count for anything. At the very least, I lost weight, surely the external measure of health in United States culture, up to a point. (It's a moving target.) I got a new summer wardrobe—fresh profesh. Kept my hair coloring on point—no roots! Was never without a scarf or a statement piece of jewelry. People commented on how great I looked. Sometimes I would thank them. One poor soul asked me what I had been doing to lose weight, and I said I had been watching my mom die.

*

>10:16 a.m., 07/28/11—Thursday. Room 6, Emergency Department, Milford Hospital. To: bboquet@email.edu
>
>From: eboquet@fairfield.edu
>Subj: Update on Mom
>We had to have her transported to hospital this am. i will update you when i have more info. She is stable. They are running tests.
>Love you.
>Sent from my iPhone

*

Reader, she was not stable.

Maybe this is a surprising contribution to a collection on embodiment: a piece about the death of the maternal body, about the fact that bearing witness to my mom's decline left me feeling curiously disembodied. Untethered in the universe. About the fact that work requires so little physical presence now, really, and caregiving requires so much.

About my mom's death, a good friend said, "Her body was doing what it was going to do." This sentiment consoled me as deeply as anything. It returned a kind of agency to my mom that her final months (and in many ways, her final years) lacked. And admittedly, it let me off the hook for all I could have done differently, some of which might have extended her time and, who knows, maybe even her quality of life. I feel, for just a moment when I really take that comment in, a healthy separation between my mom's body and mine.

*

>2:06 pm, 07/28/11—Thursday. Kitchen table at home. To: hkropitis@fairfield.edu
>
>From: eboquet@fairfield.edu
>Subj: Announcement Hi, Helen—

> Would you please contact whoever with the death notice? It should read something like
> Your prayers are requested for the repose of the soul of Patricia H. Boquet, mother of Beth Boquet, Professor of English and Dean of Academic Engagement, who passed away on Thursday, July 28th.
> We don't have any info on services or anything like that. Thanks for doing that. Talk soon—
> Beth

*

After my mom died, I continued in my full-time academic administrative role for eighteen months. I even accepted a promotion, one I had turned down when her health was declining. "Now you can take that position," one of the senior administrators said to me too soon after that terrible loss. I remember being stupefied by the callousness of that remark. I accepted the position.

The corpus of writing I produced in those eighteen months was significant. Printed and bound, it would have looked impressive, but between the covers would have been little of substance: emails (admittedly thousands of them), PowerPoint slides, assessments and evaluations (both programmatic and personnel), grant applications and reports. Nothing of lasting value and certainly nothing that hinted at the profound grief I was experiencing or the personal transformation that needed to happen for me to live in the world without my mom. A life lived on a laptop.

In those same eighteen months, as my responsibilities at work ramped up, my body was giving out. When I developed heartburn so bad I had to have a battery of tests and treatments to address it, was that a coincidence? Did watching my mom suffocate to death exacerbate my own lung problems? Once the person who carried me in her body was gone, did that mean my own body needed to bleed and bleed and bleed until it could bleed no more? Did missing her gimp and shuffle land me in the physical therapist's office with a bum right hip like hers? Would the nerve paralysis in my mouth resolve on its own if I could just pick up the phone one more time to talk to her? I guess I'll never know.

*

> 8:12 a.m., 07/11/12—Wednesday. Home office. To: hkropitis@fairfield.edu
>
> From: eboquet@fairfield.edu
> Subj: FW: Resignation
> Good morning, Helen—
> Would you please add a cc to the President on the attached letter, print on letterhead and prepare an envelope for the Pres as well? I should send that out to him this week.

> I hear John and my dad are going to be out looking for trouble this morning. That's really nice of John to take him on his errand.
> I'm working on accreditation stuff from home this morning until just before my meeting. Call here if anything comes up.
> Thanks! Beth
> —
> Elizabeth Boquet
> Associate Vice President for Academic Affairs

*

Resignation is a process. We might mark a turning point—a time of death, a signature on official letterhead—but the journey of resigning begins in the before and extends into the after. Two days before my mom died, our attorney Jane met us at my parents' apartment to sign their advance directives. I sat on the floor near my mom's feet and started to cry. "Don't start that," she said. "I'm not dead yet." After she died, my dad told me she had been dreaming about her dead relatives for weeks—visitations, as we used to call them—and she asked him at one point whether that meant she was dying. I don't know what he told her. She was resigning but, until the end, she was not resigned.

Nearly a year to the day after my mom's death, I submitted this resignation to the president and vice president for Academic Affairs. I remained in the position for another six months because spring semester was a better time to turn over my portfolio to a successor than the fall semester would have been. I was resigning, but I was not yet resigned.

I left the vice president's office in December 2012, only a few days after the massacre at Sandy Hook Elementary School. We were all in the process of resigning then. During my spring 2012 sabbatical, I worked with colleagues on the first of what has become an annual community poetry project in Newtown, Connecticut. Then and there, I wrote the poem that opens this essay. While the "resignation" in the subject line encapsulates and characterizes much of this time in my personal and professional life, I don't want to read past the "FW." Forward, because what other choice do we have. As my mom would say, I'm not dead yet.

*

INDEX

ableism, 5, 146, 204; hyperableness, 8. *See also* disability
academic discourse, 5, 27, 144; neoliberalism and, 144
Active Assailant Preparedness, 204
Active Learning Center (ALC), 60. *See also* writing centers
activism, 71–87
ADA. *See* Americans with Disability Act (ADA)
affects, embodied. *See* emotion
Ahmed, Sarah, 8, 34, 37, 174, 222
Ain't I a Woman: Black Women and Feminism (hooks), 123
Airua, Aren Z., 62
ALC. *See* Active Learning Center (ALC)
Alexander, Jonathan, 174
Americans with Disability Act (ADA), 197
Andriamanalina, Noro, 122
Antiracist Writing Assessment Ecologies (Inoue), 35
anybody *vs.* everybody, 6, 20
Anzaldúa, Gloria, 123
appearance: judging, 81–83
Arendall, Dena, 15, 88
argument, 53
Asian students, 16; model minority, 16
assessment, 127; assessment culture, 56; distributed-grading model, 171–73; as ecology, 128
Atlas, Janel, 16, 113
audience, 114, 115
autoethnographic methodology, 99

Banks, William P., 174
Bedaiwi, Hayat, 7, 16, 97, 99
"being in question," 34
Bergson, Henri, 110, 111
Bérubé, Michael, 143
Beta Rebellion, 199–205; madness trope, 201–2
binary opposition, 41*n1*, 61, 63
Bishop, Amy, 199
Bizzell, Patricia, 170
Black experiences, 9, 15, 74–75, 97; graduate students of color, 119–30; microaggressions, 119–30; racial stereotypes, 126; safe zone, 75. *See also* race

bodies: anybody *vs.* everybody, 6; body signification, 33–41; body *vs.* embodiment, 6; centering, 82–83; diverse, 146–48; "foreign bodies," 16; individual, 6; institutional, 6, 9; marked *vs.* unmarked, 6–7; normates, 6; smell, 15, 77–78; subject *vs.* object, 237–40; visible, 143–56
body *vs.* embodiment, 5
Bolton, Sharon, 224, 227
Boquet, Elizabeth, 20–21, 248
Borderlands/ La Frontera: The New Mestiza (Anzaldúa), 123
Bourdieu, Pierre, 35
Brentell, Lauren, 8, 19, 208
Bruning, Lauren, 56
burnout, 26–29
Butler, Judith, 203

Canagarajah, A. Suresh, 99
cancer, 20, 219–35, 237–40, 241–43
Carey, Triauna, 17, 18, 97, 119
Carroll, Lewis, 110
Cedillo, Christina, 34, 40, 210
Charlton, Jonnika, 228
Charlton, Colin, 228
Cho, Seung, 200
City University New York (CUNY), 219; open enrollment, 219, 230
classroom: apolitical, 144, 153; as physical space, 122
collaboration, 18
College Composition and Communication, 143
Comer, Denise, 8, 19, 212
commodification, 143, 226, 235*n3*
composition, 57
Composition in the Age of Austerity (Scott), 143
Conference on College Communication and Composition: non-tenure track faculty, 232
consumerism. *See* commodification
corequisite teaching, 153
corporate speak, 201
Council of Writing Program Administrators, 145, 146, 149, 242
Conceding Composition, 188
COVID-19, 13, 19, 213

critical embodiment pedagogy, 34
curriculum design, 14, 18, 59–64, 169–80; standardization, 144
curriculum vitaes (CVs), 19, 20, 97; embodied, 212–15
Cushman, Jeremy, 179
cynicism, 22, 23n5

dancing, 158–61
Dangerous Writing (Scott), 171
Daniel, Joshua I., 18, 143
death, 20, 244–47, 248–53
decolonial alliances, 34
Defense of Marriage Act, 50
deficiency model, 15
de Müller, Genevieve García, 146
Denny, Harry, 73
Department of Homeland Security, 203
depression, 59, 209
developmental writing courses, 153–54
digital technologies, 146
disability, 22, 146, 210; disability justice, 197; disability theory, 9; precarity of disability, 202. *See also* ableism
discomfort and pain, 14, 52, 134; body signification, 33–41; productive discomfort, 208
discourse. *See* academic discourse
disembodiment, 105; cost of disembodied labor, 227–30
dissertation writing, 44, 90, 133, 208–11, 241–42; interviews, 133–34
distributed grading, 18
diversity, 122; bodies, 146–48; diverse faculty, 124; diversity statements, 7; local diversity, 127; productive, 145
doctoral programs, 125, 129
Doing Emotion (Micciche), 222
drawing, 26–29
Drawing on the Right Side of the Brain, 26–27

ecologies, 128
Edelman, Lee, 54
Edwards, Betty, 26
elegy, 244–47
embodied rhetoric, 4–5
embodiment: affects, 65–68, 169–80; body *vs.* embodiment, 5, 6; *vs.* consumerism, 143, 226; critical embodiment pedagogy, 34; definitions, 4, 6, 244; embodied knowledge, 4–5, 34, 131–36, 147–48; embodied labor, 176, 219–35; embodied language, 4; embodied rhetoric, 4–5, 131–36; fleshy presences, 3–5, 131, 219; incorporation, 5; institutional, 3–25, 219–35; institutional bodies conflated with institutional embodiment, 6; meaning and, 144; movement and, 40, 41; programming revisions, 177; race, 35; research, 241–43; sticking out, 8; structures, 65–68; writing centers, 71–87
emotion: affects, embodied, 169–80; emotional labor, 121, 126, 235n2; emotional pain, 17; materializing emotion, 224–27
epistemology: fleshy, 5
ESL. *See* multilingualism
ESOL tests, 76
ethics of care, 20, 219–35; visible evidence, 230–31
ethnicity, 33–41. *See also* Black experiences
evaluations, 18, 125, 159–61, 184, 238–39
Evans, Elrena, 185
exhaustion, 169, 180, 190, 229, 237, 239

Faison, Wonderful, 15, 71
Farris, Michael, 18, 169
feminism: feminist pedagogy, 176; feminist rhetorical practices, 222; feminist studies, 146; intersectional feminist research, 10; social, 226; storytelling, 72; white feminism, 10; women's leadership, 5
Ferdinandt Stolley, Amy, 228
first-year writing programs (FYW), 18, 143, 144, 149; antiracism, 152; no-credit courses, 153; orientation, 151–54; revisions, 169–80
Fish, Stanley, 170
Fleckenstein, Kristie, 5
food choices, 77–78
Foucault, Michel, 52
Freire, Paulo, 176
Freyd, Jennifer, 209
FYW. *See* first-year writing programs (FYW)

Garcia, Romeo, 39, 41n1
Garland-Tompson, Rosemarie, 6
gaslighting, 125
Gatten, Alex, 9, 14, 59
gay marriage, 51. *See also* queerness
gender norms, 158–61
gender studies, 146
Gerdes-McClain, Rebecca, 8, 20, 238
Glenn, Cheryl, 178
Gonzalez, Laura, 15, 71, 75
Gouge, Catherine, 171
Graben, Tarez Samra, 228
graduate students, 7, 15, 16, 97–109, 198; financial hardships, 16, 102, 103–4; health insurance, 102; inclusive space,

16; life-work balance, 101–3; Muslim, 99–101; neoliberalism and, 143–56; scholars of color, 119–30; sexism, 104; as writing program administrator, 61
Gramsci, Antonio, 144
Green, Neisha-Anne, 37
grief, 15, 88–90, 113–15. *See also* discomfort and pain
Grimm, Nancy, 73
Gross, Morgan, 7, 16, 97, 105
Grosz, Elizabeth, 239
Grumet, Madeline R., 237
Grutsch McKinney, Jackie, 73
Gunner, Jeanne, 174

habitus, 34, 35, 128; definition, 35
Hardt, Michael, 220, 224
Harper-Mercer, Chris, 200
Harvey, David, 144
Hawai'i, 33–41
Hawaiian Creole English, 35–36
Hawhee, Deborah, 247
Hayles, Katherine, 5
Held, Virginia, 20, 220, 221, 230–31, 233
hero narrative, 228
Hester, Vicki, 171
heteronormativity, 5, 84
hierarchy, 125; graduate students of color, 119–30
Hijazi, Nabila, 8, 17
Hochschild, Arlie, 225
Hoermann-Elliot, Jacquelyn, 8, 19, 184
honi, 37
hooks, bell, 123, 143, 176
How Stories Teach Us: Composition, Life Writing, and Blended Scholarship (Robillard and Combs), 9
humor, 99–100
hybrid course, 171

identity: body signification, 33–41; food choices, 77–78; gender, 60; intersectionality, 18; lesbians, 74. *See also* transitioning
impostor syndrome, 159
inaccessibility, 8–9
Inayatulla, Shereen, 10
inclusion, 122
Indiana, 33–41
individualism, 144
Inoue, Asao, 34, 35, 127, 128–29, 152
institutional betrayal, 209
international students: food choice, 77–78. *See also* multilingualism
International Writing Centers Association, 37

interpersonal labor, 219–35, 238; materializing emotion, 224–27
intersectionality, 9, 105; identity, 18; intersectional feminist research, 10; theory of, 4

Johnson, Maureen, 8, 20, 241, 244

Kanaka Maoli culture, 36
Keller, Elizabeth, 15, 71, 77
Kelly, Shannon, 179
Kemp, Fred, 172, 173, 179
Kennedy, Tammie M., 152
Killingsworth, Jimmie, 173
Kim, Dae-Joon, 41
King, Thomas, 71, 86
Kirsch, Gesa, 13
Knoblauch, A. Abby, 4, 34, 244, 245, 247
knowledge: *a priori*, 6; embodied knowledge, 4–5, 34, 131–36, 147–48
Korean Americans, 104–5
Kotzeva, Elitza, 16, 110
Kuzawa, Deborah, 55

labor: cost of disembodied labor, 227–30; interpersonal labor, 219–35; material *vs.* immaterial, 220–35
LaFrance, Michelle, 20–21, 238
language usage, 85–86; language statement, 86; pronouns, 60, 86; vernacular, 126–27. *See also* multilingualism
Lanza, Adam, 200
Lazzarato, Maurizio, 220
Lee, Jasmine, 15–16, 91
lesbians, 15, 72; identity, 74; outing, 72
Leverenz, Carrie, 146
Levy, Daisy, 244
Lewis, Lynn, 18, 143
LGBTQ community. *See* queerness
life-work balance, 16, 91–94, 101–3, 110–12, 137–40, 188–91, 195–211
liminal space, 15–16, 143
Lindquist, Julie, 210
linear time, 110–12
listening, 161; rhetorical listening, 38–39
literacy classes, 131–36; functional literacy, 135
literacy narrative, 147
Living a Feminist Life (Ahmed), 37
Living Rhetoric and Composition: Stories of the Discipline (Roen, Brown, and Enos), 9
Lorde, Audre, 123, 128
Lorey, Isabell, 195, 196

McGrath, Alyssa, 7, 16, 97, 101
McKinney, Jackie Grutsch, 37

INDEX

McRuer, Robert, 174
male faculty, hostile, 184–87
manipulatives, 84–85
Manthey, Katie, 244
marginalization, 40, 41, 53, 122, 124, 202; marginalized embodiments, 61
materiality, 5
MBSR. *See* Mindfulness Based Stress Reduction (MBSR)
meaning: embodiment and, 144
mental health, 209
mental illness, 200–202
mentorship, 149–51; goal setting, 150–51; reflection, 150–51
Mercado-Lopez, Larissa, 123, 124
methodology: autoethnographic, 99; case study, 20
Metzl, Jonathan, 202
Micciche, Laura R., 179, 222
Michigan State University (MSU), 83–84, 208–11
microaggressions, 9, 119–30; definition, 120
Middle Eastern students, 15, 17, 131–36
Mills, C. W., 225
Mindfulness Based Stress Reduction (MBSR), 214
motherhood, 19, 196, 197, 198, 206; breastfeeding, 163–66; newborns, 44; working class, 14–15. *See also* pregnancy
motivation, 90
Moxley, Joe, 171
multilingualism: deficiency model, 15, 75–77; students, 15
Muñoz, José Esteban, 54–55
Muslim students, 15, 17, 99–101, 131–36; hijab, 83, 100

Nagle, Angela, 201
Napoleone, Anna Rita, 14–15, 65
narration and narratives, 123; hero narrative, 228, 234–35, 235*n1*; literacy, 147; martyr narratives, 228, 234–35, 235*n1*; overcoming narratives, 11; tenure narrative, 239; theory of narratives, 4
Nassar, Larry, 209
National Council of Teachers of English (NCTE): conference in Missouri, 126, 127
National Writing Project, 65
Native Americans, 245
NCTE. *See* National Council of Teachers of English (NCTE)
Negri, Antonio, 220, 224
neoliberalism, 18, 143–56

neurotypical diagnosis, 84
Nicolas, Melissa, 3, 10–12
no-credit courses, 153
No Future: Queer Theory and the Death Drive (Edelman), 54
non-tenure track faculty, 232
normates, 6
normative education. *See* standardization
Northeastern Writing Centers Association Conference, 85
Novotny, Maria, 244

Oklahoma State University, 143
Olson, Bobbi, 41
Oluo, Jicoma, 53
oppression, 53
Oregon shooting (Umpqua Community College), 200
other. *See* outsider
Our Body of Work (Nicolas and Sicari): audience, 11; authors, 10–12; call for papers (CFP), 11, 23*n2*; overview, 12–21; themes, 12–21
outcomes, 145–48
outsider, 8, 15, 122. *See also* marginalization

painting, 26–29
panic, 208–11
passing, 34, 37, 38; nstitutional passing, 16
patriarchy, 10, 244; and intersection, 4
pedagogy, 238; critical embodiment pedagogy, 34; feminist, 176; queer pedagogy, 14; writing and writing pedagogy, 175–76
Pence, Mike, 106
people of color, 34–41, 41*n1*. *See also* race
Perryman-Clark, Staci, 125
Philadelphia Inquirer, 199
Pidgin, 35–36
Portland Resolution Guidelines for WPA Positions, 232
post-traumatic stress disorder, 209
power, 35, 53, 125; empowerment, 123; graduate students of color, 119–30
Prebel, Julie, 8, 20, 237
precariousness, 195–96
precarity, 19, 195–96, 203; of disability, 202
precarization, 195–96; privileged precarization, 195–211
pregnancy, 8, 14, 16, 19, 101–3, 184–87, 205, 206; incarceration and, 43; loss, 16; newborns, 44; postpartum body, 43–45; stillbirth, 113–15; stories of loss, 113–15. *See also* motherhood
Price, Margaret, 3, 202
Pritchard, Eric Darnell, 174

privilege, 11–12; privileged precarization, 195–211
Promise and Perils of Writing Program Administration, The, 155
publishing, 66, 188–91, 197, 209–11; as commodification, 235n3
Pukui, Mary Kawena, 37

queer academics, 49–58, 210; queering program administration, 173–74
queerness, 9, 14, 72; disabled queer person, 210; gender norms, 158–61; "hate-the-sin-love-the-sinner," 52; oppression, 106; outing, 72; queer *milongs*, 158; transitioning, 59–64; voice, 78–79
queer pedagogy, 14, 50, 63
queer theory, 9, 54–57
Quinn, Ed, 230

race, 74; Black Lives Matter, 22; embodiment, 35; people of color, 34–41, 41n1; and space, 35. *See also* Black experiences
racism, 120–21, 127, 129. *See also* Black experiences
Ratcliffe, Krista, 38, 152
Reid, E. Shelley, 149
relationships, 18–19
repurposing, 55–57
Repurposing Composition (Stenberg), 55
research and scholarship, 110, 114, 115, 208–11; audience, 114, 115; black scholars, 97; boundaries, 115; data, 115; embodiment, 241–43; feminist, 10; immateriality of, 235n3; intersectional feminist research, 10; methodology, 222–24; retraumatizing research, 211; "stickiness," 222–23; students of color, 123; transformative research, 13
Research Is Ceremony (Wilson), 124
resignation, 254
resilience, 16
Resource Center for Persons with Disabilities (RCPI), 84
rhetoric: embodied rhetoric, 4–5, 131–36; feminist rhetorical practices, 222; racially-charged rhetoric, 120; rhetorical listening, 38–39
Rhodes, Jacqueline, 50, 57
Rice, Jenny, 180
Rich, Adrienne, 55
Robinson, Heather, 10
Rodger, Elliot, 200, 202
Rodriguez Carey, Rebecca, 14, 43
Royster, Jacqueline Jones, 13
Ruiz, Iris, 146
Ryan, Kathleen J., 228

scholarship. *See* research and scholarship
Scott, Tony, 143, 171
Seacrist, Scotty, 15, 71, 78
Search for Education, Elevation, and Knowledge (SEEK) programs, 220, 228, 233
security, 202–3, 204; lockdown, 204
seeing, 27
self-care, 234–35
self-worth, 126
Shaughnessy, Mina, 8, 20, 219–35
Shipka, Jody, 179
Sicari, Anna, 3, 10–12
Silva, Mary Lourdes, 18, 158
Sirc, Geoffrey, 174
Skinnell, Ryan, 8, 19, 188
Smith, Carly, 209
Smith, Trixie, 15, 71
social collectivities, 144
Solnit, Rebecca, 202
somatic mind, 5
somatophobia, 237–40
space, 19, 36, 37, 84; across and between spaces, 114; brave space, 86n2; classroom as physical space, 122; collaborative, 144; inclusive space, 16; kairotic space, 5; movement and, 40, 41; safe zone, 75, 87n2, 125–26; taking up space, 119–30; unsafe space, 125–26; writing centers, 60, 62–63
Standard English, 8, 36
standardization, 8–9; curricula, 144; standards, 144
Stenberg, Shari J., 55
storytelling, 9, 71–87; stillbirth, 113–15
Stryker, Susan, 62
students: black experiences, 9, 15; first-gen, 67, 159
surveillance, 14–15, 52, 56
Syrian refugees, 131–36

Tang, Jasmine Kar, 18, 122, 163
tango, 158–61
teachers: of color, 123–25; white teachers, 123–25
Teaching Queer: Radical Possibilities for Writing and Knowing (Waite), 59
technologies, 146, 178–79
tenure-track positions, 15–16, 91–94, 160, 195, 197, 210–11, 237; publishing, 66
Texas Tech University (TTU), 18, 169–80
Thatcher, Margaret, 144
theory *vs.* practice, 122–23
time: emotional, 110–12; linear time, 110–12
Titchkosky, Tanya, 210
Touster, Saul, 228

toys, 84–85
transitioning, 59–64; nonlinear, 60; pronouns, 60
trauma, 19, 199–211; panic zone, 208–11; post-traumatic stress disorder, 209; research, 208–11; retraumatizing research, 211; survivors, 208. *See also* violence
Trimbur, John, 143, 155
tutors, 67

Umpqua Community College (Oregon), 200
university: corporate speak, 201; institutional betrayal, 209; neoliberalism and, 143–56; precarization of academic life, 195–211; queer academics, 49–58; R-1 university, 65–66; repurposing the institution, 55–56
University of California, Santa Barbara (UCSB), 160
University of Nebraska: English Department, 51–52

Vidali, Amy, 227, 229
violence, 20, 23*n4*; gun violence, 19; lone gunman mythology, 202; mass shootings, 7, 20, 199–211; mental illness and, 200–202
Virginia Tech shooting, 199
Volpe, Edmund, 233
vulnerability, 184–87

Waite, Stacey, 9, 14, 49, 59, 63
Walker, Kelsie, 7, 16, 97, 103
Walters, Shannon, 7, 19, 195, 210
Wang, Isaac, 8, 14
WCDs. *See* writing center directors
Weeks, Kathi, 224–25
Weinman, Paula, 7, 16, 97, 104
Welch, Nancy, 143
White, Ed, 145
whiteness, 5, 17–18, 40, 41*n1*, 105, 129, 147,
152; navigating, 74; white racial habitus, 34, 35; white teachers, 123–25
Wilson, Shawn, 124
Women's Ways of Making It in Rhetoric and Composition (Ballif, Davis, and Mountford), 3, 9, 198
work-life balance. *See* life-work balance
WPA. *See* writing program administration
WPA: Writing Program Administration, 3
writing as embodiment, 170
writing center directors (WCDs), 14, 15; graduate students as, 61
writing centers, 59–64; active learning, 62; culture and, 38; embodiment, 71–87; Indiana compared to Hawai'i, 34–41; multimodality, 62; racial formation, 122; space, 36–37, 60, 62–63, 178; technology, 178–79. *See also* Active Learning Center (ALC)
Writing Instructor, The, 50
writing pedagogy, 175–76. *See also* pedagogy
writing program administration (WPA): antiracist goals, 146, 152; definitions, 23*n1*; exemplar, 219–35; feminist, 5, 222; listserve, 145; neoliberalism and, 143–56; outcome statement, 145, 146–47; pregnancy, 184–87; privileged precarization, 195–211; queering program administration, 173–74; racial tension and, 129; responsibilities, 228, 232; transition into, 197–98; white feminism and, 10. *See also* embodiment, insitutional

Yamamoto, Kaoru, 149
Yancey, Kathleen Blake, 144, 145
Yergeau, Melanie, 8, 146, 210
Young, Jennie, 17, 137, 155
Young, Vershawn Ashanti, 126

zones: discomfort zone, 208; panic zone, 208–11; safe zone, 75, 87*n2*, 125–26. *See also* discomfort and pain